BROKEN SILENCE
E. G. Miller

Copyright © 2017 E. G Miller
All rights reserved. No part of this book may be reproduced or transmitted in any form or by any means, electronic or mechanical, including photocopying, recording or by any information storage and retrieval system, without permission in writing from the publisher.
Published by Praise Ministries Inc, East St. Louis, IL
ISBN 978-0-9988208-1-1
Card Catalogue Number: 2017944122
Publisher's Cataloging-in-Publication Data
Miller, E.G.
Broken Silence / E.G. Miller. —East St. Louis, IL
Praise Ministries, Inc
Formats: eBook | Paperback distribution

ABOUT THE AUTHOR

E. G. Miller is the fourth of nine children, bible born and bred, to God-fearing parents in a small Midwestern city in Illinois.

When the fears instilled in her to remain silent by her abusers, became overwhelming from the unspeakable experiences she endured and could no longer be contained in her frail frame, she developed an enthusiastic zeal for writing.

Through writing, she found the courage to break the silence.

DEDICATION

This book is dedicated to all those who have suffered hate crimes, abuse and domestic violence both in and out of relationships… in life is hope!

INTRODUCTION

Fear is a powerful motivator or inhibitor, but never both simultaneously. For me, fear has dominated more years of my life, than many people have lived. Broken Silence is an attempt to reclaim the power that was stolen by the horrendous experiences suffered at the hands of those, committed to love by oath, nature and nurture, as well as, those empowered to protect and serve.
Hopefully, the result will be to inspire others who have suffered similar or exact experiences to Speak Up and Out!

Chapter One

It was a cold snowy day in the windy city of Chicago, as Robin Watson left work to return home, after taking sick on the job. Waiting for the southbound rail to come was difficult, as her body was rippling with pain at the CTA north station, seemed a little more than she thought she could bear. She considered taking medication, while waiting on the platform, but decided against it since she was so far from home, she needed to be alert. It was the sixties and crime was no stranger to the bustling city. If I can just make it home, she thought, I will head straight for the kitchen take my medicine, then to the bathroom and soak in a hot tub for an hour and I may have time to rest before my husband comes in from work, she thought, then I'll fix him a light supper and lie down, while he eats alone.

Her thoughts were interrupted by the sound of the train approaching, what a welcome sound and site, she thought, as she prepared to board. It came to a stop in front of her, the doors opened and she looked for a seat close to the front, not only because most of the problems seem to take place in the rear, but the closer she sat to the front, the less steps she had to take and it would allow her to exit in front of the exit ramp at her stop.

Robin, spotted an ideal seat, she reached it, fatigued and desperate, she placed her belongings down, to lighten the load from her ailing body, turned sideways on the seat, seeking a small measure of comfort and tranquility for the duration of the ride. It will take about sixty-five minutes to her exit, ramp and the stairs leading to the street. Robin was in position and endured while drifting off into a, much needed, power nap state to awaken just in time for her stop. She arose from her seat and slowly exited the doors relieved that in less than seven minutes, she would be inside her apartment, taking the necessary steps to heal. While descending the stairs from the platform, she stopped to look for her keys, it was her nature to be organized and it was always her habit to have her keys in hand before reaching the apartment building, as it was just a short distance to home.

As Robin turned the corner, by Joe Louis' old milk company, she had an uneasy feeling but dismissed it as part of her ailment and continued to the building. She was ambivalent for snow was on the ground leading to the building; it was clear no salt had been placed on the sidewalk and nothing had been done to clear a pathway. So, she treaded carefully to the entrance of the family owned building, deliberately trying to maintain her balance to prevent falling. Robin made it to the door without incident and with a sigh of relief she unlocked the door and climbed the stairs to the second floor, where she and Russell resided, with her sister-in-law, Louise, and her husband, Walter. Sticking to her plan, she unlocked the door.

Once inside, checking to verify that Russell had fixed the lock, she locked the door then reopened it and locked it again. It was clear that Russell had not fixed the lock, as he had stated, the night before, it was still difficult to open from the inside. She took off her snow-covered clothes, shook and placed them on the hanger next to the door with her shoes, put on her slippers and headed for the kitchen. There was a long hallway to the kitchen, but today, it seemed twice as long, for she had begun to perspire and her legs became heavier to lift.

As she passed the bathroom, she thought she heard a sound, but dismissed it and took another step in her slipper dressed feet, as she held on to the wall for support. As she approached her bedroom door, the noises became louder and she could not dismiss the sounds anymore, so quietly, she walked up to the door and stood still. No one is supposed to be home today, she thought, her hand slowly touched the door knob, she thought perhaps she should call the police, as she looked at the phone mounted to the wall, her heart began to beat rapidly, then without thinking, Robin opened the bedroom door and to her surprise she saw legs in the air in her bed. It took her a minute to fully grasp the magnitude of the situation, shock does that, then she found her voice. "What is going on?" she asked.

Her husband sprang from the bed saying, "Robin, it's not what it looks like!"

Robin didn't say a word the adrenaline was flowing. It is said that adversity either breaks you, or makes one stronger. She gave him a look; saw the woman's clothing neatly folded on the table by the window. Robin knew the woman had been there for some time. There was nothing on the floor to indicate it was a moment of passion preceding the act. She calmly walked to the window, opened it, picked up her clothes and threw them out. Robin turned to the woman and said,

"If it's not what it looks like or before someone says I'm dreaming, you get out of my bed and go get your clothes before I do something I may or may not regret tomorrow, depending on whose scenario is correct!"

Without hesitation, she got up, her naked body openly exposed, mascara running, lipstick smeared with a fearful and equally shocked look on her face. Her husband Russell got a coat from the closet and threw it across the bed to her and said, "Wait for me downstairs."

"I'm sorry," she said, while trying to cover her nakedness with his coat as she ran out of Robin's bedroom.

Not once did he call the woman by name. Robin didn't know if that was part of his plan to convince her that she was dreaming, but the chill from the opened window could not be denied nor the snow blowing through it wetting both the bedroom furniture and floor. Russell, standing in his birthday suit and socks calmly stated, "We'll talk about this when I return." As he picked up his pants and shirt and walked past her.

Robin was in shock, perhaps in a trance, only hearing what was going on around her while frozen in the same spot. Robin heard Russell as he came out of the bathroom and walked down the hallway, the door opened and closed and then reality slapped her across the face with the wind blowing from the open window filled the room. Anticipating Russell's next move, she walked to the window to watch the show. As she looked out, she only saw Russell picking up the woman's clothes and return towards the building. She listened and her fear was realized as she heard an inside door downstairs open and close with no footsteps to the outside entrance door. She knew he entered his sister's or uncle Books apartment, where miss or Mrs. X was waiting. Robin felt open shame for the entire family building knew their horrendous secret.

The snowflakes looked larger and were falling at record speed; the chill of the winter's day pierced her fragile body, but what she felt most was numbness. Instinctively, Robin closed the window picked up her medicine bottle from the table and opened it. She took out her pills and too numb to care, she swallowed them without water. Robin sat down on the sofa in the bedroom and stared at the bed. Time seemed to stand still, but it had not. She looked at that bed and thought, with all the hotels and motels in Chicago, how dare he bring a woman home to our bed to have sex. Her pillow cases were stained with the nameless woman's makeup and lipstick, and Robin didn't even wear lipstick. How was he planning to handle that, she queried? Her satin sheets were now stained with the semen of some woman she didn't even know. Robin had just changed the bedding that morning before leaving for work; now, she had to change bedding again. When she thought by that time, she would be peacefully lying between her own clean sheets. She was in no hurry to make the necessary changes; she just didn't want to move or touch the bed for the thought of it was worse than sleeping on a used mattress picked up in an alley. How long had he been doing this, she questioned? There was nothing to indicate that this was a new relationship, as she reminisced. There was no freshness, that she observed, no spontaneity, instead, they seemed comfortable, something she felt she would not feel again with him for a long time, if ever. She thought the woman failed to say the most important words, after saying she was sorry, like, *"I thought he was single,"* or *"He never said he was married!"* There was a trick to opening the door from inside of the apartment, but Russell didn't warn her nor did she need help opening it. She had been here more than once and opened that door more than twice, Robin reasoned. A myriad of thoughts invaded Robins mind, but, none of them were comforting. Since it was a family building, Robin was certain that everyone knew what Russell was doing but her, they were laughing at her behind her back.

Robin had a flash back and the regrets, doubts and paranoia took over. If only she had listened to her father, she thought. If only she had not married him. Robin's father stated Russell would do her the same way his brother had done his wife. He walked away from their marriage after all those years and five small children. It did not take that long for Russell to show his true colors. She was warned by his friends that she should reconsider marrying Russell; because he was leaving her parent's home and going to his woman's house on the next street and she was expecting his child. Robin thought maintaining her virginity was an honorable thing; it was her desire to be a virgin bride and since she was not putting out, she knew he had someone. But it never once occurred to her that he would not stop his shenanigans when he was married. After all, who gets married without quitting the girlfriend? Naïvely, Robin, truly believed that Russell would be faithful.

She was wrong—was an understatement!

The way a relationship begins, is more likely than not, the way it will end. It is difficult enough to maintain a relationship when love is thought to be the key factor. There are others just as essential, among which respect and trust are crucial keys for every marital foundation, love alone is not enough.

Chapter Two

Delayed Clouds of Doubts

Was Robin ever in love with Russell, or was he just someone to talk to in her loneliness while she awaited the return of the one person she waited for to return to and for her, she pondered. Thinking of the one love she threw back into the world as a fisherman does a minnow. Escaping from the present pain she took a stroll down memory lane to a time when she could now face and perhaps find answers to the whys standing out like a pink elephant in the room.

Robert was a slim good looking, well-spoken young man, the son of the Pastor. Her father had promised her hand in marriage to Robert after she completed her education. Since she had known Robert since she was eleven years old, she had grown to care for him. They sang in a gospel group together and he would often attend choir rehearsal, and both looked forward to those occasions. He was six years her senior, but that did not bother her, besides; her father was sixteen years older than her mother. Robert was not just comfortable to be with, he knew who he was and what he wanted to do. That is not to say that he always used wisdom and discretion, because he too, had hurt her in a similar fashion. Now, Robin was beginning to wonder if it were her fault that the two men in her life committed the same infractions? She had to be the blame, she reasoned there must be something about her that drove the men in her life to do these things. She must confront it to resolve it, she thought.

Robin was appointed musician of her first choir at the age of eleven, at the church Robert's father was the pastor.

Four years later, she was still musician and had built a great membership of committed and gifted individuals who were respected for their ability to touch and inspire congregations, but it took hard work. While Robert and Robin would see each other in group rehearsal and at their weekly and monthly evening church services; they never had one to one experiences. They were always surrounded by family and friends, chaperoned. It seemed ironic, now as she recalled the incident that it too, was in winter, however, Robin knew her name.

Gloria Dean was a very tall lovely young woman, who came from his hometown, in Mississippi, with her parents and siblings and united with the church. She dated other young men, so Robin was surprised when she was informed indirectly, that Gloria and Robert were a couple in Mississippi and she remained close friends with his sisters.

It was the night of one of the choir's regular weekly rehearsals. Robin had a habit of not dismissing rehearsal until she was satisfied that the choir was genuinely prepared to render spiritual excellence in the worship experience. Located in an undeveloped area, the church had outdoor lavatory facilities; therefore, it was often mandatory to call for a break, ten to fifteen minutes, giving the choir members an opportunity to utilize those facilities then return and resume. That night, as they reassembled, Robin had an emergency, which was rare for her, for the members often commented that she must have an extra bladder, the way she never left the sanctuary during rehearsals. It was cold and so she hurried outside to the restroom totally focused on the trouble spots during the rehearsal that needed to be corrected. Humming the melody and making mental notes for improvement, she was trying to hurry, go and return to the warm building. As she exited the restroom, she observed Roberts car parked on the opposite side of the street. Immediately, she digressed from her set course, as if compelled, she seized the moment and crossed the street. The closer she came to the car, the foggier the car windows appeared but she kept going not thinking, as any naïve sixteen-year-old, who had only experienced kissing for one month three days, she was clueless.

Robin knocked on the window, and then wiped it expecting to see Robert in the front driver's seat. She was surprised when her peripheral vision caught a flash of movement from the backseat of the car. She rubbed the rear window and to her surprise, Robert and Gloria were trying very hard to be still. Robin turned and walked back to the church to see a crowd had gathered.

"Are you alright?" asked the president.

"Yes," she replied. She pretended to be unaffected by what she had seen and tried with all due restraint, to carry on. However, she could not convince herself to short change God with pretense. The melody was gone; consequently, she concluded rehearsal and as protocol, turned the choir back over to the president. Before dismissing, the president asked all members to remain on standby for a special call rehearsal subject to the musician's discretion. The choir agreed. After they were dismissed, they waited for Sis. Hogan to drive them home, but Robin's brother, Thomas, eased out of the church. When Sis. Hogan blew the horn for them to come out, Thomas was seen standing talking to Robert. He came over to the car and Sis. Hogan stated,

"It's not as bad as it seems, Robin. You're young, you'll get over it."

"Yes, ma'am," Robin said.

Robert tried to see her early the following morning, but she put him off until the following day. After all, he had work and she had school, but the following day was group rehearsal, so they would see each other then. It was a long day and a longer night and morning. Going through the motions, Robin mechanically made it through the day.

When time came for rehearsal, Robin's brother and sisters announced that in lieu of rehearsal, they were all going to the movies. Thomas, Freddie and Elijah who was soon to be her brother-in-law; Ruby and Arthur who were dating for years and of course, Robin and Robert. Sitting in the rear of the theatre, Robert and Robin talked, making their own movie from the silent era, as the screen version movie played. She knew that her siblings and their dates were gone, except for, Thomas; she waited for Robert to speak.

Robert and Robin sat in the rear of the theatre in an awkward silence. Slowly he raised his arm and placed it on the back of her seat, but Robin did not move or speak.

"Robin," he stated. "Can we talk?" he asked.

She looked him in the eyes and said, "I thought that was the point of calling off rehearsal tonight, please, speak, I want to hear every word."

He took his arm off the back of the seat and took her hand.

"Robin, I could tell you that I did not invite her into the car, which would be true, but it would not change the facts; however, you deserve an explanation," he whispered. "No one in that small rural area locks their house doors and everyone knows my car doors are always unlocked. Gloria opened my door and came inside while I was napping. That is what happened, Robin, but it does not absolve me of responsibility for what subsequently happened," Robert replied.

"What happened then?" she asked.

"While I slept, she straddled me and I was aroused. I was weak and gave in to my desires," he admitted. "I have no one to blame but myself. I lacked the courage to say NO!" he exclaimed. "I gave it much thought and if I had known what she planned, I cannot honestly say I would have turned her down, but it never would have happened there, near the church. I hope you will believe I have far too much respect for you than that."

"Robert, I believe you," Robin stated. "I also know that the two of you used to be a couple and you're familiar with each other in the most intimate sense of the word. When we started kissing, one month and five days ago, I stated, I would kiss because I wanted you to teach me, but we would have to wait for marriage before teaching me about intercourse and we agreed. I know you're not a monk," she said, "But I do expect you to be respectful, considerate and discreet. Now all your business is out and mine, too, because two adults behaved as children," Robin stated.

"I apologize, Robin," he said. "Do you think we can make it?" he asked.

"I would like to try," she replied.

"So, would I," Robert stated. Still holding her hands, he lifted them to his thin lips and kissed them. That was the turning point for them, when they both realized how much they thought they wanted each other. Just as that relationship never went any further, than the hot and heavy petting and the aching desire for fulfillment, but did not end because of his unfaithfulness, choices dictated they move past that moment but never move on together. Now, here Robin was faced with the same circumstances with one clear exception, Russell is her husband. As much as she had endured, because he could neither keep his appendage in his pants nor his marital vows, with two children outside the marital bond, that she knew of, women were calling and boldly asking for him and the calls where no one speaks and hangs up on her, how does she face the family there in that building, has she had enough or does she give him one last chance? These are the questions which plagued Robin and must be answered.

Robin heard the front door open and the door to Louise and Walter's bedroom, yet, she did not move. Louise had a habit of playing music or turning on her television upon entering her bedroom. Robin knew her routine, she counted to three and then it began to play. That was usually followed by a trip to the restroom then her greeting, as she passed the bedroom, entering the kitchen. Robin heard everything except the greeting followed by Louise's footsteps into the kitchen. Robin braced herself; she knew Louise was not going to pass the bedroom door.

Chapter Three

An Unwelcomed Knock

There was a knock on the bedroom door, but Robin sat quietly and didn't answer.

"Robin, are you sleeping?" Louise asked. Wondering why she asked if she thought it were true.

Robin answered, "The door is unlocked, come on in, Louise."

The door opened and she entered.

"Can I get you anything, Robin?" she asked.

"No. I don't feel like moving," Robin replied.

Louise turned on the light and took a seat.

"Robin," she said. "I heard you came home early because you were sick and met with an unpleasant situation. I just want you to know how sorry I am you had to experience that. I am so disappointed in my brother, Russell, he disrespected not only you, but my house, in bringing another woman here and I am certainly having a conversation with him. I have not experienced my husband doing that, but he has been unfaithful and I know that," she said. "It took me years to put it behind me; I just don't know how I would have handled it, to catch him in my bed with another woman. I just don't think I could forgive that, as many motels and rooming houses operating in this city, there is just no excuse for bringing a woman to my home and your bed to have sex. Whatever you decide to do, please know you have my total support. I know what you're thinking," she said. "Yes, he is my brother, but right is right and wrong is wrong. I refuse to support anyone that is that far to the left. If I support him in this, he'll bring someone here for my

Walter and I certainly will not stand still for that. That is a poor example for all the young men in this building, his nephews and uncles."

Robin listened, because Louise never had a serious conversation with her the entire time she lived with her, that wasn't related to a recipe she didn't know how to cook. So, Robin was trying to decide whether she was just trying to find out her plans to report back to her brother, or if she was sincere. So, Robin asked.

"Louise, are you saying you did not know Russell was seeing this woman or who she is?"

"That's exactly what I am saying, Robin," she replied. "My sixteen years old nephew met me at the CTA track station and told me as we walked home."

"What did he say?" Robin asked.

"Christopher said, 'Uncle Russell brought a naked woman to the house and asked mother if she would help her get dressed.' He went on to say that Russell went outside and picked up the woman's wet clothing from the snow and returned with them and asked him to put them in the dryer. Mother asked him why they were in the snow and he told her, Robin came home early from work and found them in bed together in the act and threw her clothes out the window."

"Christopher added his mother, Vera, told Russell they were lucky Robin didn't kill them both and as soon as her clothes dried, give them to her and take her home. She didn't want to jeopardize her relationship with you."

Robin said, "I appreciate Vera saying that."

"Everyone is appalled at his conduct and uncle Book told him the same thing," Louise said.

"I don't blame you for not trusting or being skeptical about us, because he is our brother, uncle and nephew, but believe me, Russell must answer to the family in this building for his indiscretion," Louise said. After hearing Louise out, Robin, let down her guard and asked "Louise, would you mind taking the bedding off, I just don't think I can clean up that bed now?"

"Sure, Robin, I will change it and if you like, you can sleep in the small bedroom until you are ready to deal with this mess," Louise said. "The person who should change it isn't here," she said. "Do you want me to move you in the front bedroom when I finish?" she asked.

"No!" she exclaimed. "Move him in the front bedroom and place those sheets on the bed up there" Robin exclaimed. "But if you really want to help me, let's turn the mattress over and place the bottom end to the headboard," remarked Robin. Just as Louise was about to turn the mattress over and around, the front door opened.

"Don't get upset, that's not Russell, it's Walter," she replied. She stopped and went to the door and said, "Walter, come to Robin's bedroom and give me a hand, please."

Walter came immediately.

"What do you need?" he asked.

"Turn the mattress over and place the head at the bottom of the frame, Walter," Louise said. He did.

"Do you want any furniture moved around?" he asked. "You'll have to ask Robin that question," Louise replied. "Well, Robin?" he asked.

"Now that I think about it, Walter, it would be less stressful to open the door and not see the bed in the same spot; can we move everything to the left that is on the right side of the room?" Robin asked.

"I don't see why we can't," he replied.

"Robin, you really saw them in the raw, in the act?" Louise asked.

"Yes, Louise, I saw far more than I would have desired," Robin said.

"I heard about it when I entered the door," Walter said. "What I don't get, is why he did it here," he said. "I don't mean I, understand him doing this period, but I certainly don't understand him coming here, after all, it's not like anyone in this building can keep a secret. He really has a set on him," Walter proclaimed.

"Yes, he came within an inch of losing them, too. Any other woman would have left those two peas, wrapped in her clothes, in the snow for the birds this spring," Louise shouted.

"Robin, I can't tell you not to worry about it, but I can tell you this, one day, Russell will regret he ever pulled a stunt like this," Louise remarked.

"One must be human with a beating heart, to have a conscience to regret anything," Robin said.

"Don't let it stress you out," Walter said.

"I admit I am thrown by the entire situation, but I refuse to let this drain both my marriage and my health," Robin said. "When his things are out of here, I will sleep like a baby," she said.

"Are we taking his things somewhere?" asked Walter. "Yes, we're taking them to the front bedroom," Louise said.

"Louise, now you know how much Russell dreads that bedroom, he has said repeatedly that there is just too much noise from the streets up there," Walter said.

"He'll figure it out and I am sure, he'll be glad to have that room, trust me," Louise said.

"What do you want to eat family?" she asked.

"Nothing for me," Robin said. "But you two are free to help yourselves."

"In fact," Robin added, "I made that delicious dinner yesterday and Russell didn't come in until late, why don't you two help yourselves and I may fix a turkey sandwich later," she suggested.

"That would be lovely," Louise said. "I'll just take the food out of the refrigerator and warm it, set the table and complete the job in here. I'll get all that water up, as well," she said. "By the way, who threw the water?" she asked.

"No water was thrown, I opened the window and threw out her clothes and for the life of me, I didn't remember it was open for far too long. That's snow, Louise," Robin stated.

"I see, it will leave a stain in the carpet it should have been dried with a towel and heater. I will do what I can, but I'm sure it will become musty if left wet," Louise commented.

"Take the food out, Louise, so you two can eat before it gets late," Robin said.

"It's out, I must warm it," she said. "I will warm all the food, then when we are done eating, I will put it in plastic containers and place it in the freezer, if that's alright with you, Robin," Louise stated.

"That will be fine and you might want to slice some turkey for your lunches tomorrow, too," Robin said. "Someone should eat that dinner and if nothing else, I know I'm an excellent cook," Robin said.

"I second that," Walter said, as he walked out of the room.

"Thank you, I'll even put dinner and lunch for Russell in a container. Do you think you'll go to work tomorrow, Robin?" Louise asked.

"No, Louise, I don't," Robin said.

"Okay, Robin, Walter and I will take care of everything," Louise said. "I'm going to clean up in here so you can rest in your own bed, then, the food will be warm and we'll eat, clean the kitchen and go to bed ourselves," Louise said. "When Russell comes in, we'll show him to his room until you're up to talking to him, okay Robin," Louise said.

"I'll trust you to do that," Robin said.

Walter returned and stated he had fixed up the room for Russell, clothes and all. "I am headed into the kitchen to check on the food," he said. "It smells better today than yesterday."

"Turkey and dressing always smell and tastes better the day after than the day it's cooked," Robin said. "I apologize for not offering you dinner yesterday, but you had prepared yours and I didn't bother to eat since Russell wasn't home to share it. I fixed more than enough for an army, so please, be my guess," Robin said.

"We will," Walter replied. "I'll set the table, honey."

"Thank you, Walter. I'm almost finished," Louise said.
"I just want to help clean Robin up before she gets in bed," Louise said.

"Take your time, I can take care of the food," he said.

"What do you want to sleep in, Robin?" Louise asked.

"My gown was placed under my pillow for the night and I don't recall seeing it on the bed, when you took off the linen, Louise, so look in the top drawer and take the flannel pajamas out for me. It's cold and I have no reason to look sexy, they're warm," Robin said. "You did a wonderful job, Louise, my limbs are weak, so I'm staying in this bed, hand me a bottle of water, please, for my medicine and you two may go," Robin voiced.

Louise handed Robin the water and medicine. She took the medicine and Louise asked, "Would you like lights out or not?"

"Out," Robin said.

Louise turned out the light and left the door slightly ajar then went into the kitchen.

Walter and Louise completed their sumptuous, southern meal of turkey and dressing, macaroni and cheese, potato salad, string beans and cornbread with sweet potato pie and both cleaned up, fixed their lunches, placed Russell's meal and lunch in the frig, fixed a sandwich for Robin and put the food away. They turned out the lights and walked slowly down the hallway to their bedroom. They were full and Louise said,

"Walter, there is absolutely no way we can rest in bed, but sitting in a chair on the sofa would be best until the food digests. We ate too much!"

"Well," he said. "That food is to blame, it was just too good to resist; that's why we both had thirds."

"Did we really eat three servings of everything each?" she asked.

"We really ate three," Walter exclaimed.

"Well," Walter continued. "Russell should be in soon and we can talk to him, so yes, we'll sit up for a while."

Robin fell asleep and slept soundly until she heard a commotion pulling her out of her sleep back to reality. Robin was awakened by the sound of loud voices. Russell was home and Walter and Louise were talking to him. She heard him say they couldn't stop him from going to his bedroom, when there was a knock on the door. Sound carries in old buildings and vents. Uncle Book lived downstairs on the first floor, so he heard Russell not only come in, but the kerfuffle that ensued shortly after he entered the apartment. Uncle Book was respected by everyone, so when he took an interest and became involved, his word was the last word. Robin laid in the bed and listened.

Uncle Book said to Russell, "It is unthinkable what you did today, you totally disrespected your wife, your home, your sister and husband, your sister Vera, her family, me and my building," he said. "Now, you 're demonstrating that you have absolutely no regards for anyone, to raise your voice to the extent no one can sleep and with no remorse. I was going to wait until tomorrow to speak to you, but you left me no choice but to do it tonight, if anyone is to have rest this night. Should you desire to remain in this building, then, you must follow the rules: There will never be a repeat performance of the bad play you rendered here today, no encore, is that understood?" he asked. "You will apologize to your wife and try to make amends of what marriage you have left and give her the time she needs to process this situation and decide what course of action she wants to take or not. That is not negotiable. Since Louise and Walter went to the trouble and courtesy of fixing up the front bedroom for you, I suggest you smile and take it or make other arrangements. Do I make myself clear?" he asked.

"Yes, sir, crystal," Russell said.

Uncle Book continued. "There are children in this building and we have sacrificed to give them a decent way of life and we will not tolerate your misguiding them. Is that clear Russell?"

"Yes, sir," he answered. "Uncle Book, I am sorry I hurt everyone please forgive me."

"Russell, you need to grow up! You have a lovely wife; you knew she was ill before you married her. Frankly, the reason you married her was because of her illness to keep you from going to the military. So, since that was accomplished, it seems to me you owe her some appreciation for saving you, but instead, you demean her. Well, I will accept your apology when and if she does. You are a disgrace to manhood," Uncle Book stated. "Do everyone a favor and go to your new bedroom and sleep on those sheets that you slept on earlier with that strange woman. I am going to bed, people in this building go to work and school later this morning. How is Robin, Louise?" he asked.

"We put her to bed, she'll be home all day," Louise replied.

"Please tell her I asked after her, thank you. Let's all go to bed, rest well," Uncle Book said.

"You too," they said and walked him to the door.

Robin didn't hear Russell's voice anymore. Relieved that Uncle Book had come to speak to Russell and give him some perspective regarding his path in life, the house was peaceful. Robin thanked God for sending Uncle Book, as she closed her eyes and slept.

The sunlight streamed through the window, it was another day, still cold and windy, but a new day. Robin was awakened by the pain and the light. She tried to move but could not. She began to sing part of a Dr. Watt, "Father I stretch my hands to thee" when there was a knock on the door. Praying that it was not Russell, she said, "Come in."

Her prayer was answered, for in walked Louise.

"Good morning, Robin, are you feeling worse?" she asked

"Not worse, about the same," Robin replied.

"Good because if you were worse, I would suggest you go to the hospital," Louise said.

"I cannot move right now and I have a couple of needs," Robin said.

"What do you need?" Louise asked.

"I need a couple of bed pads under me and will you call in for me?" Robin asked.

"Yes, and yes," Louise repeated. "Is this the call-in information on the table here?" she asked.

"Yes, it is," Robin replied. She took the information outside the door and called from the wall phone and returned.

"Robin, they said they didn't expect to see you today nor tomorrow, they are praying for you," she said. "Relax and get better or would you like me to call the doctor for you?" Louise asked.

"Yes, just to report that I am having difficulty with my mobility but, since I saw him four days ago, I can't see him doing anything," Robin commented.

"Let's get those pads under you, do you need the bedpan first?" she asked.

"Yes," she replied.

"I can do that," Louise said. She took the bedpan out of the cabinet and placed it under Robin. "I'll be back in a few," Louise said.

Robin nodded, "Okay."

Robin had held her urine since early morning and was relieved. Louise returned with body wash cloths wet and warm. She gave Robin a quick wash with them and emptied the bedpan and returned with it clean.

"Robin," she said. "I have no idea how you're going to manage to get on and off alone. Are you sure you don't want me to tell Russell to check on you, before I leave?" "No, Louise, if he comes in and I need something I will ask, okay?"

"Okay," Louise remarked. "If you're sure. Gerri may stop by, I called her, since she's home every day. She has a key so she'll just come in."

"That will be nice," Robin said. "Thank you, Louise, for all the help, have a wonderful day. Did you fix your lunch?" Robin asked.

"Yes," Louise said. "I'm leaving now".

"Okay," Robin said. Louise left the room and suddenly the house seemed lifeless. Perhaps everyone is gone, she thought. There was nothing she needed at that time, so Robin, meditated until she dozed off to sleep. Robin slept soundly. Her body needed the rest to heal. The silence made a sound, which resonated throughout the house.

Robin was fully awake, when she realized someone was trying to enter the door. She could move a little and she tried to sit up, but the first attempt failed. She heard footsteps in the hallway, and they were unfamiliar. She pulled herself up, when the door to the bedroom opened and in walked her sister-in-law, Gerri.

"Robin, I talked with Louise earlier and she told me you needed help today and maybe tomorrow, so I stopped by. What can I do to make it easier for you?" she asked.

"Gerri, will you give me my medicine and a bottle of water?" Robin asked.

"Certainly," she said. "Please tell me that Russell didn't cause this, Robin?"

"Russell didn't cause it, Gerri, but he did make matters worse!"

Gerri brought in a bottle of water and opened it, put in a straw, gave Robin her medicine and took a seat. Robin knew Gerri wanted to discuss what transpired yesterday, but she didn't.

"So," Robin said. "Gerri if you know something about this situation, then feel free to speak."

"No, Robin," she said. "I only know what I was told. I know Russell has issues but I never thought in my wildest of imaginations, which everyone who knows me, knows they can be out there, that he would do this. That said, please know that everyone here is with you on this, and that's a first!"

"Have you felt like this before and if so, how long does it last?" she asked.

"I have and it lasts two to three days without stress," replied Robin.

"So, this too, shall pass, right, Robin?"

"Right," Robin said.

"First things first," Gerri stated. "Let's deal with the health issue and get you back to work, Robin."

"Okay," Robin said.

"You really need a change of scenery Robin."

"What did you have in mind, Gerri?" Robin asked.

"I thought you could come home with me for those three days, so that I can take care of my children, husband and you. What do you think, Robin?" she asked.

"I don't think that would be a good idea considering the weather and all," Robin continued, "I appreciate the offer, but it's too soon to go out. I must move forward, Gerri," Robin said.

"Okay, alright then and yes you will, I promise," Trust Gerri.

The next two days were challenging, but Robin struggled through. Russell obeyed his uncle and respected Robin's wishes as he remained in the front bedroom. It took five days for Robin to recover, but once she did, she tried to make up for the time she was incapacitated. Robin filled that time with church, work and developing her social skills with the illiterate. One month had passed since the incident. Russell was on the first floor talking with Uncle Book, when Robin came home from work. Uncle Book stopped Robin before she started upstairs. "Robin, come in for a moment, please, I would like to talk to you and Russell," he said.

"Is Russell inside?" she asked.

"Yes, he is," he answered. "Have a seat. There is no one else in the house, so we can be candid. Russell has something he wants to say; will you listen or do you want to wait?" he asked.

"I'll listen," she said.

"The floor is yours Russell," he said.

"Robin, I was very wrong for both cheating and bringing it to the house, will you think about forgiving me," he said.

"Think about it, are you serious, Russell?" she asked. "What did I say wrong?" he asked.

Uncle said, "Wait Russell. I don't think you understand."

"Robin, go upstairs, he isn't ready yet," Uncle Book urged.

Robin climbed the stairs and talking to herself, she said, "Russell has never been ready for anything!"

Robin turned around and went back down the stairs and knocked on Uncle Book's door. He opened it and said, "I hoped, please come in Robin."

She looked at Russell and asked, "What do you want to do, Russell have you played the field long enough, yet, are you ready to settle down with one woman or what?"

"I'm ready to settle down, Robin," repeated Russell.

"Since you have made that statement in the presence of uncle Book, then I'll make this statement. As of this day, we will give our marriage one last attempt, if you do anything to brake the marital vows, it's over," Robin spoke with authority.

"Okay," said Uncle Book. "Russell what do you say?" he asked.

"I agree," Russell replied. Uncle Book took their hands and bind them together with a cord. They thanked him and left. Robin was still naïve, instead of demanding he see a doctor for a comprehensive examination, she said nothing, but asked if he would spend that night in the front bedroom and put his things in place the following day. He said yes. The next morning as Robin was getting ready for work, there was a knock on the door and in walked Russell with his belongings.

Robin was sitting on the bed preparing to put on her pantyhose when Russell took them out of her hand and placed them on the dresser.

"I don't want to be late for work," she stated. "Let's wait until tonight," she said.

"Okay," he said, as he pulled her close to him. "We can do now and tonight," he resolved.

"Well, Russell, that sounds like fun but let your imagination keep you busy until tonight," she whispered as she leaned close to him and gave him a kiss. She tried to pull back, but Russell had his mind made up, it was happening this morning. He pushed her back on the bed, and raised her slip pulled down her panties and he was on top of her then inside her more forceful than ever before and she lost interest, as she lay there wishing he would finish and get off her and finally it was over. Robin got up went into the bathroom cleaned up and put on her clothes in there.

She walked to the door, put on her coat took her briefcase and purse and closed the door without saying goodbye. Robin was operating from a repetitive mode; she was in a state of shock but was functional. She didn't know how she made it through that day. She was waiting for the train to come but she dreaded going home, even though she thought her husband was at work. Psychologically, she had begun to feel powerless in her bedroom, loathing the sight of her bed. Something had to be done but what? Robin didn't hate Russell, she just did not like him, but most importantly, she did not know who she married. Neither of them married for the right reason and there were no signs of love, trust or respect. Void of all the fundamental factors of the ties that bind, Robin saw little chance or hope for a workable marriage so she looked for different signs for a way out.

She even filed for dissolution of marriage, but still, Robin endured the bedroom abuse. Russell slipped back into his pattern of staying out late, with little attention paid to Robin. However, she viewed his absence as a blessing; for those were times she did not have to submit to his perverse sexual experiences nor his verbal abuse. Robin was never a large girl. She was very attractive, with her large bedroom eyes and winning smile. She had an infectious personality that people found refreshing and positive, mixed with genuine candor. Robin had a small frame of one hundred-ten pounds soaking wet, she had a figure of thirty-five, twenty-two, thirty-five, slim hips and very slim legs. Russell was attracted to women who had large breast and full hips. He knew Robin did not meet his specs and he never let her forget it.

After intercourse, he would comment you're a little light on the butt side, maybe you can do something about that soon and if that didn't work to destroy her self-esteem, he would say, a man needs something he can hold on to. Only a dog wants a bone, he would say.

"Do I have to buy you cakes and pies to fatten you up or feed you every hour?"

"My brother saw you in the bed and asked me if I had trouble finding you next to me. Do you know how embarrassing that is?" he asked.

"About as embarrassing as this conversation," replied Robin. "You forget, Russell, I saw that woman up close and personal in all her nothingness and I was not impressed, at least you don't have to cover my face when you bed me!" she said as she closed the door.

"What did you say?" he asked.

Robin didn't dare say another word, she just left the building.

Robin had not seen Louise or Walter the previous day and the week-end was beginning, Robin thought it would be comforting to have a nice dinner and play bridge or any game, so she left a note in their door for Louise.

Chapter Four

A Different Type of Education

It was Friday, the beginning of the weekend approached, Robin returned home to an empty house. Not concerned, for that was often the case and as she saw the note was still in the door, she removed it thinking she would talk to them in person. She washed out the bath tub and turned on the water, went into the bedroom and picked out some clothing, a long red three- piece lounger with matching slippers, poured a diet Pepsi carried it into the bathroom with her bath oil, washed her hair and soaked in the smell of aromatic perfume as it filled the house. The water was turning cold, so she reached for the towel and dried off. She proceeded to lotion her body as the feel of satin enriched her skin. She dried her hair and the sound of the dryer drowned out all noises outside the room, she combed her hair and stepped into her lounger, zipping the skirt and top leaving the jacket open, she twirled around and for the first time in weeks, she felt beautiful she smiled at herself and put on lip gloss. As she placed the dirty clothes into the hamper, she heard the door open, thinking it was Louise, she hurried out to meet her to discuss the plans she had in mind, when she realized it was not Louise, but Russell. He had come home drunk. That was the very last thing Robin wanted in her life at that time. He told her to fix him a meal and bring it into the bedroom. Robin asked.

"Why can't you eat in the kitchen?"

"I don't want to," Russell said. "I'll be waiting in the bedroom," he repeated. "And I don't have all day," he said. Robin went into the kitchen and took out the cold lamb sandwiches she had made, added the lettuce and tomato with a touch of Dijon sliced them diagonally and placed them neatly on a plate with a slice of pickle to help cut the fat. She sliced the sweet potato pie and placed it on a plate, because he was on and off about the whip cream, she sat the can on the tray instead of adding it to the pie, in case it was one of his off days. She poured his favorite beverage into a glass, cut a slice of an orange and placed it on the rim, napkins and silverware in place; she took the tray into the bedroom only to find him sleep. Robin turned to take the tray back into the kitchen, when a voice said.

"Bring that damn tray back and sit what ass you have down next to me," Russell commanded.

Robin was reluctant, but she turned and took the tray in sat it on the table besides the bed, in that she did not like food crumbs to fall into the bed. She left the tray and walked toward the door to get her bottle of water she left.

"Didn't I tell you to sit down beside me? I don't want to tell you again," Russell roared.

Robin looked at him and asked, "May I get my bottle of water, Russell?"

"Hell no!" he said. "Come here now and lock that door." Robin locked the door and asked if he planned to eat his food or if he wanted her to put it up until he had an appetite? "I can do both, as I please," he said. Now come here," he reiterated. Robin sat down on the bed.

"Who told you to sit down?" he asked.

"You did," she said.

"Well, stand up and turn on the radio, it's on my station," he stated. Robin stood up and walked to the radio, turned it on and the music was loud.

"Is the music too loud?" Robin asked.

"It's just the way I like it," Russell responded. There was a song playing that was unknown to her. She looked at the carpet she had purchased to match the bedspread and thought she had better move the carpet and take the bedspread off before he ruined them. She moved towards the bed. Robin was afraid not knowing why but she knew who.

"Where are you going?" he asked.

"I think you'll be more comfortable if I take off the bedspread," she said.

"Don't move," he said. He got up pulled the bedspread off the bed and threw it across the room to the sofa. He took the new matching rug and threw it, too. Robin knew she was in trouble. She didn't move a muscle nor say a word. She just stood still as a statue. Russell sat back on the bed.

"What kind of sandwich is that?" he asked.

"Lamb," she uttered. "Remember not as boring as chicken nor chewy as roast beef."

"Good! Take off your clothes!" he said in a menacing tone. "Dance to the beat of the music." Robin had never learned to dance, but now she was doing a life- threatening command performance and she was concerned.

"Start with that skirt and remember the beat to the music," he said. Robin turned the skirt around to unbutton and unzip, when Russell yelled.

"That is not sexy, turn it back and do it from behind." Robin quickly turned the skirt around and unbuttoned it, unzipped it, from behind and slowly slid the skirt down. Russell laid back on the bed then.

"Now the top," he said. Robin unzipped her top and to the beat slipped out one arm then the next and the blouse fell to the floor. "The bra," he said. She unsnapped the bra and let it fall. "Panties," he said. "Now I want you to sit on that chair." Robin rolled down her panties and as they were falling, Russell said "throw them over here," she picked up the panties twirled them to the music and let go, they landed right on him, he picked them up and smelled them, she didn't know what to expect and was afraid to refuse to do more. He stood up and she noticed that his pants were already unzipped, he raised his legs and they fell to the floor. Robin was still standing awaiting instructions. He didn't have on underwear. Robin was nervous and moved. "Didn't I tell you to sit in the chair?" he said. She walked over to the chair and sat down. Russell said, "You are not sitting at your piano, lose that posture thing and open your legs wide,

I want to see it," he said. Robin followed his instructions, she opened her legs wide. "That isn't good enough," he said. "Move that chair closer to the sofa," she moved the chair.

"Now open those legs wide and take one leg and put it high on that sofa," Russell insisted. She did and it was so uncomfortable that she frowned.

"Wipe that frown from your face," he said. "Touch it, your clitoris," he said. Then a light flashed, he had taken a picture of her with his Polaroid. She quickly pulled her legs together and the bedspread off the sofa and wrapped it around her. She looked at him.

"Russell, what is this all about?" she asked.

"It is about to be your first real ass beating if you don't get back in position," he exclaimed. "I'm not playing with you, Robin, if I lose the mood because of your prudish attitude, you'll pay dearly, I promise you!"

Robin did not recognize him; the man on the bed was a stranger, not a perfect stranger. She looked for a way out, but the door was locked by her own hand.

"Okay, Robin, it's beginning to leave me, you better do something quick or the alternative will be worse than you can imagine," he said. She threw the bedspread down, posed in the chair with one foot on the sofa and her legs spread. She touched her vagina and began to play with her clitoris the music filled the room, but his voice was thunderous.

"Put some feeling into it," he cried. She tried but for the fear of it all, she could not relax. He came over with that camera and snapped and snapped picture after picture. "Oh, we have the house to ourselves, for now, Louise and Walter are gone for the weekend to give us alone time!"

"They didn't tell you, it was my surprise!" he uttered. Robin's heart dropped. She thought that was her sure way of escape knowing they would be home sometime; but now, she was at his mercy for the entire weekend. "Why did you have me to lock the door?" she asked.

"So, you would feel secure, thinking I didn't want anyone to disturb us by opening the door," he acknowledged.

"The family knows that we're honeymooning and pledged to respect our privacy," he stated,

Russell is a sadistic bastard who beats, rapes, abuses and misuses her, and he has obviously planned this for a long time, she thought. Whether Louise and Walter returns early or not, she had to obey the worthless piece of scum, but she was certain of one thing, he was not going to kill her this weekend.

"Where did they go?" she asked.

"To Vegas," he said. "Why?"

"I was just curious," Robin said.

"Well, get curious about this," he said, as he shook his penis in her face.

"What's next?" Robin asked. The music stopped.

He said, "You keep playing with that thing and get it all juicy for me." He walked over to the radio and found continuous music, reached in the cabinet and took out a bottle of Hennessey and two glasses, he poured some in one glass and added a little of his favorite beverage to it.

"You are not ready for yours yet," he sneered.

"I don't drink!" exclaimed Robin.

"You will," he said.

"This will be a weekend of firsts that you will never forget; I'm breaking you in, turning you out. You will never be a prude, again. Here's to you!" he proclaimed as he turned up his glass.

"Why are you so desperate to change me? Why not just leave me or let me go?" Robin asked. He did not answer her.

"Is it wet, yet?" he asked. She didn't answer him, but she kept playing. He walked up to her and with the back side of his hand, slapped her in the face.

"I must be careful, no visible scars," he said. He picked her up, "Light as a feather."

He complained, and carried her to the bed, turned her over and took a towel twisted it with wire inside.

"If you holler or scream you'll regret it," he warned. He hit her with that towel about ten times with each hit he said, "Learn to love it!"

He took her and tossed her on the floor spread her legs and penetrated her from behind, it was excruciatingly painful. "Learn to love it," he said. As she groaned from the pain! It was his new phrase, "Learn to love it!" He got up, left her in a fetal position on the floor groaning in pain.

"Learn to love it," he said. As he poured another drink, this time straight. He returned with another glass this one was for Robin. He filled it with straight Hennessey. "Open wide," he said.

"It will help dull the pain."

She didn't resist him. She just opened her mouth and swallowed. It was burning as it went down, she began to gag, it was stronger than any diet Pepsi she had. She began to feel woozy, her defenses and inhibitions were beginning to vanish. Russell gave her another drink and gave her more instructions too hideous to repeat. He took the camera and picture after picture, he took was with gloated satisfaction. He had his way with her every foul and demeaning way his perverse imagination could conjure, he explored with her. He gave her beer and alcohol, knowing she was ill. He poked and plowed every orifice she possessed and photographed it. She began to vomit, unaware she was in the world, and she hurdled and groaned until she was covered with vomit and only God knows what else. He unlocked the door and took her to the bathroom and placed her in the shallow water in the bathtub. He even raped her while she was in the bathtub, lingering between two worlds. Robin would never be the same in whichever world she remained.

She was hospitalized for five days, but the scars inside, would remain a lifetime. Russell's secret was safe. He claimed he found her in the house, alone, and she was unresponsive so he rushed her to the hospital rather than calling an ambulance. Of course, Robin was unable to neither confirm nor deny the information given.

That was a small example of what was to come for, Robin, a small-town girl, with a big heart was broken and threatened with physical consequences to rival the wildest imagination. It gave new meaning to the Italian word Omerta, to which the mafia gives as a code of silence.

Since Robin had no idea who she was dealing with, she had to watch what she said to everyone, for as Walter initially stated, "The people in this building can't keep anything to themselves."

Uncle Book came up to visit and asked how the honeymoon went?

"I just don't see the glow in you that I expected," he commented. "Is everything alright?" he asked.

She looked at him and said, "It will be alright, uncle Book." That answer is more than enough information:

"I will be watching," he said. Robin didn't know what information he received from her statement, but one thing was certain, she was determined to find an exit route, alive.

Robin checked his pockets and waited for him to make a mistake that she could use to escape his tyranny.

Russell informed her his hours had changed and he was working second shift, now. She changed her routine to accommodate him. One evening, her sister-in-law, Gerri came over and suggested that the three of them go out for a drink. Louise was game and she convinced Robin it would be a nice change of pace, rather than sitting in the house, so Robin agreed. They went to a lounge not far from the apartment, but not in walking distance. It was a nice place that catered to an older crowd; it was peaceful with the sounds of Louis Armstrong and Frank Sinatra. There were some Aretha Franklin and Freda Payne's song 'Band of Gold'. Both Louise and Gerri were much older than Robin, so it was understandable that they fit in more than she.

They chose a nice booth and placed the order for everyone. Robin went to the Jukebox and found a song by Aretha Franklin entitled 'Sad Song', she played that song five times and Louise and Gerri voiced their objections. Robin sat with that same Tom Collins the entire time.

"It's a shame to waste that amount of money on a drink," Gerri said. "Push it over here and I'll drink it."

"That drink is nothing but water now," Louise said. "We've had three drinks each and that's her original and only. It's time to go," they announced.

"So, what do you think about tonight and this place?" asked Gerri.

"It was a change, I must admit and I liked the fact that it was a mature crowd," Robin remarked.

"Would you like to return?" Louise asked.

"Yes, if I can play Sad Song?" Robin asked.

"We will plan for Friday night, get all dressed up and sing and dance to the oldies," Louise said.

"You, missy Robin, must loosen up and have a good time. You haven't been the same since we returned from Vegas," she said.

"We're going to restore those once bright lights in those eyes of yours Robin, we miss you," she confided.

"If you want to talk, we can do that too," Gerri said.

Robin smiled and said, "Thank you both, we should leave now." On the way home, they sang Fly Me to the Moon.

They arrived home and Gerri dropped them off. When they entered the door, they were met by both husbands.

"Girls night out," Walter said. "How was it Robin?"

"It was a nice place," she commented.

"Yes, she sat with the same drink the entire time we were there," Louise said. "We must take her out of the house more often and try to restore that light in her eyes. So, we are going out Friday night and will not be in early, any objections?"

Walter said, "Have fun ladies."

Russell did not say a word in their presence. He got up and went to the bedroom.

Robin excused herself and went to the bathroom cleaned up and put on her gown. She looked in the mirror and the person looking back bore a slight resemblance to the bright eyed young lady, she once knew, but the light that once lit up her eyes, was no longer lively, but was dim, dull and lifeless.

There was a time when it mattered to her how she looked in bed and out, now, she showed no interest in her appearance. She brushed her teeth and went to the bedroom.

"Good night, Russell," she said as she pulled back the covers and climbed in bed.

"Good night," he said.

Robin hugged the side of the bed she was on to avoid touching him. As she drifted off to sleep, she felt a hand on her body and froze. She remained still, hoping he will give up, but she knew better. Suddenly he reached for her and turned her around under the covers.

"What do you want?" she asked.

"I want you," he said. Robin didn't exchange words with him; she just followed his instructions and prayed that he didn't have the stamina to endure long. She knew he had other women and could not comprehend the need to control her, possess her and dominate her, when he had them. The duration of that romp lasted longer than she wanted, but not as times past and he had the audacity to slap her on the butt and say, "You're learning. Now go clean up."

"You first," she said. Hoping he would tire out and not come in the bathroom on her but complete his shower and go to sleep. He turned and pulled the covers off her and said, "Do as I say and keep the fresh mouth to yourself and I'll let you keep your teeth."

She got up and went back into the bathroom and cleaned up as soon as she finished, the door opened and it was Russell.

"I thought we could have a water session," he said. She almost asked if he was kidding when he took her gown and pulled it over her head, turned on the shower, stepped in and pulled her into the bathtub.

"Want a drink?" he asked.

"No thank you," she said. "I'm good."

"Not quite, but you're getting better with every act, I think I've accidentally made something I really like," he said. "I can't seem to get enough of you." After twenty minutes of torment that seemed like an hour, he had an orgasm.

"That was aces," he said. She sat down in the warm water and cried for a minute, then dried off and put on her gown, that had become wet in the fallout. She straightened up and returned to the bedroom. She opened the dresser drawer to get a dry gown.

"Step out of the one you have on and get in bed," he said. Russell was standing by the cabinet staring at her as she got in bed and she was praying he was done for the day. He poured a shot of Hennessey then another and got in bed. Robin had heard about men with a white liver, who seemed to be insatiable, but she never gave the thought much credence unto now, it was not normal for a man to be that sexually aggressive nonstop.

"So, you plan to go out on Friday without asking me?" he asked. "I suppose you met someone tonight you plan to meet that night, well, let's see how much of you will be left by Friday." As he pulled her naked body close to his, then under his. Jealousy, she thought. No, that must be a pretense. Her insides were so sore, she cried but he never stopped to ask her why, he just plowed her body like a horse a field. With every thrush, he told her how well he knew her and what she was thinking, what she would do before she knew what she would do. He controlled her mind, he said. Robin was listening as he tried to psyche her out. Then mercifully, he climaxed and rolled off her. She laid there hoping he would turn out the light so she could rest, but he didn't. She covered her head and tried to sleep, but Russell's words resounded over and over in her mind. The bed moved and she held her breath. Under the covers, she could not tell if the light was out, but she stayed under the covers. It wasn't that she didn't like sex; he had ruined it for her. What was meant for procreation and pleasure, Russell had distorted for her into a source of pain and torture. In excruciating pain, she felt detached during the act and prayed he would leave her alone the rest of the night.

Robin slept under the covers, in her own way she was creating a safety shield for herself. She could not utter a word of her abuse to anyone for fear of retribution, but under the covers she could be whomever she wanted, she was not helpless or weak, but strong. Robin did not know the game he was playing nor him, as it were, but she had to do something, before he tore her frail body in to and she had to think quickly, for Russell invaded her space and she was open prey.

Robin moved to get out of bed and go to the bathroom to get ready for work. The alarm did not go off and it was set to give ample time so the one who had to leave first for work would have the privacy needed to shower and dress. Since Robin was the last one to leave the house, she had an opportunity to remain in bed until Louise left. She looked at the clock and saw that she still had fifteen minutes before her bathroom time, but she heard the front door and knew Louise had just left. Robin reached for the alarm clock to make sure it did not go off, to keep from awaking Russell, when her arm was grabbed. She knew three things, Russell was bipolar, he had not left and the game was afoot.

"What time do you leave?" she asked.

"I go in late today," he replied. "I think we should finish what we started last night."

"Well," Robin said. "I have a new boss and there is a meeting this morning that I cannot miss. We can table it for tonight with a candlelight supper."

"I must work late, tonight," Russell stated. "Besides, if you were to stay home like any good wife, we would not have these issues."

Thinking it would not be wise to make him angry, Robin said, "Fine Russell, I can take fifteen minutes."

Russell was shocked; he looked forward to her predictability of rebellion and protests, until he was not prepared for her acceptance. Robin was trying to think ahead of him. She had placed her outfit on a hanger that she planned to wear, but because of his predictability, she went into the closet and took out an even nicer suit than the one she had. She took out different pantyhose and shoes also satin underwear and went into the bathroom. Robin was determined that she was going to turn her situation around. Russell wanted to play, she was not a game player, but it was time to either learn to play his game where he changed his rules at will, or make up her own game and rules.

Robin was taking a shower when the door to the bathroom opened and in walked Russell, in his birthday suit. He stepped into the shower and she handed him the soap and loofah. He took them and lathered the loofah and began to wash her and instructed her to do the same with him. She did remembering to remain silent regarding the time or he would deliberately prolong it. He told her to open her legs and he began to wash her and suddenly he stopped.

"You're going to be late, Robin," he said.
She looked him in the eye and asked, "What do you suggest we do, Russell?"

"We can wait until I come home tonight," he said.

Robin looked at him and said, "If you think that will be best, Russell."

He took a towel and handed it to Robin then took one for himself. He dried her off with his and she dried him off with her towel. He left her in the bathroom and returned to the bedroom. Relieved, Robin finished dressing and went into the bedroom to get jewelry and Russell said, "You look very nice in that suit. Are you sure you're going to work?"

"That is where I go in the mornings, Russell."

Robin finished dressing and her makeup was flawless, she put on her best jewelry and wore her good Sunday coat and lightly sprayed perfume.

"I have time, I can drive you to work this morning," he said.

"No, thanks honey, I don't want to get used to something that will not continue. You just rest and we have a date for tonight. What do you think?" as she slowly turned around.

"I think you look beautiful. I think I must have forgotten what a beautiful lady you are." Robin threw him a kiss and started up the hallway to the door and before she could open the door, Russell, had arrived at the door and said, "I think I can use a breath of fresh air, so if you do not mind, I will walk you to the train."

"I don't mind at all," Robin said. They walked out of the building together and all eyes were on them, he took her hand and bag and accompanied her to the train like any other husband would. It was so confusing. Robin went with the flow and so did everyone in eye view, but they were secretly wondering what Russell had planned.

Russell did everything correctly, he purchased her ticket, transfer and walked her up the stairs carrying her bags. He waited for the train, took her bag inside and seated her then kissed her on the jaw.

"Until our date tonight," he said and walked out the door, stood and waved until the train pulled off, and every woman on that train envied Robin, but little did they know they were only seeing the public persona of a bipolar, perhaps mentally unstable man, they only thought they would like to have.

Robin had a breakthrough that morning, she learned to flow not fight. Yet, she knew the situations would change, where it would be necessary to fight. Resistance seemed to fuel his fire and she had to learn not to feed the flames.

CHAPTER FIVE

Changes

It was an overall good day for Robin; everyone was surprised to see this Robin. Some of the older employees had seen her as an intelligent, vivacious and attractive woman but the new employees had never seen her as she was now and she had a twinkle in her eye of confidence. Robin would be the top subject around the water cooler this week and perhaps the next. Most people are stereotyped anyway, so are people who perform their duties with excellence, are deemed nerds and that is how they perceived Robin until that day the ugly duckling had turned into a beautiful swan. Robin's attire was simple yet elegant, fitted perfectly with just the right amount of leg showing, she was poised and confident with not one hair out of place and her work ethic was above reproach. Men and women stopped by her desk all day for one made up reason or another, but she handled everyone with a personal touch. When a person is noticed like that, the question comes to mind, how is he or she going to hold that interest? The theme for the office was 'there is something different about Robin!' Robin was the same delightfully confident woman she was before Russell abused her into believing she was not.

Robin left work with numerous offers of help and rides home, but she declined. She did as always and took the train home. However, where she once would not socialize or communicate with more than one person during the entire ride home, she chatted with everyone who spoke to her, she was coming out of her shell. Suffering in silence is a terrible way of life and Robin was a charter member of that club, with usually only one way out, borne of six; but Robin had another plan which did not include an oblong box or six people carrying it, she was striving to walk away, doing whatever it took. On her way home, Robin thought about the date night, although she considered the likelihood Russell may have last minute plans, she was going to prepare for their date, to lull him into a false since of control.

She arrived home and went to her chest where she kept her lovely gown sets she had not worn in such a long time. She chose the blue and white set. She laid it out on the bed, and fixed shrimp and a light fruit salad with strawberries, grapes and mango juice. She had salmon filet and a slice of German Chocolate Cake with two forks. Louise asked her what she had planned and Robin told her that tonight was to be their date night. She offered Louise and Walter a filet each and they accepted with chips, fruit salad and cake. They decided to take it to their room and have a date night of their own with wine and vowed not to come out until morning. The phone rang and Robin answered it, it was Russell informing her he would be home in twenty minutes.

Robin had everything under control, starting with the intimate meal in the bedroom, four movies two favorites of both, his silk blue pajamas (that matched her set) slippers and of course the bed and the tiger rug in the center of the floor. Robin thought of everything but she knew the order of which was out of her control.

Robin put on the robe to the gown set and put a flower behind her ear as she lay on the bed with her skin showing through the robe and the opening. The door to the room opened and in walked Russell with flowers already in a vase. She moved the flowers on the table and replaced them with his. She asked him if he wanted to change into his pajamas now or eat first, he said he would change and he would return shortly to eat a light meal. He took his pajamas and slippers and went into the bathroom. Robin checked to see if she left anything out. Everything was on the table and Robin placed his favorite movie in the player on pause. Russell entered the room looking refreshed, he pulled a chair for Robin and turned on the music very softly and took his seat. They ate and fed each other and began to talk to one another he Robin asked to dance with him on I've Been Loving You Too Long to Stop Now. It was interesting as they passed the strawberries to one another. Robin got up and went to bed, with her robe on while Russell took the bowls of fruit and food into the kitchen and refrigerated them and finally, he washed the dishes, a woman's job, he would say.

He re-entered the room and slightly increased the volume of music got into bed and held Robin.

She let down her guard to play the game and dozed off to sleep. Suddenly she opened her eyes to see him staring at her.

"What is wrong, Russell?" she asked.

"Nothing, I just like watching you sleep," he said. He bent down and kissed her and she stirred but didn't feel threatened at all. He kissed her neck and opened her robe and kissed her chest, breast so gently that it pierced her and was titillating, she moaned and turned towards him. He removed her robe and caressed her body. Robin was surprised that her body was responding in a positive manner to her husband's advances. Russell pulled off his pajamas top and bottom there was nothing between their bodies as passion began to build to the point of explosion. Robin was holding her legs and thighs together, but Russell did not behave improperly. There was no force only lust and desire mixed with heat and emotion and when it seemed as if nothing was going to happen, her legs relaxed and thighs went limp, game or not. It was as if a South wind blew and a whirlwind of lust filled the atmosphere. Robin was caught up in the whirlwind, fully under its' control but Russell never missed a beat or opportunity, the moment she caved in, he was inside of her and together they reached a crescendo and the cymbals sounded in unison! As they lay there basking in the afterglow, Robin was more confused than ever, as she rested in his arms not sure what to expect next or which Russell would reveal himself, she surrendered and fell asleep, uncertain what happened as the whirlwind dissipated.

The next morning was many things, excluding nothing. It is one thing to know what to expect because you know who you're involved with, but it is a totally different story when one has no idea with whom he or she is involved or what role an individual will choose to play for a day or even an hour. With Russell, that was the question. Robin lay in bed wondering why Russell was still trying to make a fool of her. No one makes a genuine hundred and eighty degrees turn in two or three days. While it is most unlikely, it is not impossible. However, likely, it was a con game at work or in play. Robin reflected on the night before and the contrast between the man she was with and the man who had been residing in the house with her for the past years were as different as night and day. But how does she prove it, she thought? Everyone wanted Russell to behave responsibly and respectfully; and this Russell, who was in the room with her at that very minute, was a keeper for them and for her to some degree. He made her feel more than pain and that is something the other Russell was incapable of achieving.

She turned with longing in her heart and eyes to be loved and looked at him, but he wasn't there. He must have gone to work early and did not want to awaken her, she thought. The door opened and in walked Russell with a tray of food.

"Good morning," she said. "And what do we have here?" she asked.

"I thought we could have breakfast in bed this morning after such a breathtaking date night," he said.

Robin said, "Absolutely, Russell, what a lovely gesture."

"Should we use the table or in bed?"

"Which do you prefer?" he asked.

"But I would prefer the bed, if it weren't for the syrup for the pancakes."

"The bed it is," Robin said.

"I'll hold the tray until you get in," she continued. Russell handed her the tray and got into bed and they had breakfast feeding one another. Russell took the tray and sat it on the table and returned to bed. The chemistry was so overwhelming that as soon as he entered the bed, Robin embraced him and this time she didn't hold her legs together, but let go. She felt his hands on her body, she felt his tongue on her breast, she felt the tingling sensation as he rubbed his body against hers, she felt him as his manhood rubbed her vagina, she felt her moisture flowing from inside and he lubricated himself with her juices, she felt as he penetrated her, she felt as the flood gates burst loose and spilled from them both they felt as the bed shook and bodies trembled, they felt. Robin gasped and he made an obscene sound and held her so tight he took her breath away.

"Woman, what are you doing to me?" he asked. Then he took her face in his hands and kissed her long and hard and they both fell back on the bed exhausted. The telephone rang and he said he would answer it; she remained in bed but listened to his side of the conversation. It was clear he was talking to Celia, who identified herself as Robin's new assistant and she told him there was a problem on the office floor and Robin was not to come in to work until next week, as all the offices will be closed until the fire department found the cause and the bosses decided where they will work. Robin asked for the phone, but Celia stated she was calling from an official phone so she had to call when she had a landline. Robin, unfamiliar with the name, Celia, called her office and received a message that the number she was calling has been disconnected, no further information is available. Robin then called the fire department and was informed that there was a four-alarm fire at the office and all personnel are asked to call the affiliate office for instructions beginning the following morning at six. Robin hung up and the phone rang, this time she answered and it was her boss, Mr. Marshall. He informed her that the offices were under water and fire and he was working on acquiring a temporary facility and if possible, he would like for her to be on call and come in as soon as he had secured a facility to get things organized for the following week. In the interim, she was to cancel all appointments scheduled for today through Monday and by Wednesday it should be business as usual was his goal. Robin agreed so he would messenger over contact information and to make a list of those, she recommended who were qualified to get the job done and to contact them after she received his instructions.

When Robin concluded her conversation, she informed Russell she would be working from home today, but is on call for tonight until a duplicate office is established.

"I may need a ride if it is late honey," Robin informed him.

"No problem," he said. "If I am off work or can get off. I am sure he will arrange transportation for you since he has given you so much responsibility, but whatever I can do. I have your back. Now, what must you do?"

"I must get my briefcase and cancel all appointments scheduled for today through Monday and draw a replica of the offices as they looked yesterday," she said.

"I'll help you with the latter," he said. "You make the calls and we'll do this. Here is your briefcase."

Robin had all the information she needed inside, she cancelled the appointments and put the clients on alert for rescheduling after Tuesday. Russell had been to her office three times and knew the layout, if he did the big sketches she could fill in the minute details. Working together, they accomplished everything in two hours. Robin had her reservations regarding Russell and every fiber of her being resounded he was not to be trusted, but she needed his help and since he was using her, she justified her actions with all is fair in love and war, though love making would be part of the spoils, this was war. He was the General and called the strategy for the games and he recognized his opportunity and would not fail to siege the moment.

Robin may not be ready for Russell and his games, but she was ready for her boss' call.

Chapter Six

The Work and Games Begin

People and puzzles have one thing in common; they must be handled to figure them out. Robin with the assistance of Russell had accomplished a monumental achievement for the work force, however, the major work was yet to begin and it is not a minor undertaking. Robin planned to take one step at a time and verify every step upon completion. She had a plan. Since part A was now complete, she knew how to fill the time waiting for her instructions for part B.

That done, she turned her attention back to her husband, she wanted to enjoy whatever it was they were doing and hopefully discover more about him, even if it were a game. Gamers may have hidden agendas or goals as to strengthen vocabulary, increase brain power, reveal I Q, and other tests but they were supposed to be fun too, she thought. Russell had game and it was obvious that his Game was afoot. He was in play mode.

"Russell, what would you like for lunch and dinner?" she asked.

"Don't worry about me and food," he answered. "Food I can get anywhere, just make time for me."

"You're on," she replied. "Why don't we lie down and relax a while?"

"I'm ahead of you, honey. The bathtub awaits with your bubble bath, let's go," he said.

The water was perfect; they splashed around in that bathtub and had a whale of a time. Russell helped her to feel and that was awesome, she said. They seemed to get closer, at least he wasn't verbally abusive to her as in the past nor was he physically abusive. Robin looked good and her confidence level was exceptional, she was radiant and it was obvious that Russell played an important part in her newly found role of ecstasy.

They dried off and put on their bath robes and went back to bed.

"Do you want a sandwich, honey?" she asked.

"Only if you're having one," he responded.

"Well, let's see what we have that is fast to work with," she replied.

"We had such a large breakfast and we haven't really worked it off, yet," Russell stated. "Let's work that off and then eat. I know what I want, how about you?"

"You like to play games, Russell, let's play show and tell," suggested Robin.

"You must teach me that game," he said.

She pulled off her robe and said, "Do what I do."

"Ok," he said. He took off his robe and they were so engrossed in their activities, that one would think they were the only two people in the world. He found a hot spot on her body and every time he touched it, she moaned and she found his hot spot, she was very busy with him until he began screaming.

"No, not yet, don't, stop, don't, stop" but she kept working it. And finally, he said, "Don't stop, don't stop are you ready?"

"Yes," she said. "Don't stop," and they yelled in sync as their bodies trembled and shook. They fell back on the bed and stayed in each other's arms for what seemed like forever. Robin wanted to convince herself that Russell had changed his mind about the needing something to hold on to and he was satisfied for the moment with her bones and her being light in bed. She believed she had him as much as he knew he had her. Robin had five orgasms that morning and she thought something was different about the last two, she suspected she became pregnant. She decided she would keep that information to herself, for if their marriage was going to work, she wanted it to be based on the two of them and not out of a sense of loyalty or duty to an unborn child. She told no one. She was even reconciled to the fact that she was being played by Russell, subconsciously, but she had the satisfaction of knowing that being played and knowing it, is so much different than being played and not knowing it. Robin was in the know.

Her boss called and said he found a secure building two blocks from the other building and he needed her to choose the personnel she wanted to work with, to meet at the office in two hours as well as repair, contractors and cleaning crew to come in later to have the building in shape by Monday.

"I'll leave it up to you, Robin, and I will meet you at the new location on Saturday evening, expecting everything to be complete. Have all the providers to bill the office and for those who must have money in advance, I will give you the business bank book and petty cash box," he said. "Everything will be delivered to you at the new site, you must sign. The keys will be separate and yours to keep make sure everything is locked up until the alarm is installed. Are we on the same page, can you handle it?"

"Yes sir," she said, "I can. What time Saturday?"

"Five P.M," he replied. "Thank you, Robin, we're depending on you."

Robin called all her staff and gave them instructions, specific titles and the address and time to be at work. She chose employees who would work even if it took to working around the clock to accomplish the jobs despite the length of time and they had two days to complete the building. Yes, it was a tall order, but the old Robin could never resist a true challenge and this was a challenge!

"Russell, I need to be there at four-thirty, if you can take me, I can pay cab fare. I just need a receipt," she said. "I can probably get an employee to take me home."

"I can help you Saturday until your boss arrives and check the details," said Russell. "And take you home when he let you go."

"Please tell Louise that girl's night out must be moved to Sunday or next Friday. I don't anticipate being home until Saturday evening. I have work clothes with me for three days and an overnight bag," Robin said.

Russell and Robin worked well together, he waited for the delivery service to bring the packages sent by her boss, opened the door, turned on the lights and looked for a command post for Robin to conduct business and to rest in with a door that locked for privacy. He went upstairs to see what was available for the boss and how many restrooms were available. Russell found the perfect space, so that was the first room to be completed. Everyone showed and assignments were given and performed. Everyone was clear regarding their positions and the work began. Russell took care of the interior design for the cubicles and the waiting room, after giving the information to the contractors, they were told where to go for the supplies while Robin called the stores, confirmed their orders and had all bills sent in duplicate, one by the worker contractor and the other by mail. Everyone worked diligently and Robin had food brought in only to the door no one other than those on staff was permitted inside, but Russell. Robin left when the painting began, until the building was aired out, she took a room in a motel, two blocks down, over-night. Robin left Russell in charge and he was well received since he knew his wife's vision, who better to carry it out. But she checked every two hours via phone. He had the cleaning crew to come in Saturday morning and it took them three and a half hours to complete the entire building and remove all debris. Russell picked Robin up as soon as the fumes ceased to be a threat. She contacted the florist who put the final touches on the interior and the dining area would be humming Tuesday morning with luncheon, donuts and coffee daily and a vending machine on two floors water cooler in waiting area and end of hall one on second floor in president's office was nicely furnished. Celia took care of time cards and receipts. They tallied all suppliers' bills and everyone agreed to wait for payment until Tuesday. Petty cash was not touched. All checks were to be written on Monday with payments on Tuesday. It was the largest project Robin had handled single handedly or as a team effort. She was very proud of the results.

The boss, Mr. Marshall, arrived at five PM on the dot. He used his own set of keys to make sure they worked on the doors. He entered the waiting room and voiced his approval, the floors were squeaky clean. The wall coloring was positive. He entered the work area and exclaimed we captured the essence of the old building and just brightened it up. He was very pleased. He checked the storage closet and approved the lavatories met with his approval both men's and woman's. He checked the supplies and was satisfied. He checked his office on the second floor and was elated, it wasn't luxurious but it was very nice and comfortable and efficient even a small refrigerator and stove, dishes in the apartment. He went through the bills and Robin asked to make out the checks for payment. The laborers were to be paid and the employees were to be paid. Robin asked if the employees could receive a bonus for their work above and beyond the call of duty. He insisted that they be paid triple time for three days instead of two and for a twenty-four-hour day. He also insisted that Russell receive the same pay as the other employees plus a substantial bonus for his design work. Robin stated he didn't have to do that, Russell considered it a privilege to help the business and his wife. Mr. Marshall stated that in that case, he insisted he be paid double the amount for the design and the salary.

"No Sir," stated Robin. Mr. Marshall sat down and took out his checkbook and wrote out a check for the amount he decided on and handed it to Russell and stated to him, that he could have a job with his company as Supervisor any time he wanted. Mr. Marshall turned to Robin and asked.

"Robin, will you write out his payroll check please?" he asked.

"Yes, sir," she said, as she took Russell's check out of his hand.

Mr. Marshall smiled.

"I wanted to tell you to put it in your pocket," he laughingly said.

Russell said, "We're one, so we're good, Mr. Marshall, thank you."

"Robin, will there be refreshments on Tuesday?" he asked.

"Yes, sir, there will, however, I wanted to ask you about the drinks."

"Four cases of champagne, six cases of wine and sparkling grape juice and club soda. The number is in the petty cash box and charge it to my account," he said.

"Anything else as a special request?" she asked.

"Have them deliver a leg of lamb, as usual and trimmings and you like diet Pepsi two cases and Seven up two cases," he said.

"Robin, will you come to my office as soon as you can?" "I must return," he said.

"Certainly, Mr. Marshall, I'll be there in three minutes," she replied. She dropped the hanky, picked up the keys to his office and went there. She knocked on the door.

"Come in Robin," he invited.

"These are the keys to your office, Mr. Marshall," Robin stated.

"I hope you kept a set?" he asked.

"No, I didn't keep a set, but there is an extra set," she replied.

"You keep them, Robin," he responded.

"I just wanted to thank you personally for proving to be as reliable as you are punctual and professional. You have no idea how much it means to me to know that we met the deadline with time to spare, and that is because of your organizational skills and gifts to choose the right people, as well as, to know how to talk, motivate and treat them. It is for these reasons that we want you to have this, and he handed her an envelope."

"Thank you," Robin said as she folded it and put it in her pocket.

"If it is not enough, please do not hesitate to let me know. Because, you are a woman of integrity, please keep the business checkbook and petty cash box, you are wise," he said.

"I would like to make you CFO and of course a raise comes with the title. Give me your answer Tuesday, I want you to rest Monday and pick an assistant for yourself someone you trust and is trainable."

"Yes, sir," she said.

"Luncheon will be Black Tie on Tuesday, no?" she asked.

"Yes, there will be important people present who said it couldn't be done; we hit the lottery on that fact alone, so go shopping and purchase the loveliest dress up out there, shoes and bag. My wife will send you gifts should she not be in attendance. Russell is invited and if you take your new assistant with you shopping, you have my permission, no limits," he said. "Now you go home with your husband, you two have been amazing. The security people should be arriving anytime now, here are the new codes and the keys to the alarm. You have your own code number, so stop and stay whenever you wish."

Marshall continued, "Until your husband joins us, he cannot enter the building alone, but he can with you. You have earned my trust, Robin, and my wife's. Go, now."

Robin calmly walked over to Mr. Marshall and hugged him.

"You are the second most wonderful man I have known, Mr. Marshall; it is an honor to know you and your wife please hug her for me. Thank you for your trust," Robin said passionately as she left the room in tears.

Robin placed water on her face and went to the first floor where everyone awaited. She looked for Celia and asked if she had left, and she was informed no one had left the building.

"Celia, where are you?" called Robin. "How is she getting home? Celia, are you ready to go?"

"Here, yes, seeking," said Celia finally.

"How many of my staff are still here, Celia?" Robin asked.

"Everyone," she replied.

"Okay, Celia, come with me and no one is to leave, yet," Robin took out the check book and wrote Celia's check and handed it to her. And finished the other nine and disbursed them.

"Russell, will you collect the supplier's invoices?" she asked. As he brought them to her, she wrote out the checks and distributed them with notations in the memo section, including the florist, which she planned to deliver. It was a good night for all the employees. Robin even wrote out the check for the alarm company and gave it to Mr. Marshall, as he entered the room. The check book was in order and balanced. Robin locked the desk and took the petty cash box, but asked Celia to get her coat for her, as she slid the boxes into the secret compartment.

When Celia returned, Robin pretended to lock the desk and she stood up and put on her coat. When she asked. "Celia where is your coat?"

"I didn't bring it," said Celia in a soft voice.

"Ok, Celia, come with me, please."

When they reached the bathroom, Robin said, "Celia, I really like you and I am so grateful you were here to help complete the work. I am perplexed that there is no information about you in the system. Now, I need you to be honest with me, do you work for the company?"

"No," she said. "I was in there trying to keep warm when you asked us to help."

"How did you arrive and what made you call me?" Robin asked.

"I took the shuttle you provided from the old building here with everyone else. Everything was destroyed in the fire and no one knew who worked where. I didn't mean to deceive anyone, I just got caught up and it was an opportunity for me to make some honest money so I took it," she said.

"Celia, I am so glad you came clean with me before someone used the information to ruin someone's life. I have hired you, but I need you to come out of the booth and I need to re-write the check whereby I will not be fired. Will you give me the check, please, but I need you to do it in front of one of the old employees or you can give it to Russell and you go into the kitchen and get that brown jacket I was wearing so you won't freeze, ok?"

"Ok, to everything, Robin," said Celia.

Robin took out another check and wrote void on the old check and the stub and wrote Celia another check with a base pay. When Celia received her check, she hugged her.

"This much?" Celia asked.

"Yes, this is a nice check, too, I know," repeated Robin. Robin called attention and everyone listened and she asked. "Those who were inside, how many of you watched Celia working these past days?" All hands went up. "Would you say she did her job?"

"Yes," shouted everyone.

"Why?" they asked.

"Well, it seems that the day I was placed over this project, was the day Celia came inside out of the cold weather. She needed a job and because she was standing with the workers, it was presumed that she worked for Mr. Marshall, so when I asked all of you to help fulfill our boss' mandate, she raised her hand to work, I gave her a check tonight based on the mean hourly salary, and she became quiet. I took her into the bathroom and talked with her and learned she didn't have a coat, which made no sense to me, so I asked her to tell me the truth and she agreed. I asked if she was an employee here and she said no. She was informed that since I hired her and she worked faithfully, she deserved to be paid but not the amount of the check she was holding. I asked her to return that check and she would receive another at the base hourly rate, she returned the check, it was marked void, and so was the stub and the check placed in the box and her true salary was written and given to her and she hugged me and I told her to hug Mr. Marshall, for it was because of his generosity of triple time that caused her to earn a nice check and she could take my brown coat to keep her warm but for a good worker, such as herself, she can work with me anytime. Now, let's help her get a room and a bed, and some clothes and give her a hand up because she's trying. I'm proud of Celia and I hope there is a way she can remain on here. Is it possible, Mr. Marshall?"

"Yes, Robin, you hired her now fill out her paper work and she's in," he said. "Hold her check until the paperwork is complete."

"Yes, sir," Robin said. "Can we pass a hat now and deduct it from the check, so she can have money for necessities? I will go with her and find a place and help her get settled so she can work."

"I have a spare room," Regina said. "She can travel to work with me and we can be company for each other, if she wants."

"Ok, Regina, you and I will have numerous discussions regarding you and Celia," Robin said. "And will bring warm clothes for you both."

Mr. Marshall spoke up and said, "Whatever Celia needs to remain a viable employee until the paperwork is processed, I am asking Russell to take care of that business with the four of you. Robin, you have the means, understand?"

"Yes, sir," she replied.

"Regina, please wait for us?" Robin asked.

"Robin, if you don't mind, you go home and Celia and I will see you at the opening and we can talk afterwards," Regina said.

"Ok, then Regina," replied Robin. "That will give you two an opportunity to become acquainted, perfect. Ok, everyone, remember Black Tie, dress to the nines and on time. Thanks again and enjoy."

She walked everyone to the door and asked, "Is there anyone else here who was not a member of the original staff?"

"The ledger will be checked before Tuesday," she said. "Goodnight all thanks again."

"You'll probably sleep late tomorrow," she said.

"No," replied Mr. Gulley. "My family and I will be in Sunday School in the morning everyone is welcome to attend."

Robin replied, "I will not commit to tomorrow, but I will say I will attend one Sunday with your family." A few more consented to do the same. It was a good night.

The Security people were finishing up and Russell said. "We should remain to help Mr. Marshall."

Robin agreed and they all closed together and watched Mr. Marshall drive away. There was no way they were going to leave him to lock up alone. They felt good as they left, so much had been revealed, it was a fresh start, new beginnings, as Russell helped her into the car.

Chapter Seven

The More Things Change, the More They Remain the Same.

Russell and Robin arrived home and they were so tired, they spoke briefly with Louise and Walter, who offered them dinner, but they begged to be excused and asked for a rain check, for they were so tired, that food and showers were not priorities, all they wanted to do was sleep. That alone was totally out of character for Russell but for games. They entered their room and Russell fell on the sofa while Robin, laid across the bed, both were fully clothed. The room was completely dark and silent as they drifted into the world of slumber.

It was the sunlight streaming into the window that caused Robin to stir. She still had on her coat. She looked and Russell was sprawled on the sofa with all his clothes on, as well. She didn't want to disturb him by getting up to go to the bathroom, so she just laid there and still exhausted, drifted off again. Robin heard a sound and looked at the clock, to her surprise; she had slept an extra two, much needed, hours. She looked over at the sofa and saw Russell standing up slowly taking off his clothes.

"Good afternoon, Robin," he said.

"Good afternoon, Russell," she replied.

"How long have you been up?" she asked.

"Not long," he replied. "I didn't want to awaken you. I know after all you've accomplished, you deserve to sleep until tomorrow, honey."

"Well," Robin said. "I did not do it alone, thank you for all your help."

"Can I get you anything? I just could not decide what you wanted to eat."

"Baked chicken for me, mashed potatoes and green beans, after my Pepsi," Robin said.

"Ok," he said. "Let me take that shower and I'll get that for you. What about dessert?"

"Jell-O sounds good to me. What do you want?" she asked.

"Chicken is fine for me, too," he said. "I'll get a large bucket, biscuits and sides."

"Do you want me to see what Louise and Walter are eating?"

"You can ask," she replied. "If they have not fixed anything, then ask if they would like chicken and double the order."

"Ok," he replied. "Maybe Walter will ride with me."

"Fine, I will get that Pepsi, shower and get dressed," she stated.

"Can I pick out what I want to see you in?" asked Russell.

"Sure," she said.

He went to the closet and pulled out this long red lounger with the dolman sleeves, deep V neck and a split in the front. He hung it up and said, "Just this and shoes."
"I'll start your bubble bath, when I finish my shower."

"Yes, dear, anything else?" she asked.

"No, but, I'll let them know that we are still tired and after we eat, will return to bed, okay?"

"Fine honey, we do need to discuss some things," she stated.

She must have dosed off again, for the door opened and Russell announced her bubble bath was hot and they were leaving, Louise was going, too.

"Good, sounds like a family affair, see you all soon, Russell."

Robin got up and took off her clothes, and went to the bathroom with the lounger. She hung up the lounger and got into the bath and soaked. The hot scented water felt so good that she just relaxed and enjoyed the peace. The water began to cool and she turned on the hot water to warm it up and it just did not work for her, so Robin got out pulled the plug and dried off, lotion on and put on the lounger. It was sexy. Robin brushed her hair and fixed her lip gloss, cleaned out the bath tub and returned to the bedroom. After spraying a little perfume, she went into the kitchen got the tray and napkins, she was not a fan of the plastic utensils that usually come with take out, so she put real silverware on the napkins and two wine glasses. She did not mind the plates, but put the vase with the rose on the tray. She sat up and turned on the soft playing music of Otis Redding, 'Try a Little Tenderness', was playing and pulled out her briefcase. Robin was looking up the personnel files. She confirmed everyone who worked with them the last two days were employees. She also acquainted herself with the names of other employees, not frequently seen. She was satisfied when the door opened and Russell and company had returned.

Louise and Walter opened the door and spoke and said they were going to their room and have another date day and night, Robin laughed and asked, "So you two, liked that, right?"

Walter answered, "Yes ma'am, it was good and if you have any more ideas please share."

"Yes," Louise said. "We'll join you youngsters."

They all laughed and Robin said, "Count on it!" She heard them open the cabinet and click their wine glasses and she thought this house is going to rock tonight.

"Are you listening to music or TV?" asked Russell.

"Music" Louise said. "We may even dance some," she said.

"That is great," they replied.

"We're too tired," said Russell.

"Ok," Walter said. "Sure, you are!"

He laughed and said, "This chicken smells delicious."

Robin asked if Russell wanted her to fix their plates. "No," he said. "I see your briefcase is out, so you're working. Just tell me what you want."

"A Pepsi, breast, mashed potatoes, gravy and green beans and biscuit," she said. He poured her a glass of wine and asked if she wanted it.

She said, "Yes." She drank the glass and handed it back to him. Russell filled it almost to the top. Robin began to drink and he interrupted her and asked if she would like her plate and she said she was getting up to sit at the table. Robin got up and sat down at the table; they said grace and began to eat. Russell went to the kitchen and returned with strawberries and another bottle of wine. Robin ate the chicken and a few green beans; she skipped the mashed potatoes and gravy. Russell ate chicken and drank wine, but wine was never the drink to impair him, so Robin did not worry. She watched him eat four pieces of chicken then he laid down on the bed and Robin got up and laid down beside him.

Robin asked if he wanted to talk about their plans and he said, "Absolutely."

"What do you want to do, Robin?" he asked.

"I thought we could take the money we made and put it down on a place of our own and since we both have good credit, we could find a great place with room for children," she said.

"Children," he said. "Maybe we could wait on that."

Robin didn't say anything.

She asked him what he wanted to do.

He said, "We could open a joint savings account and buy a new car and continue to save for another year, then we will have enough money to build a home and take a vacation or two."

Robin said, "That sounds like a plan, but our car is only two years old. We can wait a few more years before purchasing another car."

"With what I cleared and you, we don't know how much you made yet, but I'm sure it is twice what I made," he said. "We could do whatever we want. Besides, you're getting a large raise and I can work there when I'm available, so there are no limits."

Robin didn't say a word on that subject; (she knew game was on) she said, "Pour me a glass, honey, while I go to the bathroom, please."

"Ok," he said. Robin picked up her dirty clothes and took them into the bathroom. She locked the door and looked in her pocket and pulled the check out, opened it up and read it and sat down on the commode. Robin was in shock, she had no idea what she had in her pocket. She placed that check into her jacket and put it on a hanger and hung it in the hall closet, and the dirty clothes in the hamper. She thought about the things he wanted to do and she knew she had to get him out of the house for a short time. He had to work tomorrow, but because of the amount of money involved, he probably wanted to go to the bank with her. The only two people who knew about that check were Mr. Marshall and her, so she decided not to reveal it, but open a separate account with it.

Robin left the bathroom and returned to the bedroom. She drank the glass of wine and asked Russell what time he was to be at work?

He said, "I thought I would go to the bank with you tomorrow and take off."

"Ok," she said.

"How much wine do we have left?" Robin asked.

"That's it on the wine," he said. "I really didn't expect you to drink so I only bought two bottles. We have plenty of hard liquor."

"Do you want to try a mixed drink or a straight shot?" he asked.

"No," she said. "I don't want to mix drinks."

"I'm easy," he said. "I'll go get a few more bottles and a couple of chardonnay."

"That would be nice, if you really don't mind, Russell."

"Anything for you," he picked up his keys and said be right back, honey and leaned over and kissed her.

Robin said, "Good, I can hardly wait, so, hurry back."

When she heard the door close, she was up and got the coat from the closet and took out the check. She went back to the bedroom and took out the checks she had written and the blank check for herself and filled it in, recorded it in the book and put it in her purse. It was a nice check and she decided to go with that and hold on to the other check until she was alone to deposit. Robin made sure that her check was with the two checks that were made out to Russell and put them in her purse. She was ready then. She sat on the bed and waited for Russell to return. Robin didn't have to wait long, shortly thereafter, the door opened and he walked in carrying a box a case of wine and set two bottles out and placed the others in wine racks.

"What's your pleasure," he asked. "Red or white?"

"Red," she said. "I'm a little hungry and thirsty."

"We can take care of that," he said as he handed her a plate with two pieces of chicken breast and a glass full of red wine. He was going to make sure Robin drank that wine. Trying not to raise his antenna, she did exactly what he wanted. She drank a whole bottle and ate the sliced chicken. She laid down and he took off his clothes and laid down. Robin was full, but she knew what he expected of her. She was glad she was off the next day.

The Pinot Noir had made Robin very mellow, she lay there on the bed and thought how she would handle the situation and decided to let him handle it, that is what he liked, control. She brought the situation on herself so whatever he did, she was prepared. Robin stated they should try to get up early and go to the bank, in case she was needed for some reason the following day. Russell agreed, then he asked if she wanted another drink, Robin declined. He looked at her and asked if she felt frisky and Robin asked,

"Do you think you can make feel frisky, Russell?"

"Without a doubt," he answered. He pulled her to him and began to kiss her. He stroked her hair and body caressing it in the most intimate way. He touched her and her body was ready, he could tell by the fluid flowing from her vagina and how wet she was.

"That's the way I like it," he said. "I want you to ask me to penetrate you. I will not until you ask me. So, ask."

Russell took his finger and rubbed her and she moaned but did not ask. He stuck his penis at the vaginal canal and teased her, she moaned again, but she did not ask him. He rubbed against her body, but she still didn't ask, her body began to cramp and ached, but she still didn't ask, he stuck his tongue in her ear with an in and out motion and she still didn't ask, after holding it between her legs and stirring himself to the point of explosion, she still didn't ask.

"What's it going to take for you to grab it and push it in?" he asked.

She didn't say a word, she just endured, knowing that what she was feeling, he had to be feeling as well. Russell began to groan and moan, his movement was increasing and his penis was throbbing with anticipation, he stopped asking her and began to penetrate.

She said, "Not yet, Russell. You said you wanted me to ask. Well, wait and let me ask."

He groaned and said, "I don't know what you're made of, but I can't wait any longer, ask me please, Robin, ask now."

Robin just moaned and he thrust his penis into her vagina and with rapid motion, he asked her now, and went deeper, now, he asked and went deeper until finally he was all the way in and gooey juices were everywhere.

He said, "Talk to me. Robin just once say now."

She didn't but her body began to move with his and he was talking to her body and not to her. He put her breast in his mouth and she moaned, now, he slowed down and she said, "Now Russell."

He hit the headboard of the bed and yelled and both exploded in rapture as he blew a load and she pulled away.

He yelled, "No, let me back in."

She opened and he hollered, "Damn you're driving me crazy!"

And she yelled and he thrust and thrust until she screamed, "That's it right there, Russell, right there. Oh," she yelled and he joined her on the last one and collapsed on top of her.

"That was wonderful," she uttered.

"That was better than wonderful, it was the bomb," he said. "Let's try that again."

"Let me catch my breath," she whispered.

Russell got up and poured her another drink and one for himself and asked her if she could move?

"Yes," she said. "Why?"

"I want to try something," he said.

"What?" she asked.

"Drink up," he said. "And I'll show you."

She drank the wine and was warm inside and she asked, "Russell, that wine tasted different, did you put something in it?"

"I put a shot in it, but it won't hurt, just totally mellow you out," he said.

"I put two shots in mine," he said.

"Yes, but you're used to it and I don't like to mix drinks," she continued.

"Tuesday is important. I need to be at my best, don't want you to mess me up, Russell, I'm warning you."

"I won't," he said. "Not with alcohol, but I plan to drive you out of your mind. You must tell me when you want it, though, deal?"

"We'll see," she said. "Russell, I need to ask you something."

"What?" he asked.

"Have you noticed how many times you have sex, in a day?" she asked.

"What about it?" he asked.

"That's what I want you to tell me, how can you do that are you taking something or what?"

"No," he said. "I'm not taking anything to cause an erection, it's just in my blood. My father was like that, too, so it must come from his genes."

"It's unusual to have that many erections," she stated.

"A lot of women would gladly change places with you," he said.

"Ok," she said. "What do you want me to see?"

"It's more like experience than see. We've never tried it before, maybe tonight is the night," he said.

"Does it hurt?" she asked.

"You tell me afterwards and if you don't like it, we won't do it again."

"You promise?" she said.

"Yes, I promise," he said. "Drink up."

She drank the wine and she was woozy and "what?" she asked.

"Do you want another?" he asked.

"Should I need another?" she asked. "Yes, one more. Just one more."

He handed her the drink and she could tell it had more alcohol than wine.

Russell said, "Drink it down, baby, like this." And he drank his in one gulp. Robin drank hers down and it hit her. She was so warm inside and he started kissing her and she kissed him back. "Let's see if you can get as juicy as you were earlier."

He grabbed her around the waist and kissed her navel and she moaned.

He kissed her thighs and between the thighs and Robin began to moan more. He kissed her between the legs and she groaned.

His erection became obvious and he laid it at the opening of her vagina and began to rub her clitoris with it, as she twisted and turned and moaned, "Do you want it?" he asked.

She didn't answer, so he laid there and put her breast in his mouth and sucked them.

He took his tongue and licked her skin past the navel and headed south. His mouth was there on her and in her his tongue was circling inside of her and she was moving trying to get away. He grabbed her hips and drew her close to him as he opened his mouth and his whole tongue went in and she squirmed. "Oh," she yelled. "That's good."

He continued and she moved all over the bed, moaning and whimpering and he kept going until she said, "Ok, now, please, now."

He pulled away and penetrated her and asked, "Is this what you want? Say yes."

"Yes," she said. He thrust and she moaned more, he switched and his body trembled.

He said, "Cum, for me, cum let those juices run. And don't hold back."

His mouth was in her again as she pushed herself towards his face, she was begging now, Russell,

"Now that's it baby," he said. "Call daddy".

Robin couldn't believe she was crying out for him but she was. He turned over and from behind, he screwed her until he slid out then he turned her back over and then it happened she yelled, "Stop, I can't take it, stop,"

He said, "Yes, you can relax and enjoy this; I'm going to make you beg me."

He pulled out and put his fingers inside her and she started to move to the top of the bed, he grabbed her hips and in a circular motion, he moved them and she screamed now, he climbed back on and in and suddenly he said, "I can't hold it, I'm going to cum. Oh, oh, oh," he cried and lifted her behind with both hands and it was over. He lay there and said, "I'm watching you!"

"Well," he said. "Did you or didn't you like it?"

She said she liked it.

"I got you now," he said. They went to sleep in each other's arms. She wondered if this was another form of abuse or what, she enjoyed it but wondered why the alcohol was necessary if it was for pleasure. The more things change, the more they remain the same. Tomorrow is another day.

Chapter Eight

Wake Up Call

Robin awoke as it was her routine at five o'clock, and just laid there thinking about all that had transpired the past three days, and was troubled with questions and remorse. Questions regarding, the marriage and Russell's intentions. Despite the seemingly softness and appeal that had recently surfaced between Robin and Russell, the underlying facts stand in question. What made him do a hundred eighty degrees turn in one day? The mental review of her physical assets, she had not grown in breast or hip size, her butt had not taken on a Kim Kardashian fullness and her abdomen was still flat as a pancake, so what caused the pause in verbal abuse? Why would Russell not want children, if he wanted or anticipated the marriage was going to last? Why not want a place of their own, since they could afford it? Why would purchasing a new car be a priority over a home, when the current car was only two years old? Why would he lose a day's pay to go to the bank and celebrate, when the major celebration was scheduled for the following day? Was there a way to safe guard the money against Russell withdrawing the entire balance? Why would having her under sexual control be an over- riding necessity for Russell?

Russell was unaware that Robin had a savings account and she wanted it to remain a secret, so all that was required, was for her to deposit her check and forget it. However, their joint account was an entirely different matter. Robin decided to save her requests regarding the joint savings account to the time of deposit. If only she had the answers to her questions; then she would have enough information to form an intelligent opinion and decision whether to just let him deposit his checks in an account of his own, or to simply state separate accounts would be better until they solidify their marriage and both were on the same page.

Robin opened her eyes and looked around the large room and saw the disarray and was moved to clean up before getting dressed. She got up and didn't make any noise but quietly put on her slippers and a robe and began to dust the room and tidy up the room. She moved Russell's pant and shirt and a card fell out of his shirt pocket. Robin picked it up and looked at it, then stuck it into her robe pocket as she continued to clean up. She neatly placed his shoes under the shoe rack, picked out a pair of slacks, shirt and sweater, and matching socks for Russell. Since this was her day off, she picked a matching outfit for herself except for the socks. She decided not to vacuum to keep from awaking Russell. She went into the bathroom, took out the card she picked up and was surprised to discover that the card belonged to a psychic, she showered and dressed thinking about the card and how no one knows anyone. For the life of all that is holy, she could not figure out who or what this man was nor what he was planning, but he had her attention, it was becoming interesting.

He had an appointment scheduled for tonight, per the notation on the card. She thought, it should be interesting to see how he works it, to explain his absence to attend the appointment he had scheduled with his new advisor. Robin thought of having him followed and it was an option, but she needed to know what the discussion or subject matter was between Russell and his advisor/seer, and the only way to achieve that was to be in the room, have a microphone planted in the room, or pay the seer/advisor off. The major problem with the latter was a question of integrity.

If the person was on the level, the real McCoy, as it were, he or she could not be bought nor consider betraying the gift. However, a fake would; if the price was high enough or they had a relationship, a love interest.

Robin had her job cut out for her. She considered sharing the information with one of his sisters to solicit help, but thought about the tenuous position she would be placing her in and decided against it. She did, however, begin to ask questions regarding the psychic and her reputation.

Robin finished her chores, dressed and went to the kitchen for cranberry juice and a slice of toast, so she doubled everything incase Russell wanted a light breakfast snack. She put on the coffee for him, as well. While sitting there in the kitchen, she took out the checks and filled out the deposit slips and placed the card back into Russell's shirt pocket and returned to the kitchen.

"Good morning Mrs. Watson!"

Robin turned to see Russell and stated, "Good morning, Mr. Watson! I hope you had a very pleasant and restful sleep."

"I certainly did," he replied in like manner and adding. "You must have, as well, since you've been up so long and have done so much. I fixed the bed and thanks for laying out my clothes that was a nice touch."

Robin replied, "You're welcome, sir. There is toast, coffee and juice if you feel so inclined to have a bite."

"I'm inclined," he said.

"However, I feel like a few eggs, as well," he added.

Robin went to the refrigerator and took out the eggs, two additional slices of bread, the butter and vegetables and cheese and made an omelet, more toast and poured coffee and juice and he sat down and heartily ate.

"So, what bank are we going to?" he asked.

"Well, we can either go to our bank and deposit into our joint savings or if you want to open a separate account, we can do that, but either way, there must be rules," she insisted.

"What kind of rules?" he asked.

"We can discuss them now," she softly stated.

"Let's hear the rules," he said.

"Because so much is happening in the world today, it would be good to have a maximum or daily limit for withdrawals," she said. "What do you think?"

"That sounds good," he said. "What do you think a thousand- dollar daily limit, for three consecutive days, without notifying the other?"

"That sounds agreeable," she replied. (As she thought to herself, who does that without an agenda?)

"For special or emergency withdrawals, let's agree on five thousand on savings," Russell said.

(Stop the Stupidity, she thought)

"Well, honey, we really don't need the savings stipulation since we have the checking agreement. Savings should not be touched, it's savings. Do you want to do a joint checking or separate?" she asked.

He said, "Separate checking."

Robin tore up the joint deposit slip and pulled out the separate savings and checking.

"I'm making out the slips where half of the check is placed in both savings and checking?"

"That's good," Russell eagerly stated.

So, that was completed as planned.

"Russell, would you like to carry your checks or leave them in the briefcase?" she asked.

"Briefcase," he said. "But I will be making a withdrawal from checking at the bank."

Robin replied, "That is fine, Russell." (Queries increased.)

"We can leave after the dishes are washed," he said. Robin left him in the kitchen and went to the bedroom thinking to herself; she was glad he decided to do separate checking, that way she did not have to give an account to him for the decisions she would make and vice versa. She thought it would be interesting to see who fails to adhere to the checking account rules first and under what circumstances.

She picked up her briefcase and scarf and headed up the hallway as he finished the dishes.

"Don't forget to cut off the coffee pot, Russell."

"Thanks for the reminder," he said. "That's done; meet you in a second, Robin."

He was at the door helping her put on her coat and she wanted to say something to him, but she remained silent.

"Have you decided to take the job you were offered or what?" asked Russell.

"I haven't decided, yet," she said. "But of course, you will be second or third to know."

"I'll remember that," he said. His comment and questions bothered her briefly but she tossed it aside to focus on completing all her chores for the celebration the following day and the perfect gown and shoes.

She also wanted to touch base with Celia and Regina to make sure they had their attire.

"Russell, I need to contact Celia and Regina to make sure they have their attire, what do you suggest?" she asked.

"Robin, call and see if they are ready to go shopping and inform them we will be there within the hour," Russell stated.

Robin followed Russell's advice and called Regina, who stated they would be ready and waiting. They had been to the bank and were paying the bills and Celia was sealing the envelopes and putting on the last stamp. They gathered their belongings and waited by the door. "How much can we spend on the dress code?" asked Celia.

"Don't worry about it, Celia, we'll figure it out."

"Regina, thank you again for taking me in, you've made me feel as if I am a part of something and have family, a sister," said Celia.

Regina said, "Thank you, Celia, I am very hopeful for us. Let's plan to enjoy the celebration. They are here. Remind me to have duplicate keys made, Celia please."

Regina locked up and they went to the car.

Russell got out and helped them into the back seat.

"Good to see you both," Robin spoke. "Have you given any thought to the color and kind of gown you want to wear?"

"I have an idea that black or blue would be the perfect colors and matching shoes, but beyond that, I am puzzled," Regina stated.

"We're going to the Mall now, so we will find everything we need at this exclusive shop, Juliette recommended," Robin said.

Russell pulled up to the Mall and they were all helped and entered the building going to the high-end stores to browse, while Russell, went to do his thing. If he finished first, which was highly likely, he would meet them after he paged them twice. They had three gowns to locate, fit and purchase along with accessories, so they were prepared to stay awhile.

The ladies asked the sales assistant to show them three gowns in their sizes in the colors black and blue and she obliged. They had the entire area to themselves with no rushing spirits to break their concentration. Robin saw two gowns to her liking for both Regina and Celia and asked them to try them on they did and loved them. They looked at the price and Celia asked.

"Regina, can we afford them?"

"We can afford one, but we will be alright, you'll have a check soon," she said.

"Do you like the gowns?" Robin asked.

"We love the gowns!" they replied.

"Well find your accessories," suggested Robin.

The assistant said she would help them, as she led them away.

Meanwhile, Robin spotted a dress that was deemed to impress and went to try it on. Everything about the gown embraced her essence, it was a keeper. Robin smiled and thought, how blessed she was to have found the perfect gown, now all she needed were the matching accessories. The head buyer was on the floor and asked if he could be of assistance and she explained and showed him the gown and he went to the other side of the room and returned with several items from jewelry to shoes and hose, he never asked a question regarding size, style or color preference, he just utilized his expertise and appeared with the results

He made suggestions and explained why, as she inquired. He even made a call and arranged for all three to have a facial and hair styled. They were finishing their manicures when they heard the first page and knew Russell had finished shopping. Robin asked one personal assistant to find the man who was paging them and explain they needed fifteen minutes. She agreed and Regina and Celia chose Ruby red nail polish but Robin chose a demure flattering classy color.

During check out, both Regina and Celia looked nervous.

"How much did you set aside for this?" Robin asked. "How much is it?" they asked.

Robin couldn't answer because they were still getting the merchandise ready to be boxed and adding separately, so that everyone received the correct purchases.

Regina was the first to be checked out and she spent a total of twenty-two hundred and change, Celia's total was twenty-one hundred and change and Robin's total was twenty-seven hundred and change. Regina handed the lady a charge card for their purchases and Robin asked if she could have copies of the receipts and they complied. Robin gave them the charge card Mr. Marshall gave her and added a tip for everyone who helped. Robin wrote the names on the receipts and asked for an envelope which was done. Robin had everything she needed and told the women how lovely they looked with their new hairstyles, facials, makeup and manicures. Regina stated she had never had one done by someone else and Celia said she had never had a facial.

"I will submit these receipts and whatever the refund, you will receive it by the end of the week, is that okay, ladies?" Robin asked.

"Yes, they said, we expected to pay for the clothes but the extra's we didn't factor in," Regina said.

"Don't get your hair wet," Robin said. "Sleep pretty with a silk cloth bonnet."

"We'll get them now," Robin said. She purchased three and gave them two.

The store provided carryout service to the car and Russell was loaded down, too. Robin asked him to bring the car around and he said,

"They have it out front."

"Let's go, ladies and gent," Robin said. "Unless there is something else you need before we go, speak up."

"I should make a call," she was concerned about the large bill that Regina charged, so she wanted to see what her boss suggested. She called Mr. Marshall and explained the situation to him and he instructed Robin to asked to have the store remove the charges from Regina's card and everything charged to his card except for a thousand dollars. Robin hung up and asked Regina for her charge card, she took the card to the cashier and asked to speak to the manager. He came out and Robin asked to speak with him privately, after she explained, he followed her instructions and cancelled the transactions, issued new receipts and charged Regina's card as instructed and returned both cards. She wrote cancelled on Regina and Celia receipts and the duplicates, asked for the originals and handed Regina both her card and new receipt.

"There must be a mistake!" Regina exclaimed.

"No, Mr. Marshall insisted we handle it this way, until Celia receives her first check," Robin stated.

They both hugged Robin. "Does that offer still stand to get what we need now?" Regina asked.

"Absolutely, depending on what it is," Robin said. "Lotion, lipstick, makeup and night cream."

"Well you can handle that, Regina, right?" she asked.

"Yes, and we can get them right over there," Regina said.

Robin picked up night cream for herself, as well. They spent a total of three and a half hours in the Mall and it was time to go. They hurried out to the car and when they were settled and buckled in their seats, they began to reflect over the last hours.

Celia stated she had never purchased anything from that store nor thought she would ever have an opportunity to; it was so far out of her life range. She was in awe that not only did she purchase items to wear but she had a spa like experience there, as well. "I am going to work so hard and hopefully, I can shop there at least once a year," said Celia.

"I admit I never shop at high -end stores, such as that, because I've never felt the need to pay the extraordinary prices they charge," Regina said. "But the personal experience of the day was so memorable, that I will return for a beauty treatment and perhaps a full spa experience with Celia, in a few months."

She looked at Celia and said, "My treat, since we're in this together; we'll not only share the household bills, but the joys of life as well!"

The time passed so rapidly, that within minutes; they were at Regina's house.

"Do you have food fixed?" asked Russell.

"No, we were going to grab a burger later somewhere," Regina said.

"Well," said Russell, we just passed a burger place, I'll turn around."

"Do you want anything, Robin?" he asked.

"Yes, fries and grilled chicken or fish filet," she said.

"Burgers for all?" he asked.

"Yes, and fries with coke," they said.

Russell placed the orders and asked to bag them separately and gave them to the ladies. "I got you three burgers a piece and large fries," he said. "With apple pie."

"Thank you," they echoed.

"You're welcome," he replied.

"By the way, you ladies look ravishing!" he said.

"Oh," they said. "You're too kind."

Russell took them home and helped carry their packages inside and waited for them to lock up before leaving.

Robin was hungry and decided to eat a piece of chicken and a few fries and drank a Pepsi. They were close to home.

"Robin, do you want more wine?" he asked.

"I want sleep, honey, sleep," Robin said.

Russell still pulled over and went into the store and returned with a case of wine, placed it in the back seat and drove home.

"Robin," he asked. "Did you see my checking balance?"

"No," she said. "What is it?"

"It's more than I have ever put aside!" he emphasized.

"Good," she said. "I am so happy for you."

"Well, we have much more than that in our savings," he said.

Robin did not say a word. It's the money, she thought, he wants all the money. That's two answers she didn't have when she awoke that morning.

Chapter Nine

Dealing with Reality

Robin was looking for answers and she found two. So, she decided to see what the night would bring. Robin was tired but she had to hang up the gown, bonnet her hair, then lie down and think. Russell was busy admiring his clothes and looking at his bank balance, while Robin was praying that balance he was boasting about, would last him for longer than two months.

She was not going to replenish it when he spends his entire checking and start on the joint savings, so, Robin decided to work on their savings while he worked on the checking.

The rule is a thousand a day withdrawal, so she would begin the following day, only taking what was hers.

She wondered how and when he planned to make his move on her checking account, from what he had said earlier, it was clear that he wanted control over her money.

The thought of how much money he had in his possession and the anticipated savings were more than Russell could handle. He has had money before, but this was making him feel and behave differently, as it burned a hole in his pocket. Robin lay there waiting for him to make his move, then finally, Russell made his announcement.

"Robin, I must go out for a while to take care of some business. Since I took off this morning, I was informed I was placed on the graveyard shift tonight and if I don't go in, I could lose my job," he announced.

"I say go, Russell, it is job related."

"That's it, to show up for work," he replied.

"Is there anything I can do to help you get ready?" she asked.

"No, I'll take a few pieces of that chicken I bought earlier and a soda that will be enough for my lunch."

"Perhaps there is a slice of that cake left, I'll take a slice of that, as well," he said.

Robin just laid there in waiting.

"I'll fix that lunch for you," she offered.

"No, honey, stay in bed and rest, you need all the strength you can muster for tomorrow and by the way, I'll be there for the event and to hear your decision although I maybe a little late, depending on who relieves me and the time."

"That's fine, transportation has been arranged for us," she said.

"I'll be leaving early, to see what last minute changes are needed and give the place and people the white glove treatment, or inspection. So, go and make that money!" she said jokingly.

He went into the kitchen and returned within five minutes with a bag, waved to her and walked up the hall, opened the door and was gone.

Robin laid there on the bed and wondered if he thought she was that stupid, to believe that he was going to work? She picked up the telephone and called his job, spoke with the supervisor and asked if she could leave a message for her husband, Russell, when he arrived for the graveyard shift?

He told her she could leave the message, but Russell wasn't scheduled to work until Monday morning; he's been off due to death in the family, and is taking an additional three days of sick leave.

"Who did you say you are, again?" he Robin asked hung up. She didn't know it was that bad. Who died in the family, she thought and what had he done on those days off? Well, he didn't say he was fired, she thought, but she said.

"He is planning something!"

She thought about the days he worked, Friday and Saturday, for Mr. Marshall, the previous day, that day, the next and the rest of the week. She was confused, even though he made more in those two days than he would have at his job for a month, taking that many days off, was a dangerous move, he was putting his job in jeopardy.

He had a plan as sure as he was with one of his women, at that time. Robin didn't plan to be on the wrong side or be taken by surprise; she had to come up with a counter plan or plans. Robin knew something was wrong, but she never thought it was as complicated as it had obviously become.

She never let herself believe that love nonsense that Russell told her nor that he could do a hundred and eighty degrees turn overnight regarding his personal feelings, he was just not that good an actor. Robin believed then and now it was confirmed that Russell was trying to play her.

Robin knew he had an appointment to see a psychic that night and she debated whether she should go there are not and decided that her appearance the following day, was far more important and she could always follow-up with the psychic later, if not that week, then the next. She got up to go to the kitchen and her socked feet hit something, she looked down and saw a small red book that could be used as an address book, but it was not hers.

By simple deduction, she knew whose book it was, Russell's. She put the book on the table and went into the kitchen and poured a glass of concord grape juice and returned to the bedroom. As she passed by the table, she picked up the book and sat down on the sofa, took a drink of juice, placed the glass on the table and then opened the little red book. Nothing she saw was alarming or seemed unusual, Russell indeed used it as his address book and because he was the supervisor on the second shift, he would have the names and numbers of women she did not know. Robin was close to the end of the book, when she noticed something that seemed unusual, there were a group of numbers lined up as though they were to be added up, but weren't because there was no line nor rationale for the numbers to be added, they were single digits for a grand total of thirty-six, so adding them made very little sense to Robin.

She picked up the phone and dialed the numbers and after three rings, someone picked up and said hello. Robin hung up immediately and starred at the numbers until they were embedded into her memory, she took the book and placed it back on the floor, and when she saw Russell's camera, she picked the book up and took a picture of it identifying him as the owner of the book, then turned to the page with the single digit numbers and took a picture. She took the Polaroid's and placed them in her briefcase, put the book on the floor where her foot encountered it and laid down.

The phone rang but she made no effort to answer it, knowing it was Russell on the other end. Then she thought it could be anyone on the other end and decided to answer should it ring again. Surely, as air is essential to breath, the telephone rang again. This time she waited for the third ring, picked up the receiver and with a sleepy sounding voice, said hello and the caller hung up. That confirmed it for Robin, she was certain it was Russell, checking to ascertain whether she had made the earlier call, but because she sounded sleepy when he called, he was convinced that she had been asleep when he first called.

Robin could not have made the call to the number where he answered the telephone. He was relieved and in the clear, so he thought, and Robin was going to make sure he continued to feel secure, since she was not ready for him to make abrupt changes in his plans which would start a domino effect, and cause her to make changes in the timing of her plans. She knew what to expect from Russell, to prove his theory one way or the other, he would utilize his usual tactics of charm and abuse and she would be ready for him, to sway him as much as he will try to sway her to the point of total self-confidence; but for now, she intended to sleep, for it may be the last opportunity for a peaceful sleep she had before the war of the Watsons began.

Robin slept soundly that night and was at peace with herself when she awoke as a new day streamed through the window, she threw back the covers and got out of bed, said her prayers for the first time in a long time, she hummed a song as she went to the bathroom to bathe. She felt good as she filled the bathtub and poured in her bath oil. She stepped into the tub and soaked for fifteen minutes and then hastened to finish up to get dressed. Everything was laid out for her to put on.

Chapter Ten

Celebration Sincerity and Fiscal Planning

She took her time dressing, desperately trying not to ruin her hose with a run. Robin reveled in the softness of the material of her underclothes, as they caressed her body. She slipped into her robe to complete her make up before putting on her dress that zipped from the side. She put on a little blush and lip gloss touched up her eyes and she was done and gorgeous.

She eased into that beautiful gown and stood looking in the mirror very pleased. She picked up the camera and snapped a few pictures from the mirror point of view. Picked up her purse and the telephone rang, the Limo driver was waiting, so she lightly sprayed her perfume, put on her coat, picked up her briefcase and purse and walked to the door.

She unlocked the door and walked out and locked it and started down the stairs, when she was met by Uncle Book.

"I was coming to help you out," he said to Robin.

"The limo driver seemed impatient," he said. "So, I thought I would make sure you had everything you needed and how I could help."

"I'm sure he isn't impatient, uncle Book, he's being paid to wait for and help me. I can use a hand with my briefcase," she said.

Uncle Book took the briefcase out of her hand and said, "Robin, you look like a movie star, can we stop and take a picture of you?"

"Absolutely," she said. "I insist."

"Ask Maurice to come for my briefcase and we'll stop and let you take a few pictures, if you promise to give me one," she added.

"Certainly," he said.

Maurice came for the briefcase. "Maurice, will you take this to the car and return and take a picture of us together?" Robin asked.

He took the briefcase to the car and returned and took six pictures and uncle Book also took two of Maurice, who looked fabulous. After saying her goodbyes to uncle Book, Maurice escorted her to the car and helped her inside the car and as she made herself comfortable, Maurice got in.

"Robin, do you want coffee?" he asked.

"I'm good, thank you," she said. "It's going to be a tremendous and long day. However, I would like for you to be on stand bye to take me somewhere while the festivities are in process and please keep this information to yourself."

"Yes, ma'am," he said. "But what if Russell should ask or Mr. Marshall?"

"Mr. Marshall would never ask you, but should Russell ask, please, it is a matter of life and death that you not tell him anything, do I have your word, Maurice?" she asked.

"You have my word," he said. "Robin, should you ever need my help, please don't hesitate to ask," he said.

"Thank you, Maurice, I just may need to take you up on that," she said.

"Please excuse me while I make a few calls to my staff to make sure they are all well and on fire about today."

She called Regina and Celia. Regina informed her they were up and dressed waiting for her call and would be leaving in fifteen minutes.

"Fine Regina, we'll look for you," Robin said. "Oh, is Celia close to the phone?"

"Yes, she is, Robin, hold on a minute."

"Hello, Robin," said Celia. "What can I do for you?"

"What time did you schedule the help to arrive?" Robin asked.

"They should arrive in thirty minutes," she said. "And we're on our way, too."

"Fine, Celia," Robin said. "I can hardly contain myself, I am dying to see you two."

"We're on our way, Robin, see you very soon, Maurice did pick you up, right?"

"Yes, we're just about there, correction, we're pulling up now," Robin said. "Get off the phone and come down."

Robin took out her keys to the building and her private code and used them for the first time. She felt honored when the code went through, she carefully placed them in her briefcase and invited Maurice to come inside.

He checked everything and reported to her office and she asked him to let them in when they arrived.

Celia and Regina would arrive first then the crew to cook and decorate and setup. Before she could finish speaking, there was a knock and bell, "That's them" she said.

"I have it, Mrs. Watson," said Maurice and it kicked in, we're at work. Robin could continue the first name basis, as their boss wasn't around, but they had to follow protocol and do the appropriate thing.

Celia and Regina came in giggling and it was like something out of a movie or fairytale to see the two of them there dressed to the nines looking like princesses.

"My," Robin said. "You two look like royalty. We should have a camera."

"We brought one," said Celia.

"What are we waiting for?" Robin asked.

"Maurice, will you take our pictures before the work begins?" asked Regina.

"Absolutely," he said. He took pictures separately and as a group. The fun was over, the crew had arrived.

"Mrs. Watson, the crew is here, do you have specific instructions or should they be giving a free hand?" asked Celia.

"Tell them to follow the faxed instructions they originally received from me and if they have improvements, I am available for consultation," Robin said.

"Never give a freehand, Celia," she said. "Those instructions go for the cooks and decorators, as well."

"I gave specific instructions and they should arrive with everything they need to achieve the goals. There are specific instructions for every venue in my office, locate them and make sure they are followed to the letter," Robin said.

"Where is Mr. Gulley?" she asked.

"He will be in shortly," said Maurice. "He's on the lot now."

"Ask him to come to my office," she said.

"Maurice, I want you to take care of security, but you need an assistant, so what do you think about Mr. Gulley?" she asked.

"I think he'll work out," he said.

"You must find something to keep him busy when you run the errand," she said.

"I'll think of something," he said. "Will you know who will be present then?"

"Yes," she said. "He will."

"We'll handle it."

"Do you have a specific plan?" she asked.

"Yes, let me get Mr. Gulley, here he is, now."

"Mr. Gulley, you're to assist Maurice with security today. He will tell you what he has in mind."

"Since most of the supplies end up in people's cars, you keep an eye on the liquor and meats, take this notepad and keep track of everything that is opened and watch how it is disposed of and write down all bottles of alcoholic beverages and until I send for you and whomever relieves you, give them a new notepad and the same instructions," he said. "The staff will have an opportunity to enjoy themselves as soon as the serving is complete."

"Are you alright with this, Mr. Gulley?" she asked.

"Yes," he said. "I'm over the kitchen pantry and over the conduct of the people, right?"

"Right," said Maurice. "But also, the suppliers, as well. Make sure no one working in the kitchen is parked close to the exit, so that they can be seen leaving and entering their cars and leave space for the vendors to unload and make a record of what is delivered. Are we good?"

"We're good," he said.

"Alright let's get it setup. Takeover, Gulley," he said. "Mr. Gulley left in the direction of the kitchen."

"Good job, Maurice," Robin said.

"The day is still young," he said.

"Go take Mr. Gulley's picture, please Maurice?" Robin asked. He took two pictures and returned them and went to his post at the door. The florist and decorations were being completed when Maurice notified Robin via phone, that the guess would be arriving in thirty minutes.

Robin motioned for Celia and she came. Robin told her as soon as they completed their jobs, and to make sure it was soon, that they come to her office and signed off and they would be given an approximate time to return either today or tomorrow. They completed their jobs and were in her office within ten minutes.

They signed off and she asked them to double check so nothing was lying around that should not be and they could return early tomorrow to take down everything, she said seven in the morning.

"Celia," she said. "I need you to tell Mr. Gulley to get the invoices from the vendors, too, please."

"Okay, Mrs. Watson," she said.

"Tell him to keep them put the time receive on them and check the contents of boxes and bags to confirm every item is where it should be and check it off on the invoice as complete and not to give the invoices to anyone else under any circumstances, not even Mr. Marshall, he would never ask for them, turn them over to me as soon as the guest leave."

"Will do," Celia said. "Anything else?"

"Yes," Robin said. "Take Regina and the two of you meet me at the door to greet the guest. And wear a big smile along with that great look."

"Yes, ma'am," she said.

Mr. and Mrs. Marshall arrived and Robin asked Regina and Celia to wait at the door with Mr. Marshall until they returned from upstairs.

"Mrs. Marshall," Robin said. "Let me show you your special gift."

"Yes, Robin, please," she said. "But remember, dear Juliette."

"This is your modest apartment/office when you need to get away or Mr. Marshall works late, all the conveniences of home," Robin reported.

"Thank you so much, Robin, please know that my family and I are so grateful we have such a lovely, intelligent, capable, caring person like you watching out for us and the business. I have a little something for you," she said. She opened her purse and pulled out an envelope and said, "This is a small token of our appreciation and please call me Juliette."

"Juliette, I cannot accept another gift, I love what I do and I have come to love you and your family as if you were my own, so, thank you, but I cannot."

"Robin, do you know you single handedly saved our company and because of your humility, not only are we giving you the contents of this envelope, but we are giving you a share in this company, you earned every cent. I know you chose the staff to do the work, but you were close by delegating authority the entire time, we were watching how you handled things, and we are all united in saying you far exceeded our expectations in every respect. Now, put this away so no one will have ill will against you."

"I need to tell you something," Juliette said. "We have a grand-daughter, named Johanna, she's seven years old, she has experienced horrific things for the past five years and we're hoping and praying for her healing and recovery. She was taken from us and used in human trafficking," she said.

We have jumped through loops to get her back and to have her in our legal care, but she has had numerous horrific days and nights. Your capable business finesse, is what enabled us to take the time to do all we did to legally adopt her and she requires so much attention, so if we go the extra mile to do for you, it is because of the extra miles you have gone for us without a single complaint and we love you."

"It would be lovely if you could spend a week-end with us and perhaps a holiday, but you are welcome to our home anytime. You may be the one person who can unlock Johanna's years of silence, I just have a feeling," she said. "Your husband is welcome, too."

"Thank you, Juliette, that means so much to me, I am speechless, I certainly plan to visit Johanna," Robin said. She hugged Juliette and said, "we should get back to welcome our guests."

"Yes, we should," Juliette said. "But let me put these little trinkets on your neck and ears to enhance that lovely dress."

"Are those real diamonds?" Robin asked.

"But of course, they are," answered Juliette. "And they are your Harry Winston's now. The insurance papers are in the envelope in your name and the appraisal price, as well. You look so lovely dear, I could not be prouder, if you were my own daughter."

She hugged Juliette and waited for her to say, "Time to get back."

They walked hand in hand down the stairs and Juliette squeezed her hand as they let go. They stopped by Robin's office to put the papers away and as they locked the door, Russell came in. He looked very nice, but he spent enough on himself to make that a sure thing. Robin introduced him to Juliette and while she was gracious, she made her excuses to join the receiving line. Juliette placed Robin behind her in the receiving line and the guest were more than receptive but honored to meet such giving and gracious people who had achieved the impossible in less than the allotted time frame and it was entrusted into the hands of a young Afro-American mixed woman.

To witness the exceptional celebration, first hand, was awesome and to be escorted to their seats in such a unique manner was unforgettable. The receiving line was seated and the ceremony began, with music prayer and speeches testimonials and roasting. "Dunch", a combination of lunch and dinner, was exquisite and dessert.

Most events of this magnitude are usually held with people who tolerate one another, but this event was so genuine and loving, that every speaker commented on the trust and unity that emanated from the Marshall family business, which was an indicator that business was about to hit a record high, if only to discover the secret behind the Marshall success.

Robin winked at Maurice and he began to put his plan in action, then Robin whispered to Juliette that she had to leave the building for a few minutes and if she needed to know the circumstances, she would gladly fill her in, but she wanted her permission.

"You have both our permissions," said Juliette. "I take it you don't want Russell to know?"

"Right, Juliette, please don't tell him," Robin said.

"Go," said Juliette. "And you have our full support. Should there be a need, who do we call?"

"Celia and Regina," Robin said.

She excused herself and went to the office got what she needed and left by the side door, where Maurice was parked and waiting. Robin got in the car.

"Where to?" asked Maurice.

"The nearest bank," she stated.

"Three minutes," he said and three it was.

She got out and went in with her briefcase and went straight to the first empty office and took a seat, she even rang the bell, and a young lady came in.

"How can I help?" she inquired.

Robin stated, "I want to open an account a money market and a savings here is my pertinent information," she said.

"Is that Harry Winston jewelry?" asked the manager.

"Yes, Robin said, it is."

"How much longer will it take?"

"I only need your money and signature on these cards, that need filling out, and I'll make copies, tell me the amounts and I'll handle everything," said the young lady.

Robin provided everything, signed all the checks, made a withdrawal from her joint savings and left there with a substantial amount to be envied by the best of the best. She had problems believing her own worth.

Robin took her receipts and placed them in her briefcase, took her personal information and asked for a brown manila envelope, put in everything, then put away the envelop, gave the young lady a tip and left the bank. Robin hurried back to the car and Maurice said three minutes and three minutes it was. She went back through the side door, locked up her briefcase and office and resumed her place.

"Did it go well, Robin?" Juliette asked.

"It went very well, Juliette," she replied.

"Good, faithful workers should have a guardian angel to protect and serve," she said.

"You didn't miss anything but food," she said.

"We should be dismissing in about fifteen minutes, we must get back to Johanna, before she acts out. Will you be alright, Robin?" she asked.

"Yes, we will be fine, you take care of Johanna and yourselves," Robin said.

"Does anyone need a plate to go or special dessert or drink?" Robin asked.

"No, we had a glorious time and you must share your secret," they said.

They presented Mr. Marshall with an award for Man of the Year. They saved the best for last and Robin was happy she made it back in time to share that moment with him. He accepted the award on behalf of his employee's and stated there would be no award without the right team and he asked everyone to stand as he called their name and he Robin asked J. Watson to stand and everyone gave her a tremendous applause, as he called her his angel on his shoulder, and it was so moving.

No one could be jealous behind such an inclusive and open expression of genuine love and gratitude and every one of the team hugged the other as Juliette clapped with her whole heart.

The final remarks were granted to Juliette who sang the praises of the family employees and to honor those guests present whose word is their bond and finally to Robin Watson who showed them how to love more than themselves.

Then the employees and workers remaining in the building began to chant speech Robin, speech. The M. C. said, "The people have spoken, they want to hear from Robin Watson, so let's hear from her, show her some love by your applause."

The building went up in thunderous applause as Robin made her way to the Podium. She thanked everyone, and asked to give the Marshall family their well- deserved applause, for it was this family that fought to keep the business open, it was this family that went the extra mile and found another building to replace what had been loss."

"It was this family that believed in second chances, it was this family that put their trust in an unknown individual to prove that there are people in this world who can be trusted despite their differences, it was this family that granted mercy to the lonely and the once lost, for under them, they found self- worth, themselves."

"We applaud this family for being you, an example to the wise and comfort for the lonely and forsaken. To Mr. and Mrs. Marshall true lights of love and hope in a dark and demonic world may they rule in peace until the prince of peace returns. To the staff and co-workers present, words alone cannot express the joy and gratitude you brought into our lives. Shine on forever and a day, we love you from the bottom of our heats for pricking ours, we're always with you. Thank you for everything, your second family. May we close with prayer, Lord of light and love cover us and shield us from the darkness all around and heal us of our maladies and broken hearts, restore us, renew us and revive us in Jesus name we pray. Amen."

The ceremony was dismissed and the family line was greeted by all the guest and workers, Robin requested that the Marshall family be excused and granted first exit and it was done. Mr. and Mrs. Marshall embraced Robin in the presence of everyone and threw kisses to their employees with gratitude and thanks.

The guests were flattered that such an open demonstration of love and affection dominated the entire ceremony. Celia and Regina began to check on the cooks and staff and Mr. Gulley was in the kitchen and Celia asked him to report to Mrs. Watson's office with the invoices. Robin asked him one question.

"Did all the vendor's invoices and their products prove to be precise?"

"Yes, ma'am, they were all on point, he said and I didn't give any one the invoices, they're leaving my hand for yours for the first time," he said. "Russell asked for them, but I did not give them to him. He took over for me when I took over for Maurice, but I was not gone long perhaps thirty minutes. If he took anything, it was not very much."

"You did Good Mr. Gulley," Robin echoed.

"All the vendors said they were already paid, when Russell asked them," Mr. Gulley mentioned.

"You may leave now, Mr. Gulley and thanks for helping to make this a ceremony to remember," Robin said.

"It was my pleasure," he said.

"Were there any food and alcohol items left?" Robin asked.

"Yes, there were several," he said, "I would like to have a piece of that Lamb and salad, cake and a few other items, if you don't mind."

"No, I don't mind," Robin said. "Let me get Celia and Regina and have them fix every one of my staff a basket."

"Celia and Regina, please come in the office," she said.

"What can we do for you?" they asked.

"Will you two please fix all of us bags from the leftovers and Mr. Gulley wants lamb, salad and cake; please take him into the kitchen and he will let you know how much he needs for his family. Fix yourselves a basket and if you want wine please leave a bottle for Mr. Marshall, for me to put in his office and some Lamb for his freezer. He loves Lamb. Put his name on and label it, thank you."

"Ask Maurice what he wants, as well as Russell, thank you, ladies," she said.

"Did the cleaning crew return or are they to come in the morning?"

"No, it's still early, call them and ask them to come now and finish up so the building will not attract rodents and bugs," replied Robin.

"The Decorators should take down the decorations and that way, I won't have to come in early in the morning," she said. "Give them fifteen minutes to arrive. I have a change of clothes here, so I'm going to change out of this dress and shoes. I have a very nice wool purple pant suit, and that will work well for me, with that exquisite scarf I purchased."

"We fixed everyone a nice basket and there is still food left and plenty of Champagne and Wine and soda," Regina reported.

"Was there any other meat left besides lamb?" she asked. "Yes, there was roast beef, chicken, Tuna salad and Salmon. Shrimp is gone."

"I do not recall placing that order," Robin stated.

"Mrs. Marshall's grocer delivered the extras," Celia said.

"Leave a pint of Tuna salad and wrap it well, we'll put it in the fridge for tomorrow," she said.

"I'll take the Salmon, and eat it tonight, wrap it well, but cut it into three pieces and wrap each separately," Robin insisted. "Have Maurice place the Champagne and Wine in the Limo with my basket."

"Did you ladies get what you needed?"

"Yes, Robin, we got plenty," Regina said.

"Whatever remains, if it doesn't have an odor, we can eat tomorrow for lunch, so no one must bring lunch. We had plenty of refreshments," Celia said.

"We can live off them for a minute. Put chips and nuts in a plastic container and remember donuts and coffee will be here in the morning and milk, too," Gulley said.

"Has the cleaning crew arrived yet?" Robin asked.

"Yes, they're in there taking down the decorations and putting trash into the bin outside. In about thirty minutes, everything should be finished," Celia said.

"Ok, ladies, you two may leave, since you were here very early this morning. How are you fixed for cash, Celia?" Robin asked.

"We're good, Robin," they said.

"I completed all the paper work and Friday, Celia, should be clear to receive her check. Take care of those dresses and shoes/purses we may have another society party," Robin said.

"Some things cannot be duplicated, oh well, take care of them," Robin repeated.

"You don't have to worry about that," said Celia. "If the cleaning crew is done, we'll leave but not before we finish our assignment."

The cleaning crew finished and the ladies left after them. Robin went into the kitchen, dining area and restrooms and they were super clean, she checked out the waiting area and it, too, was clean. Robin looked and everything was gone, she called for Russell and Maurice and neither came. She took her clothes, locked up her office, and locked the building utilizing her code and went to the Limo and got in.

"Well," said Maurice, "You finally wrapped things up and are you ready to leave now?"

"Yes," she replied. "I'm ready to leave but I'm not sure I am ready to go home, it is always difficult to unwind behind a great event."

"Have you seen Russell?" she asked.

"Yes, I saw him about two hours ago, he got his basket the ladies fixed for him and he left."

"Good," she said. "He's probably out with one of his women, that's why I wanted him to get the Champagne and Wine. I just don't feel like getting into an altercation with him after a day like this, a person should have peace and rest," she emphatically stated.

"I must return the limo tonight at six," he said. "So, if there is some place you would like to go, let me know."

"Well, I would like to go back to the bank and see if she has my packet ready, but since we don't know where Russell is, then we should disregard that idea and accept things as they are. Besides, you have your basket, so why don't you drop it by your place, so your food can remain edible and chill your wines."

"Do you mind if I do?" he asked.

"No, I recommended it," she replied.

"Ok, I'll stop by and drop my things off and check my mail," he said.

"Do you drive, Robin?" he asked,

"Yes, I drive, I just haven't purchased a car of my own yet," she said.

"I have an idea, you can drive my car and I will drive the Limo and we can return the Limo and I won't have to find someone to drive my car," he suggested.

"How far is it?" she asked.

"About seven minutes away," he stated.

"Certainly, Maurice, I'll drive your car and we can take my things to the house. On second thought, I think I should stay with my things, so we'll take them last, but I wanted to beat him home to be comfortable, and put my things away," she said.

"I've been sitting out in the car for a long time with this food out here and we should get it into a refrigerator to keep it good," he said.

"Let me take mine in now and if you want me to, I'll put yours in the fridge, I can do that to. I think salad dressing or sandwich spread is in something, think it's Tuna salad and that needs to be refrigerated," he said.

"What do you think, Robin?" he asked.

"I think it will be too late in another hour or so," she said.

"I've been so busy, I haven't had time to really eat, think I will have a little Tuna and Salmon." He gave her the basket and she took out a container and ate Salmon and Tuna.

"Where are the kosher pickles?" she asked.

"I didn't see any pickles," he stated. "No one got pickles."

Robin ate and then she asked about the time. Maurice said he was going out that night.

"Did you get a pay check?" she asked.

"I didn't receive a pay check today," he said. "I did when everyone else received theirs."

"I don't recall writing you a check, she said, why is that?"

"Because Mr. Marshall gave me mine," he said.

"Oh," she said. "I am so glad you told, me, now I don't have to worry about it."

"Ok, so what are we doing now?" he asked.

"We're giving you a ride to return the car," she said.

"Give me your keys," she said. He did.

"Unlock the doors," he said. She unlocked the doors and he placed the basket inside and got into the Limo.

They drove to the dealership and dropped off the Limo, he got the papers and handed them to Robin who put them in her purse, moved into the passenger seat and he got in and drove to her house, they took the food upstairs and came down. Robin placed the wine in the wine rack and left it.

Russell was not home and she looked through the trash to see if he left remnants of food, soda or champagne, but she didn't see anything to support the theory that he had been home. He was probably at his girl's house. She went over by the sofa to see if he picked up the address book, and it was gone.

He felt free, she said and self-assured, finding his book. She was pleased, but something seemed off. The red book was gone, yet, it appeared he had not been home? It was part of his game to make her doubt, wonder where he was especially since this was a very special day for her. He wanted her to be lonely and long to see him, while he was spreading his oats somewhere else. He would soon know that she was not home alone, as he presumed, but this was not the way it looked. She was only receiving help with the groceries.

Maurice promised to check on her later to see if she were alright. She opened a bottle of wine and poured it into a crystal glass and drank it. She ran a bath and took the bottle into the bathroom and soaked while she drank the bottle. Robin thought about how nice it was to be in the house alone to have the freedom and privacy she so craved and now she had it. Robin dried herself off put on her robe, and walked to the front door to lock it from the inside.

Chapter Eleven

Dangerous Games

Then she went to the bedroom, took out her briefcase and looked at the papers and saw that she was close to being a millionaire twice. She decided that she had enough money to purchase her own home and the more she thought about it, the more she was inclined to do it. She had not figured the share of the company into the mix, nor the amount in the joint savings account. She didn't look at the appraisal of the jewelry. Robin took out the envelope she received from Juliette and she was amazed that she had missed a check, she was under the impression there was only one check and an appraisal paper, she was wrong, Robin had a check from another member of the family, she decided to put it in the bank the following day and make a withdrawal. She would figure it out in her uncluttered time. She would call Juliette later and stay close to them, especially Johanna. Robin packed up her papers and carefully put them back in her briefcase and put it away after which she poured another drink. Robin turned up the bottle and it was empty, she decided to open another bottle and she did. She began to feel sleepy and drifted off to sleep. She awoke to the sound of knocking on the door. She went to the front door and unlocked it, and there was Walter on the other side of the door. He asked if she had company and she replied she took a bath fell asleep and awoke to the knocking, she wasn't aware that she had locked the door.

Walter looked around, as if he didn't believe she was alone, but she said to him, it has been a long day and I'm going back to bed, but in case you and Louise wish to discuss something with me, please let's do it after work the next day, she said I brought home Lamb and other goodies from the celebration today, enjoy, and she went back to bed and didn't give Walter another thought. As she lay there waiting for sleep to return, she heard Walter in the kitchen she poured another drink and a form of sleep came, but not for long.

Robin heard voices in the kitchen that were obviously Louise and Walter. She overheard them say, uncle Book Robin said threw a shindig at work today that was extravagant, impressive and she looked like a million dollars with a Limo and driver waiting for her and they took pictures. He showed me the pictures and they were amazing. That dress she was wearing cost more than we could make together in a year, she said and we know Russell didn't pay for it. He had pictures of Russell, as well, dressed to the nines on his way to her ceremony. He told uncle Book her boss offered her a high-powered job, with a large salary, and she would be accepting it at the ceremony. All that and he's still messing up, said uncle Book. He just won't learn, he said, Russell didn't come home, yet, but she left uncle a bottle of expensive champagne in front of his door.

He said he was going to save it for a very special occasion, maybe the one when Russell decides to settle down and have a baby!

"Russell is a fool," Walter said. "That woman he's messing with in the projects is going to be the ruin of him."

"What woman?" Louise asked. "No, don't tell me, I'd have to tell Robin and she doesn't need to be hurt by him any more than what she's hiding from everyone. That look in her eyes didn't come from the 'Sand Man'. I can only imagine what he's put her through and I don't like it." And she walked out of the kitchen. Walter left the kitchen abruptly and ran after Louise. Robin took another drink and then another and the bottle was empty, she turned over and found a comfortable spot in the bed and there she stayed until morning.

Louise knocked on her door and asked if she could do anything else for her? She said she drew her a bath and it was waiting, and we never had girl's night out, she said. Louise had to leave but she suggested they could talk when she returned home, or they could meet at the lounge around the corner and she'd call Gerri.

"Let's meet there," Robin said. "No, let's come home get dressed up and we'll go out, tell Gerri, please."

"Okay," she said. "We'll do that. I'll call Walter and tell him so he can prepare something."

"There's enough food in the house already fixed, to feed a small army; let him fix something from that," Robin said.

"Get in that bathtub before the water gets cold."

"On my way," Robin said as she picked up her robe to put it on. They walked to the bathroom together.

"I know Russell didn't come home, it's not you, so don't worry about it, he's not worth it," Louise said.

Robin said, "I won't, Louise."

Robin got into the tub and the water was semi warm. She turned on the hot water and hoped it would heat up the water in the tub and it was working to some extent. She lathered and soaked, lathered and soaked and washed her face at least six times after she washed her hair. She got out of the tub, blow dried her hair and brushed her teeth, gargled and moisturized. She put on her make-up and got dressed, she had two very important meetings and she was fresh. Robin went into the kitchen and fixed a cup of tea but decided on a Pepsi, she took her medication and sat down looked over her information and when she was satisfied, she got up put on her coat and left. She walked down the stairs and uncle Book was bringing in the milk. He commented again on the festivities of the day before and said to be encouraged and to have a nice day.

Robin thanked him and said she planned to have a green day and smiled. She left for the CTA station and arrived just in time to get her tickets and go up the stairs to board. She got on and took a seat and meditated until it was time to transfer and she got off, a young man almost knocked her down as he ran past her carrying a beige purse in one hand and a knife in the other. She hurried and went down the platform looking around to make sure the man in the plaid jacket was not following her. Robin grabbed the first thing moving and took a seat still looking to make sure she didn't see that plaid jacket and large grey cap and most important, that he didn't see her.

She breathed a sigh of relief when she didn't see him, but that experience was the turning event in her life, Robin decided, that was the last time she would risk riding with CTA, she was buying a car. She made it to work and opened the building and locked herself in, checking periodically to see if she had been followed by the man. She turned the alarm on and went into her office and tried to calm down before everyone arrived. Mr. Marshall came and he unlocked the door and turned off the alarm and was surprised when he heard movement in the building. He went into Robin's office and she jumped a foot into the air.

"What's wrong, Robin?" he asked. "The alarm was on and you're as jumpy as can be, what happened?"

Robin told him what happened and her decision to buy a car and he said that was a good idea, since I left home so early and had to transfer to get here. He told her to leave it to him regarding her transportation for the remainder of the week and in two weeks they should be a little more settled and she would have time to look for the car she really wanted.

"You concentrate on the meetings that were rescheduled for this week and next," he said.

"Yes sir," she said. "How is Johanna?"

"Johanna was having an episode when we arrived home yesterday, but we had the usual long night that is why I came in early, I never went to sleep," he said.

"Mr. Marshall, you must get some rest, why don't you go to your apartment on the second floor and rest, I can bring you tea or coffee, the donuts will be here in an hour and I can awaken you then," suggested Robin.

"If you don't mind, Robin, it does sound inviting," he said.

"Please, Mr. Marshall," she said. "I will personally turn off the phone so you will not be disturbed."

"That's fine, Robin, I can do that," he said.

"Go now," she said, "rest and I'll come for you when we need you present, okay?"

"Okay," he said. He went upstairs and that was reassuring knowing someone else was in the building and that it was Mr. Marshall.

Robin had a greater incentive to be motivated, now, she went through that information and had two more diet Pepsi's and she was ready to go.

The donut delivery arrived and she took care of that, placed them in a large crystal tray with the see thru top and left them on the counter by the coffee machine with condiments, napkins and cups. She went back to her office when she noticed someone approaching the door, she reluctantly went to the door and it was Maurice, she let him in and told him, Mr. Marshall arrived early and is upstairs in his apartment resting and she wanted him not to be disturbed unless it was mandatory.

He said he understood and went for donuts and coffee. A short time later, Celia, Regina and Mr. Gulley arrived and went to their cubicles to begin the day. Maurice came in and asked them not to disturb Mr. Marshall upstairs unless it was his wife or another emergency and they all agreed. Celia was assisting Robin and Regina was hiring and doing interviews, Mr. Gulley was scheduling appointments and making contacts with different buyers in three countries.

Robin was scheduled to have the first meeting in ten minutes, she went to the conference room and set up the recording for the meeting, while Celia took notes and met specific requests.

She had a folder in place for everyone and extra paper, pens, pencils, sticky notes etc.

Robin began the meeting on time, as everyone was prompt. She made her presentation showed the graphic backup's and asked for questions.

The meeting went very well, as they had met her at the ceremony, there were no questions why Mr. Marshall was not present. She left the room after the question and answer period, allowing them time to make up their minds regarding the presentation and when they signaled a decision had been reached she re-entered the room. The presentation was well received and the lawyers were working out the details for her approval, as second in command to Mr. Marshall.

She went upstairs to check on Mr. Marshall, and he was sleeping so soundly, she didn't have the heart to awaken him, she tipped toed out and closed the door, leaving him to enjoy the most peaceful rest he had in weeks.

Robin wrapped up that deal and went back into the conference room to thank them and say goodbye to the clients and to prepare for the next presentation.

She asked Celia for another diet Pepsi and she gulped it down in seconds and Celia went for another one, she had an idea to put a small refrigerator in the conference room and stock it before the end of the business day. She left the room and made the arrangements and returned. Celia restocked the conference room with the same supplies, replaced the tape for the next meeting, put out the folders and went to the waiting room to greet the clients and bring them to the conference room.

Robin was waiting and highly motivated, she was in her element, as she made the presentation so interesting that it was contagious, everyone was on board. The presentation was followed by the question and answer period and the participation was overwhelming. When she left the room, she was more excited than she was originally, that she had almost come to terms with the scare of early morning. Robin knew it was a winner, as she sat in her office looking at the diet Pepsi, waiting for them to signal her.

Then the signal came, she went into the conference room and the lawyers were already there with the papers to be signed and a firm substantial offer, forty percent above the previous one, was awaiting her signature. Robin signed the papers and welcomed them into the Marshall family, as the transfer was being completed. She thanked them and wished them travel mercies as they journeyed home and looked forward to their continued success and growth together.

They shook hands and left for the airport. Robin wanted to awaken Mr. Marshall, but he was resting so well: She thought about the fact that he would be up all night and let him sleep so hopefully, he could let his wife sleep that night. The workers were so excited, the deal of the year had been finalized and they were starting a new era.

Robin had been at work all day and had only drank diet Pepsi, but the others had not taken one break. She went to each station and relieved everyone to have a forty-five-minute lunch break and she would hold down the fort. They didn't argue with her, even though they knew to operate all three posts effectively, required major skills and they knew she possessed them.

Robin was doing an excellent job, when a young man entered the door and stated he had an interview scheduled in five minutes. Robin asked his name and he stated Raymond Hawkins.

"Well, Mr. Hawkins," she asked. "Do you have a Resume with you?"

"Yes," he stated. "But I also faxed my Resume, as well."

"How old are you?" she asked.

"I am twenty," he replied.

She asked, "Do you mind if I take that remaining three minutes to locate your name and information on Regina's computer?"

"No, ma'am, take your time," he said.

"No, Raymond," she replied. "Time is money, we utilize time well here and that's lesson number one; hopefully, you'll be around to receive lesson number two."

"I've located you, please come in and have a seat," she said.

He came in and the light lit up in Mr. Gulley's cubicle, she said "Just a minute, we have an overseas problem I need to address, be right back."

Robin spoke four different languages, she answered the call and speaking in French she talked for five minutes and hung up.

"Mr. Hawkins, please tell me why you want to work here?" Robin inquired.

"I love action, I am passionate and young, while I am lacking in experience, I am enthusiastic, easy to engage in conversation and I am a quick study, I learn fast," he said. "I will be an asset to your company as your company increases my assets."

"That's cute," Robin said. "But we have a serious work ethic here, not to say we can't let our hair down, but everything has a place and in this building family comes first. You must fit in. I am sure you're wondering why there is only one person doing everything, that's because, we care about one another. They all worked straight through without as much as a restroom break, while two important meetings were being held, so they were relieved to have lunch a break go to the moon or whatever they need to do to return with clear minds ready to work."

"Have you eaten?" she asked.

"No," he said. "I didn't want to be late."

"Well," she said. "I don't believe that is the real reason, but there is food in the kitchen."

"May I have your identification please?" she asked. He opened his wallet and took out his driver's license and handed it to her.

"By the way," she asked. "What are you trained to do?"

"I said I am a quick study," he said. "I would like to enroll in college but I don't have the money and I still stay at home with my mother."

"How far do you live from here?" she asked.

"Ten blocks in the opposite direction," he said.

She asked, "Did you walk?"

"Yes, ma'am," he said. "But I was on time."

"Barely," she said. Robin hit a button and Celia answered.

"Celia, will you please come to the front for a minute, you can make up the lunch time due you."

"Yes ma'am, be right there," she said.

Robin turned to Mr. Hawkins and said. "There is plenty of food in there. I want you to help yourself and not come out until you're full. Meet the nice people and clean up after yourself and someone will direct you to me, I'll hold on to your license, okay?"

"Okay," he said.

"Celia, meet Raymond Hawkins, we'll call him Raymond, take him to the kitchen and let him eat until he is full, get to know him, I'm interested in what you and the team think. When he is done, bring him to me, thank you, Celia."

"Okay, Mrs. Watson," she said.

They left and Robin continued to work and at intervals, she looked at his driver's license and recalled his wallet was empty. She made a copy of his license and put it in her pocket and continued to work. Regina returned and Mr. Gulley and Robin filled them in and asked Regina to look at Raymond's Resume and give her personal recommendation and fax it to her ASAP. Regina said she would.

Robin had made up her mind that it would be good for both Raymond and his mother, as well as, the community to help one of our own. She went into her office and opened the petty cash box took out two fifty dollar bills and left an IOU with Raymond's name on it. The fax machine beeped and Robin knew Regina had an answer. She went over and retrieved it. Regina wrote in the margins and Robin paid special attention to her suggestions. It seemed they were in sync regarding Raymond. Regina checked his references and they checked out, however, Robin wanted to speak with his teacher.

She called the number provided and it was his former high school. They informed her she would call as soon as she came to the office. There was a short wait and the phone rang it was his teacher. Robin introduced herself and explained why she called. Raymond applied for a job and Robin wanted to know what light she could shed on the pros and cons of hiring Raymond Hawkins.

Miss Edwards stated that Raymond was a very promising student who maintained good grades and was eligible for a scholarship, but had no one to help him. He never knew his father and his mother was sickly but did the best she could.

"He was good outside of school as well," she said. "There was never a problem with drugs or alcohol or even dating, because he had to be the man and adult of the household. If I had not had the responsibilities for my own children, I would have invested in his life to send him to college, but my pay check would not stretch that far. Raymond learns fast, so if there is any position open for him, I implore you to give him the opportunity.

"Thank you, Miss Edwards, you've been quite insightful," Robin said and hung up.

Robin walked over to the cubicles and asked Regina and Gulley what they thought of Raymond, their opinions were favorable and she informed them he would be joining the family, but not to mention it to him.

"I just need to test him," Robin said. "But I'm certain he will pass, so I'll run his papers through. Speaking of which, Celia's information came through, so she'll receive her check tomorrow, Regina."

"Do you have any immediate claims on any part or does she have a checking account, how do you want me to handle that?" she asked.

"I know you wrote up a rental contract, may I see it, and then I will know how to help," Robin said.

"Yes, I have a copy here," Regina replied.

"Fax, it over, Regina. I'm going to approve this application for Raymond, please try to expedite his license to chauffer status, Regina, yesterday. Then I can prepare for you two after I check on Mr. Marshall, he really needed the rest," Robin stated.

Robin walked back to her office and started his paperwork at base pay with education stipulations. Celia walked into the room with Raymond and Robin asked if he were full.

Celia said, "Yes, I even fixed a basket for he and his mother."

"Good Celia. We have a little business to take care of and I'll call you when I'm done. Bring in the papers for employment, Celia."

Raymond looked at her and asked, "Seriously?"

"Did you seriously want a job?" Robin asked.

"Yes," he said. "I need a job."

"Well, this is the thing, Raymond, we do not have a position open for which you qualify."

"I'll sweep, mop and clean," he said.

"Good to know, Raymond, that's what we have in mind for you, to begin," she said. "You'll start at the base pay entry level and with each periodic review, you'll receive an increase. You must be here at seven every morning and report to Maurice for your detail and instructions. If you see that you're running late, call Maurice and notify him before your due time, understood?"

"Understood," Raymond replied.

"Here is an advance for your transportation; I need you to sign an IOU for it with today's date. You start in the morning, and if you do well, then we will finance your education. Are we on the same page, Raymond?"

"Don't let anything stop you, this could very well be the best opportunity you have and you can contact Miss Edwards, and thank her after you thank God," she said. "Fill out your papers in the waiting room and return them with the IOU, okay?"

"Right away," he said. He took the papers to the waiting room and filled them out.

Robin went upstairs to check on Mr. Marshall with copies of the contracts from the meetings that morning along with tapes of the meetings and she was prepared to leave them. She opened the door and she could hear him snoring, so she placed everything on his desk and left the room.

When she returned, Raymond had completed the papers and the IOU and handed them to her. She looked over them and said, "Seven in the morning."

"I'll be here," he said.

He left and she watched him walk off in the opposite direction and she said, "Tomorrow, he'll be headed in the right direction for life." She smiled and went to her office. Filed the papers and went to the fax machine to pick up Regina's document.

Robin read the document Regina prepared for Celia's maintenance in her home and as she reviewed it, she thought this is an inclusive document. She didn't have to worry about the utilities, insurance on her possessions, food, gas, credit card payments (which she questioned)

For the sum of nine hundred dollars a month. Robin decided to put that contract on hold for a moment. She needed to talk to Celia before paying this, after all, Regina was given money from the hat and Mr. Marshall, there should have been notations regarding that money on the paper. Everyone knew that Robin was the overseer for Celia, so that should have warned everyone that everything would be scrutinized. Celia was making enough money to pay the nine hundred per month, but helping someone out doesn't mean that the individual should pay for everything, but half of the expenses, whatever they maybe. Robin thought of Raymond and whether he had the inclination to do snooping or detective work. Robin thought she would give this to him to ponder and research. She had to get him a cell phone. She stopped everything and ordered a cell phone and had it special delivered to Raymond's home address, she made copies of the information and blacked out the names on his copy and wrote a request for information on the property of Regina with a fair rental and expense amount include all utilities even gasoline to work and or fun and food. Submit a fair and reasonable monthly amount. Before messaging the information to Raymond, Robin asked both Regina and Celia into her office.

They entered the office and Robin asked them both to have a seat. She apologized for not doing this before now, but she explained she wanted to have all of Celia's paperwork in and then do what Mr. Marshall instructed, but if they felt better with him doing it instead of her, she was willing to inform him. They both stated they would rather she handled things since he had so much on his plate.

"Okay, then let's get to it. Celia, you are a very capable woman, so how is this relationship working out?"

"Regina is a wonderful person and it occurred to me that since the two of you work together and live together, that is a lot of togetherness, so how are you getting along? You can speak freely and you don't have to worry about anything because in this house, we're family. How is outside this house and in Regina's house, Celia?"

"Well, I figured it out and I think we can do a little better than twelve hundred dollars a month," she said. "Explain please, Celia?" Robin asked.

"Well, the Rent is five hundred a month; the food is three hundred a month; utilities are three hundred a month and gas is one hundred a month now we have the credit card bills and insurance and taxes, and I think we can trim some of the fat," said Celia.

"What do you say Regina?" Robin asked.

"I'm open to whatever we decide in this room," she said.

"That is good," Robin said. "How much did you deduct from the hat passing money, Regina?"

"That amount was thirteen hundred dollars and no, that has not been deducted yet."

"Well, we can get rid of the credit card thing now, Regina."

Mr. Marshall had all but a thousand dollars charged to his account. He was paying all of Celia's expenses, since she had not received her check, and he paid Regina's because Celia is living with her, except for a thousand dollars, that he felt Regina could pay especially since her bill was a thousand dollars more than Celia's. The thousand dollars that was charged to Regina's card, is hers and nothing from the hat will be deducted for Regina's credit card payment," Regina continued.

"Celia still has a credit of thirteen hundred from the hat. Rent and utilities will be three hundred fifty dollars a month and food will be one hundred fifty a month, for a total of five hundred dollars a month is what will be deducted from Celia's check beginning two months from now, monthly, and written to Regina for room and board. The balance will be held by Regina until Celia requires it.

"Do you have new furniture of your own, Celia?"

"No, ma'am. I was thinking about buying a bedroom set, but I must wait," she said.

"Why do you have to wait, Celia? Is your bed uncomfortable?"

"Yes."

"Regina, do you want Celia to wait for a special reason?" "No, she never shared with me the bed is uncomfortable. It is old and second hand so if she wants a bedroom set, then we can do that."

"Okay, since I promised the boss I would take her under my wing, then I will take you two tomorrow and buy it and open an account for you which either the boss or myself will check weekly."

"A thirty-day notice of termination of rental agreement must be made by either party to be legally binding and without a thirty-day notice, the party initiating the termination, (either wanting to leave (Tenant) or wanted to leave(Landlord)) will relinquish their money to the other without a thirty-day notice. Are these terms agreeable to both?" Robin stated.

Regina and Celia said, "Yes."

"So, the check you will receive tomorrow is clear and you can purchase a very nice bedroom set, but not before tomorrow. I'll fill Mr. Marshall in and there will be no discussions about this at home and any changes must come through us. If it is not agreeable this is the time to speak and we can take care of the issues. Is there anything?"

"No," Regina said and Celia.

"Okay then. We are done. I am going to awaken Mr. Marshall and ask Maurice to stay until he speaks with him. Thank you, ladies. When you clock out make sure all food is put up. See you in the morning."

Robin was pleased that went well. She was happy she caught Regina in time before she took every dime Celia had to pay all her bills plus whatever else she wanted. Celia was the Golden Goose. People don't change overnight and the threat of Mr. Marshall discovering Regina's plan to rob Celia, would only last just so long and Regina would begin again. Robin had to find a solution for Celia as soon as possible. Greed is a powerful motivator and consuming fire. It is extremely difficult to extinguish without imprisonment or death. Celia must be protected.

Robin went upstairs to check on Mr. Marshall and she was torn between awaking him or allowing him to sleep. She opened the door and there was no snoring, so she knocked and a familiar voice said, "Come in, Robin?"

"How did you know it was me?" she asked.

"Who else would keep such a close watch on me?" he asked.

"I called Juliette," he said. "And explained what happened and she said, 'bless you Robin, someone could sleep.'"

"Now, you can carry the bulk of the night and she can rest, right?" she asked.

"Right," he said. "And only you would have thought of that."

"I watched the videos of the meetings and read the contracts, Robin as I told the Mrs. I could not have handled either any better. Now, I have decided for you to have a car and driver at your disposal around the clock and Maurice is taking care of that. I only want you to think and continue to take care of the business and our employees the way you have in the past, Robin."

"I should have taken care of that issue long before now, is there anything you need, Robin, my wife and I will gladly do anything for you," he stated.

"I will do anything for you two and I would like for you to ask her if I can spend the week-end with the three of you and let me know tomorrow," Robin said.

"I can tell you now, Robin, that will make her week-end, and Johanna's, not to mention mine," he said.

"That makes me happy," she said. "Now you go home to your number one family and I will clean up here, I just don't want a lot of people around your things; if something happens, I want to be able to defend or explain it."

"I appreciate that, Robin. I'm going," he said. "And you wait for Maurice."

"I will, but I almost forgot, I hired some young man this afternoon, named Raymond Hawkins. He doesn't have experience; he is twenty years old and desires to go to college. We don't have a position open for him, but there is something hungry about him that will be beneficial to the company, as well as, he and his mother. I had his license expedited and changed to chauffer status effective tomorrow and he begins work at seven in the morning to report to Maurice for detail and instructions. I spoke with his teacher Miss Edwards who highly recommends him and stated when he graduated from high school, he received a scholarship but had no one to help him. She stated she had too many children for her check to stretch or she would have helped. He has never been arrested or in trouble with authority or drugs and alcohol and what he needs is guidance and a hand up. Besides, it will really send a positive message to the community about this company helping one of our own."

"His mother has been ill for years, but 'did what she could', quote the teacher."

"Robin, I am with you one hundred percent," he said. "Your instincts are on track, it was the right thing to do."

"He had no money in his wallet and walked the ten blocks here, we fed him and sent him home with some of the leftovers from yesterday for he and his mother and gave him one hundred dollars from the petty cash fund and he gave me an IOU receipt, so he can at least ride the bus to work. He was five minutes early for his appointment."

"Thanks for sharing that with me and I'm proud of you once again you did the right thing," he said.

"Wait until I tell my wife all of this, Robin. Every day you give us another reason to be thankful and confirm that you were God's gift to us and we don't intend to lose you. Since we know the business is in good hands, I am leaving and you must wait for Maurice."

Robin walked with him down the stairs and looked-for Maurice. The building was empty, as she watched Mr. Marshall leave. Robin went back upstairs and pulled off his covers and changed the entire bedding. She took the dirty bedding and placed it into a bag to be sent to the laundry. She tidied up the room, locked the door and went downstairs. When she reached the bottom, there was Maurice waiting for her.

"Well," he said. "Everything is ready and your carriage awaits."

"I am sorry if I kept you waiting, but I had to clean up Mr. Marshall's apartment before leaving. Who knows, he may need to return and rest and it would be very disappointing to discover an unkempt room, I know I would, Maurice, let me get my briefcase, coat and purse."

She put on her coat and went outside she saw the new car and said, "Maurice that is a sleek car, how did you pick it?"

"It was part of a package, Robin."

"Package?" she asked.

"Package, Mr. Marshall arranged for it, until you have time to choose the car of your dreams, it is leased for a month, Robin."

"Oh," she said. "I thought you picked it."

"I picked the package, Robin," he said.

"So, you picked the color, Maurice?"

"Yes, I love red," he said. "I thought it would be a pleasant change in your life to brighten it up a little."

"Okay, is it too late to change it, Maurice?" she asked.

"No, what did you have in mind, Robin?" he asked.

"A lot more room," she said.

He laughed, "I see, I can stop by the dealership now."

"Good. Call them and let them know I want to stretch my legs out and read my reports and think, it's just not a good environment for me to do my best job on a continuous basis, for my work."

"I get you," he replied.

"He called the dealership and asked if we could exchange cars and was placed on hold. A short while later, the owner came on the phone and asked if we required a mid- size or larger and Maurice stated she needs something large enough to spread out her reports, think and not be distracted nor disturbed to maximize her travel time for work and entertainment."

"He said hold please and when he returned, he said the car would be ready for pick up in twenty minutes they needed to wash it, you can leave the other car out front and the keys will be in the new car well stocked and enjoy," he said.

"Don't we need to sign something?" asked Maurice.

"No," he said. "It has been taken care of, as a matter of fact, this is the initial car that was ordered."

"Thank you," said Maurice and he hung up.

"Robin, the original car ordered, will be ready for pickup in twenty minutes that was five minutes ago."

"Ok," she said. "This car is so small." She heard everything.

"I have a girl's night out, tonight and need to be home to change ASAP, but since we need to kill a few minutes, take me to this address, there is someone I want you to meet, Maurice."

She pulled up her briefcase, but it was so uncomfortable trying to open it, she stuck her hand in the pocket of the briefcase and pulled out the paper with Raymond Hawkins address and asked Maurice, you see what I mean?"

He replied, "I wasn't thinking, Mrs. Watson, I thought you just wanted to get from point A to B." She handed him the paper.

"This address is on our way, three minutes," His timing was always spot on.

Robin said to him, "Maurice, I hired this young man this morning and I don't have a position for him, but I'm entrusting him to your care, train him and delegate positions to him and make them diverse. Pay attention to his surroundings and when we leave, give me your candid impressions of all we encounter."

"We're here," he said.

He helped her out of the car and they went to the door and knocked. A woman answered the door, in pajamas and a robe, "Hello," she said. "It has been busy around here today."

"We're sorry to disturb you," Robin said. "But this is Maurice and I am Robin, your son's new boss and this is his supervisor."

Suddenly, a figure appeared in the doorway and said, "Please come in." It was Raymond. "Have a seat over here. Mother was resting on the sofa,"

"We stopped by so Maurice would know who to expect in the morning and to get the phone number to the new cell phone I sent earlier," she said.

"I knew it was you," he said, "I have been trying to work it and I don't know how to activate it."

"Good we stopped by, may I see it," she said. He passed the phone to Maurice who in turn, passed it to Robin. She opened the phone and scrolled down and asked, "Have you owned a cell before?"

"No," he said. "And we don't have Wi-Fi either, it may not be able to work here."

Maurice said to Robin, "If you don't mind, Robin, I'll add his phone to my work plan."

"That's an excellent idea," she said. "Just give me the number."

Maurice took the phone and went outside with his cell and then returned and called Raymond out.

She heard Raymond say, "Yes sir," and knew they had hit it off.

They must have been outside five minutes, when they returned, Maurice said, "Raymond, is good to go and we called your cell from his, so you have the number, but he wrote it down for you, too."

"Thank you, both, but is everything good, Mrs. Hawkins?" she asked.

"Yes, things will be much better now," she said.

"That is our prayer," Robin said. "We must go now, but Maurice will see you, Raymond, at seven; have a blessed day Mrs. Hawkins, it was very nice to meet you."

"What should I wear tomorrow?" asked Raymond.

"Whatever you wore today will be fine. You're about a thirty-two shirt and twenty-nine waists and thirty-two long inseams, right?" Maurice asked.

"Yes, sir, size thirty-four jacket," Raymond added.

"Seven in the morning," repeated Maurice. "May I see your license?"

Raymond opened his wallet and took out his license and this time there were bills in his wallet, Maurice took a picture of it with his cell and handed it back to him.

"Tomorrow, so get a good night's sleep; do, you have a problem working nights?" he asked.

"No sir, whatever it takes."

"That's a no," his mother added. "He's available any hours."

We left and Maurice said, "He's a very nice and pliable young man with limited experience, which is a plus for the company. He doesn't have a lot of habits to break and he is eager to learn which means he is programmable. He is open and honest and it will be an honor to train him. He has a lot of promise. He grasped the phone in two minutes. He doesn't have much, so, I will pick up a few uniforms for him socks and shoes, for tomorrow."

"Good," she said. "He is the companies first human investment and we're sending him to school, in six months or a year depending on his evaluations."

"That's wonderful," he said. "We're here and that must be your car, just wait and I'll drive over to you."

He got out walked over to the car, got in and drove over and opened the door for Robin, opened the door to the back seat of the Limo and helped her in. He entered the car and started it up and asked her what time did she want him to pick her up.

She said, "There will be three of us and we're going to a local club to have a night together as sister-in-law's."

He stated that he knew this upscale club that had a special for women tonight.

"There is a dress code," he said. "But they have everything and since you have a driver, you should take advantage of what I know and the safety of being driven."

"Yes, sir, Mr. Maurice, we will try it."

"Besides the business has a tab there, so, it won't cost you anything, just bring your I.D. and after tonight, you'll be in the system," he said.

"What is the dress code?" she asked.

"Elegant," he said. She was excited, he got her home and she went in and unlocked the door, to find Louise sitting in the living room in a pair of slacks and top, ready to go.

"Louise," she said, "I'm going to change into something more appropriate for our night out; call Gerri before you change and ask her to wear something nice and sexy and we'll pick her up in an hour, no driving tonight."

She said, "Okay."

She called her and went to her bedroom to find something elegant and Robin did the same.

Robin did her makeup, combed her hair out, put on her lip gloss, slipped into her perfect black dress with pearls and a split in front, with the matching bolero jacket, put on her high heel shoes and put on the earrings Mrs. Marshall gave her, picked up her clutch bag and added a few items with her I. D. and charge card and took her briefcase up front and Louise asked if she would lock it up until they returned.

Louise said, "Of course." and she did. This was to be an evening to remember, for Louise was not a feminine looking woman. She had a nice-looking face, but her body was more masculine looking and the way she walked, seemed to enhance those assets.

Louise had on a lovely lavender and beaded dress with a matching jacket and Robin said to her, "You look perfect, sis, put your I. D. in your purse."

"Okay," Louise said, "What time are we leaving?"

"In five minutes," Robin said.

"Five minutes?" she asked. "It will take us that long to get downstairs."

"Are you ready?" she asked.

"Yes."

"Then, let's go," she said.

They went to the door and Walter came in and said, "I know you're not going out in the neighborhood, with all this glamour going on and what's downstairs, but do have a good time ladies."

"Thank you, Walter, we plan to."

Downstairs they went and out the door and there stood Maurice, waiting to help them into the Limo. Louise had large eyes, but hers were twice as large and she was silent, that was a first for her.

"Louise, give him Gerri's address, please," and she did.

Maurice said. "Six minutes, Mrs. Watson."

"What did he say?" she asked.

"He just gave the approximate time it will take before we arrive at Gerri's house," Robin said.

"Oh," she said, "this is nice."

They were pulling up, when she said, "It usually takes everyone else at least fifteen to twenty minutes to drive from my house to Gerri's."

"Does he know a shortcut?" she asked.

"Sit back and relax, Louise," Robin said.

"I am relaxed," she said. "How can I not be, in all this opulence."

"We're here," he said. "Who is calling her?"

"Will you please, Maurice?" Robin asked. "Just say your ride is out front."

She came out the door looking very elegant, Maurice got out and opened the door for her and closed it. He got in and said, "You ladies will fit right in."

"Oh, Louise and Gerri, this is my driver and friend, Maurice."

He said, "She is my boss, who signs my checks and friend."

"Glad to meet you," they said.

"Do you have your I.D.'s?" he asked.

"Yes," we said simultaneously.

"Mrs. Watson, let them scan yours first then their I. D."

"Yes sir."

"Let go and enjoy yourselves, I know the boss needs this," he said.

He opened the door for us and said, "If you need anything, call me and I will be here in a minute. I will introduce you and then take off and get something to eat, unless you want me to join you."

"No, Maurice, girl's night, remember?" Robin asked. "We'll be fine after you show us the ropes."

"Speak for yourself," Louise said, "I'm a little out of my element."

"Relax Louise, we're here to have fun," Robin said.

Gerri said, "I'm game, let's go in and girl game."

"Let me park," said Maurice, "and I'll escort you in, find a good seat and introduce you to the boss."

Maurice parked and joined them. He took them in and found a very nice table in the center of the room, seated them and went over to the door that said "Private", he knocked and said a few words and returned to the table.

A short time later, a well-dressed man appeared at the table and asked Maurice if he "wanted to introduce these lovely ladies"

And he said, "Certainly, this is my boss, the CFO of the company, Robin Watson, and her two sisters in laws, Gerri Murphy and Louise and they're out for girl's night. I would appreciate it if you took excellent care of them and show them a great time."

"You know I love to show the lovely women a great time, so don't worry and leave them in my very capable hands, I'm Felix, and at your service. Now, if I may have your hand first, Mrs. Watson," he said.

She extended her hand and he scanned it and her I. D., then Gerri's and Louise's.

"You're in the system now. You're welcome here anytime and can order anything in the house. We're at your service, if there is a problem or you're not satisfied, just ask to see Felix, okay ladies?" he asked.

"Okay," they said.

"We'll send someone over to assist you for the night, would you prefer male or female?"

Maurice said, "Male."

"Male it is," he said.

Felix beaconed to a man and he came over and introduced himself as Ralph D., "What will you have tonight?" he asked.

Maurice said, "Bring them a magnum of your best champagne and you decide after that. I'm going out for a while and leaving them in your care, take excellent care of them."

Ralph D. brought them the Champagne and strawberries and the band began to play, Ralph said, "Always keep one person at your table if you're asked to dance or must use the ladies room. Always take your purse with you. Because this is such an exclusive place, there are people who frequent here to find vulnerable women to seduce and steal from."

Two men came over and Louise asked and Gerri to dance and Robin persuaded them to dance. Then one man came over and asked if he could sit and talk with Robin until they return and maybe all could have a drink or dance. Gerri and Louise seemed to enjoy dancing to the oldies and the attention.

"Tell me what makes this such an exclusive place?" she asked Ralph D.

He replied, "The individual services the atmosphere and the quality of our food and drink. Would you like to order food?"

"Is there a menu or is there a house special or a how does that work?" she asked

"We have a menu, but many people love our shrimp, fish, lobster and chicken," he said, "our reputation is beyond reproach."

"I'm waiting to see why it so highly recommended," she said.

"It seems as if your sisters in laws are having an enjoyable time," he said, "I am certain that Maurice would never have brought you here if he were not sure it was a place you would enjoy."

"You're probably right," Robin said. The lights began to dim and the band played on, even more sensual music combined with the champagne made everything more interesting.

Another man Robin asked to dance and she started to refuse when he said, "We only have something to gain, by dancing, if only a few moments of warmth, excitement and tenderness we may never experience again, so why not?"

Robin looked at him and she saw these blue eyes that she wanted to explore deeper and said, "Yes, let us seize the moment."

He took her hand and as he led her to the dance floor, she felt a spark of life and he whirled her around on the floor and drew her closer to him and whispered, "My heart is racing too. It could be the newness of our touch or it could be the secret desire to know each other better or it could simply be we won't each other. Whatever it is, it is exciting. I haven't felt this type of emotional turmoil since my high school days, and I love it."

"Me too," Robin said. They danced and danced until the music ceased and he led her by the hand to the table.

Louise and Gerri said, "You danced like you've been dancing together all your lives."

He looked at them and said, "I met this lovely lady for the first time tonight, but I am a determined man and I have made up my mind, that it will not be the last dance nor the last time we see each other."

He kissed her hand and said, "I don't want to know your name tonight, but the next time we meet, I promise I will know everything about your life from conception and all your friends at this table, too."

She nodded her head and smiled. He walked away, and looked back then walked forward until he was out of sight,

Louise said, "I was so surprised because I've heard you say a thousand times that you cannot dance and I know that to be a fact. But watching you and that gentleman on the floor dancing, it seemed you were born to dance together. You two fit together and you two said you never met before tonight...that is most unusual."

Robin replied, "Louise, are saying you don't believe me and him? I have absolutely no reason to lie about anything, not to mention this trivial dance, I don't even know his name and believe me, I would like to know it."

"I don't mean that Robin, it's just when you see two people dancing like that, a person knows that there is chemistry between them," Louise said. "No one could blame you if you had a friend, you wouldn't be doing anything the other one isn't doing."

"Well," Robin stated, "if I planned to follow in my husband's footsteps, I certainly would not bring his sisters along! We will never run into each other again; the odds are against it. However, in case Russell and I do not make it, I would like for us to make a pact right now, that the three of us shall remain friends, sisters and close, can we agree to do that?" Robin asked.

Gerri said, "I certainly have no problem with that."

And Louise said, "He hasn't been home in two days or even called has he Robin?"

"No," Robin said. "He's too busy with his new or old woman, the same one he brought to my bed."

Louise said, "He is my brother, but the things he's doing, I would have been gone, if Walter did that to me. We'll remain sisters and friends and if one needs the other, we'll be there for her."

"Good, now that is out of the way, would you ladies care to go to the dining room and eat?" Robin asked. "Ralph D., I believe my sisters would love to try Lobster and appetizers, can you help us?"

"That is my job," he said. "Would you like light or is this table suitable?"

They asked him what was the protocol?

He answered, "The customer is always right, but VIP's call the shots and you're on that list. Tell me what you want and I will make it happen."

In that case, they agreed to have a sampler platter brought to the table with another bottle of champagne and chardonnay.

"Be back in a few," he said. He returned with a gold pan, soap and towels to wash their hands and dried them and left packages of towelettes on the sides of the plates. He received a beep and went off and returned with a portable table loaded with a buffet. He then took individual plates and filled them with a little of everything and placed a bib around our necks and in our laps and poured the champagne.

"Let me know if you require seconds or specifics," he said.

Louise said, "The Lobster is delicious."

"It is the specialty of the house, designed to make one return for more," he said.

She ate the Lobster and requested more. Ralph D. did not hesitate; he gave her two servings, with special butter.

Gerri said, "I'll have more shrimp and a glass of Chardonnay, please."

"Right away," he said, and he fixed her up.

Robin ate fish treats lobster bites and shrimp with a glass of Champagne and asked, Ralph if he could eat and drink.

He said, "VIP's call the shots, but I can only do that after you're served."

"Well get a glass and pour yourself a glass of your choice and eat whatever you like," Robin said.

"Yes, ma'am," he said.

He made sure everyone was served and went out returned with another tray with Roast and steak and hard liquor, Hennessey. He sliced the meat and said, "Try this with your lobster."

And he fixed ate and drank. The table finished off the trays and alcohol and Ralph D. was full, but highly functioning, he brought the gold pan with warm water, soap and towels and they all cleaned up and he provided hand cream, removed the trays and ropes and our table was open again to receive callers. Men came over and asked Gerri and Louise to dance and they did it all, from waltz to the roaring twenties to slow dance. They were popular and loved it. Robin looked for Maurice. It was after one in the morning, so Robin beeped him.

Maurice was there within five minutes Robin asked for the bill and Maurice came over.

"Are you ladies ready to go?" he asked.

"Yes," Robin said, "I'm waiting for the bill."

He said, "No, Mrs. Watson, I'll handle this part." He went to the door and knocked.

Felix came over and said, "You're in the system, Robin. May I call you by your first name?"

She nodded yes, and he continued, "You just give approval for your assistant Ralph D. and say tip and you're ready to go, no muss no fuss. We look forward to serving you again. Perhaps you'll schedule a sauna and massage next time. Thank you for your business and please come again."

Robin, thanked him and said, "Sooner than you think."

Maurice made sure Ralph helped them to the car with all their belongings and closed the doors, he entered and said, "ETA for Gerri, six minutes. Is there someone you can call to meet her at the door?" he asked.

Louise said yes and called to inform them. When they arrived, her husband came out and helped her into the house, she turned and said, "Thank you for an exciting night, call you two tomorrow."

She walked inside and her husband was behind her. Maurice stated, "ETA, six minutes."

Louise said, let me get the keys out and I think we can make it inside."

Maurice said, "I must walk my boss to the door."

They arrived and Maurice turned off the ignition, opened the door and helped them out, closed the door and locked the car. Louise placed the key in the lock and unlocked the door. Everyone went inside. He took the keys out of the door and handed them to her. He asked both to take his arm and they walked up the stairs and came to the door. Louise unlocked the door, thanked Maurice and said goodnight. Robin said good morning and she would be ready waiting for him to pick her up. She thanked him for a great experience and said,

"I hope you can sleep."

He left and they locked the door, hugged good night, and went to their rooms. Robin opened the bedroom door and thought about her briefcase, but said she would be up before Louise left and she would get it then. She took off her clothes and hung them up, then put on her gown and got in bed, reached for the alarm, set it early, placed it back and went to sleep. When the alarm went off, she jumped up and went to the kitchen to get a drink of water and a diet Pepsi, took a quick shower and heard Louise walking down the hallway. She said, "Good morning" and Robin reminded her to get the briefcase out of her safe before she left, she said, "okay".

Louise told Robin she forgot to turn on the alarm but heard her and that's what awoke her. She thanked her for that and last night.

"It was worth it," she said. "We haven't had a time like that ever."

She went back to her room and came back with Robin's briefcase. She thanked her and she went to finish dressing. Louise returned dressed and ready to go out the door, she asked if Russell had left any signs of being home and Robin didn't hesitate to answer.

"No," she said. "There are no signs he has been in the bedroom, bathroom or kitchen, so he has clothes wherever he is or he took clothes on Tuesday, knowing he was going to stay."

Louise looked at Robin and said, "You should check your accounts and freeze them and when he comes home, don't leave anything out and around he can use or have another woman use pretending to be you. Ask your bank to require three forms of identification or a paystub. He is up to something. Be careful."

"Thank you, Louise, and don't worry about your rent I'll take care of that on Friday, but I will move his things into the small bedroom when I return tonight."

She said, "Robin, I'm not concerned about the rent, especially after last night, but I don't think I would move anything right now, it may be more dangerous for you than you think. Think about it, he's trying to get you to react, to make the first move, so he can countermove, that is not a good thing. Don't fall into his trap. Roll with it if you can."

Robin said she would and asked how much is the rent, he never told her.

Louise said, "He pays three hundred a month, but until you decide what you want to do, give me a hundred and throw in a few meals like you've been doing and we'll be good."

"Okay," she said. "Go to work and I better finish dressing Maurice will be here shortly." She finished dressing and was about to go downstairs, when the phone rang, she picked it up and said hello. A voice said hello, it was Russell, there was a knock on the door and she knew it was Maurice. "Russell, I must go, who did you want to speak with?"

"You," he said.

"You called too late," she said. "My ride is here. Talk with you later and have a great day." She hung up, went to the front door and gave Maurice her briefcase and purse and told him she had to move something and would be right down. He asked if he could help, she said, "I need to hide something."

She went to the bedroom and took her jewelry and placed it in the corner of the small bedroom up front, changed her mind and put it in her pocket, locked the door and went downstairs to the car. Maurice helped her in and said, "Just a moment Mrs. Watson."

Maurice entered the car, started it and drove off, he said, "Your uncle was watching you all the time and I can't figure out why."

"Maurice, Russell didn't come home the night before the celebration and hasn't been home yet, as we were leaving, the phone rang and it was him. I told him I had to leave, we'd talk later," she said. "It was clear he was calling to find out if anyone was home, he's planning something. I went to get the jewelry, Mrs. Marshall had given me to hide it, but wasn't satisfied with that so, they're in my pocket."

"I have the phone number where he is, but not the address. He left his little red book on the floor, it fell out of his pocket in his hurry to change clothes the day of the celebration, when he sneaked in late and tried to get to the office in time, he didn't notice he left it. I found it in the dark that night on the way to the kitchen in my sock feet, I kicked it picked it up and went to the kitchen. When I returned to the bedroom, I opened it and there were a lot of numbers in there but one next to the last page looked suspicious, it was lined up as if to be added but they were single numbers and could be added in a person's mind, there was a line under them but no total. I picked up the phone and dialed the numbers in their order the phone rang three times and he answered it, I hung up. I knew he was going to call home so I let the phone ring the first time he called. Then he called again and after two rings, picked up the phone as if very sleepy and he hung up. Pictures were taken of the book and the page, they are in my briefcase. But he doesn't think I'm wise to him. Three weeks ago, before the fire, I was sick and left work early and came home and found him in my bed with some woman, I threw her clothes out the window into the snow and told her to get out of my bed and go get them, He gave her his coat and told her to wait downstairs. He asked his sister to help her and she did, but told me she had no choice and didn't know he was doing something as crazy as that, to bring a woman home. Louise was furious and so was Uncle Book. He told everyone that he was going to try to make his marriage work and he was planning a honeymoon at home for the entire week-end and that was what everyone wanted to hear, clueless, no inkling he trapped me, locked me in and raped me over and over. He beat me and plied me with alcohol until I didn't know where I was or what I was doing but he abused me so I wanted to die and he threatened to kill me if I told anyone. The next day he changed, he was a different person for seven days and then this. I knew he was messing with me, but I was looking for a way out alive, so I played his game with him, and I've been playing, ever since. This morning Louise told me to be careful, that when a man is gone this long and comes back, it isn't good. She told her to hide her papers and anything he can use to try to take her money, notify the bank to put a freeze on the account they have together or move the money. She started on that the day of the celebration but now she must step it up and withdraw all her money and leave his. She knows they will be there today looking for paperwork or her I.D. so some woman can pretend to be her. Now you know the whole story," she said. "What do you think?"

Maurice said, "I am so sorry this has happened to you. I think you should leave him, it can't end well," he said.

Robin asked Maurice if he thought Raymond would make a budding detective. He said he would need a little time to determine if he has the instinct for it.

"I have the instinct," he said, "what do you need, Robin?"

"First, I need to get to the bank and withdraw all my money from our joint account and close the accounts he knows about and open new accounts or place the money in the new account I just opened," Robin said.

Maurice said, "Close out the accounts he knows about and put the money in the accounts he doesn't know about until you open new accounts. Call the bank and ask them to send a financial consultant to the office, he suggested and go from there," said Maurice.

"That's the best idea I have heard," Robin said. Secondly, she needed to find out the name of the woman he was with and her address to include her name in divorce proceedings.

"We need something to help find out that information," he said, "what about her phone number?" she asked.

"That will be a good start," he said.

She passed him the number and he said, "I'll have her name and address before noon."

"Check out his spending habits for the past two weeks, after all, he has not been to work in that length of time and if he has taken out any insurance policies on me," she said, "these are things I need to know," Robin said. "As well as, if he has been to the doctor or clinic lately for STD's."

Maurice said, "These are doable things. I'll let you out and you unlock the building and I will park and return before you check out the building."

Robin opened the building and before she stepped into the waiting area, Maurice was there, he checked out the building and Robin went into the kitchen to put on the coffee and open the slot for the donuts. She took out the crystal platter, washed her hands, put on plastic gloves and took the pastries and neatly placed them on the platter and covered them with the glass top. She got a diet Pepsi out of the refrigerator and walked to her office. She saw Maurice talking to Raymond and suggested they use the conference room.

They left the area and went to the conference room. There was a room off the kitchen that was small, but had potential it could hold a desk and two chairs and needed and extra entrance, but since it was close to the kitchen, it was located easy and close the restroom. She contacted the contractor and asked him to come out and fix up the room for security. It took him two hours to fix up that room and it was ready for occupancy the following day, with phone, file cabinets monitor and ceiling fan with brick flooring. It looked very nice, but needed an additional smaller desk and phone, so the contractor added a wall desk to pull out and push up when not in use with a floor lamp and chair. Robin had name plaques made for Mr. Maurice E. Merry, Supervisor of Security and Mr. Raymond Hawkins, Trainee. Security Department were outside the door. She wanted the approval of Mr. Marshall first before unveiling it to the family so it was covered and locked. Mr. Marshall came in briefly and said he would work from home, he just wanted to stop in and see if there was anything he needed to know and she asked him to follow her and give his suggestion or disapproval. "Since Maurice was holding meetings all over the place, he needed an office," she said.

Mr. Marshall said he approved until they branched out, then he could have a larger office. "You're always thinking, Robin," he said. "The improvements you have made were all necessary and prudent."

"Well done. Is there anything else?" he asked.

"Mr. Marshall, your apartment is clean and the bed is too, why don't you go upstairs and rest, did the Mrs. get any rest last night?" she asked.

"Yes, thank you, she did. I was up with Johanna all night, but it was not as bad as it had been because I rested yesterday," he said.

"Well, sir," Robin said, "there is nothing hindering you from resting today as well," she said.

"Maybe an hour or two," he said.

"Yes, sir," she said, "it is so comforting just knowing you're in the building," she said. "Go upstairs and let me know what you need and I'll have it for you in twenty minutes at most and thanks for the transportation, we had girl's night out last night."

"Wonderful, Robin, you need a balance in your life. You're very welcome and my wife said she will make the arrangements for your arrival and stay and contact you today, she said, 'just bring yourself,' she has everything there that you will need."

"Yes, sir," she said. "I am excited about it."

He went upstairs to his apartment and went to bed. That was good enough for her, inspiration was in the building. Since Mr. Marshall approved the Security Department, Robin beeped Maurice, but it took a while for him to respond. While she was waiting, she called the bank and asked Regina if she could borrow her car to run an errand.

She said, "Of course, but I need to see your driver's license."

Robin said, "Fair enough."

Robin got her briefcase and jacket, took out her license and showed it to Regina and she approved it and gave her the keys to her car. Robin drove to the bank and made a withdrawal from their joint savings leaving one dollar in that account and had her checking account closed and a new one opened, while there.

"They were the accounts Russell were aware," she had. Robin drove across town and deposited the money in her new savings account and asked for a balance. She put a password on her account to protect it from fraud and made sure that if any inquiries were made into her accounts, they would be brought to her attention immediately. She opened a checking account while there and she made the same security arrangements with a password and numbers. She had just completed everything, when Maurice beeped her and she called him and told him she would be back in the office in an hour. She went to the bank she opened a money market account and savings and asked for a balance and password protection added to her accounts, it was done and she purchased traveler's checks for everyday use and to pay Louise. She was all set now; she filled Regina's tank up and returned to work feeling so much better. She asked for a balance on Russell's checking account and was surprised that he had less than fifteen hundred dollars total left. He had spent quite a lot of money, but none of it was on her. Robin was not concerned because she could purchase what she wanted. The question was not on whom he had spent his money, but where he thought he could get more?

"Sad to say, he had to go to someone other than her," she said. Robin wrote out her rent payment to Louise with a traveler's check and notation, photo copied it and all them to have a record of the traveler's checks. She put Louise's in an envelope and sealed it. She took two traveler's checks and put them in her purse in case of emergency.

Maurice came in and asked if we could go to her office.

Robin said, "Follow me please."

She picked up the keys and placed them in her pocket and walked towards the kitchen, she got a Pepsi out and walked over to the side and Maurice asked, "Where are you going, Robin?"

She answered and said, "give me a hand please."

Maurice noticed it was a new steel door, Robin removed the paper and the sign on the door said Security Department. She opened the door and said come into your office, he looked surprised and she handed him the keys and took a seat.

"What is going on?" he asked.

"Your desk," she said. "And your assistant's. We can speak in here it is sound proof."

He cried a little and caught himself, "I'm emotional," he said.

"That's fine," she said. "You deserve a moment. Now you wanted to talk to me."

"I found out the name and address of the woman. Her name is Ebony Kane and she is twenty-nine years old, she lives at the address on the paper in front of you, she is having a baby never been married, but was living with a man when she and Russell met three years ago, with one child. She moved to her present address two years ago, with him as a co-signer with their sixteen-month-old daughter Classy Watson and her other daughter Shelby. He has made major purchases in the past two weeks, a new bedroom suite for adults, a plasma television, computer and games also clothes. The neighbors state they have been partying for two weeks and had a lot of people over the past week-end. Said they were engaged and would be married in a few months. I am so sorry, Robin, he's been trying to make you leave him initially, but now he wants more. He has two insurance policies on you totaling a million and a half dollars and with what he thinks he will get from a divorce or God forbid, your death, they will be super rich. I don't think you should return there tonight and you need to change your beneficiaries yesterday and your will. Robin, this is no longer personal, it is deadly and we need to tell Mr. Marshall immediately because his company is at risk."

"You're right," she said. "Mr. Marshall is upstairs, I'm going to make the changes to my insurance and will and you bring Mr. Marshall up to date on everything. And I will be up as soon as I'm finished."

"Is there anything I should not tell him?" he asked.

"No," she said. "Be totally honest with him so he can make the best decision for the company. Now I know why he doesn't want children with me nor a home of our own."

Chapter Twelve

Reality

Reality set in, as Robin walked to her office and looked around, for what seemed like the final time. She gathered all her policies and change of beneficiary forms and faxed the new changes to the proper agencies, removing Russell Watson as her beneficiary effective yesterday. She then wrote her resignation, dated the same previous day. She addressed the envelope to Mr. Marshall and sealed it. It was a difficult thing for her to do, as she prepared to surrender her keys, I.D., code and petty cash box over to the owner, she had everything on the desk that was once her pride and joy, awaiting the arrival of Mr. Marshall.

Robin sat there then decided she wanted to see her staff in the cubicles and walked over to see them and say goodbye. She asked if they were making progress or marking time, making progress, they said. You haven't asked us that in a long time, they said. We've missed it. Robin turned around looked for the new employee, Raymond Hawkins, and she wondered where he was, but she wondered if she would see him again. There was so much happening, it was overwhelming and her mind was hanging to sanity with a thin thread.

Robin did what she needed to do, so she went back to the office and locked the door, with her resignation in hand, she walked upstairs to the awaiting audience with all her dirty laundry on the line.

She walked upstairs to the apartment of Mr. Marshall and knocked on the door to his apartment, the door opened and Mr. Marshall was standing there with open arms. "Come in Robin."

She took a step towards him and he grabbed her and hugged her and said, "It's alright to cry, if you want, Robin. You have been through a lot and you've managed to be thoughtful, loving, giving, considerate and genuinely concerned about others, while suffering in silence some of the most vile and horrendous abusive acts one can imagine. You're amazing."

"We've been on the phone with my wife," he continued, "and she wants you out now. 'A woman of your class and grace, should never be forced to endure what you have with no recourse.' said Juliette."

She went into her pocket and pulled out her letter and handed it to him. "I cannot bear to see anything negative touch what you have built up," she said. "I refuse to let him take you or the family down with me. I must submit this to spare you."

Mr. Marshall ripped up the letter. "This never happened, do you understand, Robin?" he asked.

"Are you sure?" she asked.

"Yes, we are sure," he said. "Who could do your job with such expertise, perfection and love?" he asked.

"I can't even do it," he said.

Maurice said, "You cannot search for a Cinderella without a shoe and a foot to try it on, without both, you can forget it. She's in a class all by herself."

"We will figure this out," he said, "however, the best way to do that is to move out and get a legal separation. We have a meeting with an attorney shortly and we're acting, immediately," he said. "The reason he hasn't been going to work, is he thinks, he'll be fired and I must support him to get a divorce. He must face reality, Robin, like everyone else, he needs proof and it seems we're the only one with it. Don't you worry, Robin, I promise you'll come out of this victoriously."

Maurice asked, "Mr. Marshall what time is the appointment with the lawyer?"

"Juliette is taking care of that now, we're waiting for her to call," he said. As soon as he finished talking, Juliette called and spoke with her husband and informed him the attorney was coming to them so that anyone looking will just think that a businessman was keeping a business appointment.

"He should arrive shortly to give us our options and his advice," he said.

Maurice stated that is a prudent move.

"Russell is desperate now, he could be anywhere conjuring all type of maleficent ideas, to close the door to the end of living a double life," he said.

The bell rang and Mr. Marshall went to the door, opened it and said, "We will be more comfortable in the conference room, follow me."

Everyone entered the conference room and the discussion was underway. The lawyer was a high powered criminal lawyer, Robert E. McAfee, Esq. and he informed them that since no police reports were made, no pictures were shown and Robin confided in no one during the abuse and there was little chance Russell would confess, which meant they either had to get evidence, which would be extremely dangerous and potentially deadly, but doing nothing had the same potential consequences without the possibility of Robin being rescued.

"The other choice is to find the weakest link in his second life and convince that person to help us betray and convict him. While you're thinking about your options, let's make sure he can't get to your funds, as beneficiary or investments as husband of the late Robin Watson, where this seems to be heading, therefore, I need all your accounts and a list of any assets you have," he said.

Mr. Marshall said, "She owns ten percent of the business but has not received the papers, yet. How much would you say that is worth and does Russell know?" he asked.

"Yes, he knows and about ten million dollars," he said. The room was quiet even Robin's mouth was opened.

"Who else knows about this, everyone in the business and the family knows, perhaps the value is off a million or so, but it was Juliette's final decision after Robin made the company more than that in six months' time, and she put the business back together after the fire and increased the stock value with her unique strategies for the work place and the staff. We want to adopt her, but we'll settle for her moving in with the family and all our children support our decision!" he exclaimed.

"Well," said the lawyer, "it seems Russell has more than ample motives for murder, let's prove it."

Mr. McAfee said. "We need small cameras and a good story to keep her alive tonight until we can get the camera's in place, Robin, how good of an actress are you?" The Plan will hinge on how convincing you can be under stress and I'm sure manipulation, in the event Russell returns home tonight. Are you willing to endure whatever comes?" he asked.

"I don't know," said Mr. Marshall. "We think she has endured enough at the hands of Russell.

"We'll need your participation, too," said Mr. McAfee. "Your wife said you two are willing to do anything and spare no expense, to keep Robin safe, did you mean it?" he asked.

"Yes, we mean it with all our hearts," he said.

"Alright," he said. "It may take a week or two, depending on how fast Russell spends what he has remaining. So, let's hope he can't control himself and it could be over sooner. Is everyone on board?" he asked.

"We are on board," said everyone in unison.

Chapter Thirteen

The Best Laid Plans

"We need those cameras and a few microphones," said Mr. McAfee.

Maurice said, "I have them in the trunk of my car. I haven't had time to stock my office, Robin surprised me with, yet."

Maurice got up and went to his car and returned with the items Mr. McAfee wanted. "How do we utilize these?" asked Maurice.

"We will install one or two on her coat and purse as decorations and microphones as well," he said. "Do you know how to disguise them, Maurice?"

"Absolutely," he replied, "it will take me six minutes, he said. He took the purse and some material from a bag and placed them in a design surrounded by stones and rhinestones.

"It is impressive, you pull it off," said Mr. McAfee.

"I thought I would have to bring in my expert to do the job," he said.

"He did the same with her coat using the points on the collars to form a unified look, the color of the buttons on the coat and sleeves."

Maurice informed Robin that the best positions to place the microphones and cameras in the house, would be in the bedroom, directly in front of the bed, with the color of furniture flush with the color of the equipment. Microphone behind the bed or under the table next to the sofa, in the picture and on the door facing the room.

He suggested that a microphone be placed on top of or under the medicine cabinet or vanity, since he liked to play water games or behind the commode, where she can easily retrieve it. The hallway was a good place to add one or two and a camera.

"Do you think you can do that?"

"Yes," she said. "I can."

"You'll be on film," he said. "Whatever he wants to do to you, will be on film until the film is destroyed or not.

"I understand, Mr. McAfee, I will be memorialized; but, Russell may not show up," Robin said.

"But in case he does, I will be prepared to endure if it means I'll get justice," she said.

"Great," said Mr. McAfee. "We're all set but announce you ordered a plasma television and you're looking for it to be delivered tomorrow while you're at work."

"Is there anyone you can ask to let the deliveryman in to install it?" he asked.

"Gerri has a key and so does uncle book, we'll try them after telling Louise and she may have a suggestion," she added.

"Do you think she's home, now?"

"She may be; however, she will be more receptive if there were something in it for her," Robin said.

"Immediate gratification," she added.

"Tell her you'll leave the television with her should you move, but until then, you're considering renovating the bedroom and kitchen and that should incite and invite her to help in any way you see fit," he said.

"You're right," she replied. "And it is drab in the rear of the house, so, that should work fine."

Robin called and Louise answered the phone. "Louise, this is Robin, I have a problem and need your help."

"How can I help?" she asked.

"I just purchased a plasma television, but it won't be delivered until tomorrow while I'm at work, can you recommend someone to let the installation man in?" she asked. "Perhaps Gerri or uncle book?"

"Well," she said, "Gerri has a key and she is home during the day. Do you have a specific time?"

"Between eleven and twelve-thirty," Robin said.

"Okay, I'll call her and ask and call you back," she said.

"That will be great and should I move, I want you to have the television," she said.

"Really?"

"Really, Robin said, but until that time, I am considering renovating the bedroom and kitchen if it is alright with you, it's a little drab and needs brightening up. I won't contact anyone until you give me the okay," she said.

"Okay, Louise said, I'll let you know and Gerri will be here so you can tell them the time is perfect, okay?" "Okay, Robin said, but if she can't make it, please call me back."

"If she can't make it, Uncle Book's wife can let him in, so, if I don't call you in the next five minutes, it's a go."

"Thank you, Louise, you won't regret it and I have your rent, too, see you later," she said.

"Okay."

"Can we make it happen by that time?" she asked Maurice.

"Absolutely, a couple of twists and the camera will be recording whether on or off," he said. "Before you turn it over to Louise, we'll receive a repair call and remove the equipment, however, that contracting job is all on you."

"Didn't you get the memo, it's part of the plan," Robin said.

"Once the Plasma television is in place, it will pick up everything from every direction in the room and some of outside of it," said Maurice.

"You must really know what you're doing to have such advance technology," she said.

"Why do you think he is such an asset, he wired my entire estate. If he says he can do it, he can. Just as another leader of my team," said Mr. Marshall.

"There is a lot of talent and experience in this room, if we can't pull this off with Russell, then we all need to hibernate for the next twenty years, or go back to school," said

Mr. McAfee. "We would never live that down, to be beaten by a novice."

"Well, she hasn't called back," stated Mr. McAfee, "so, that means she has someone on standby for tomorrow."

"Why did you doubt she would?" asked Maurice. "You were the only one of us who doubted.

"My experience is people are unpredictable, the one's you think will are the ones who won't and vice versa," he said.

"We've all been there, said Mr. Marshall, but this seemed to be a sure thing. It is the one who unlocks the door tomorrow that is the wild card."

"We'll, be prepared to give that person a gratuity," he said. "First ask what is the fee and if he or she declines to say, give that person fifty dollars for their trouble and be done."

"That is not to say that they didn't let someone in before you arrived or will after you leave, but we should plant someone in the area two hours before arrival time and two hours after or until that person leaves," he said. "Better yet, change the bedroom door lock and lock the door before leaving the house, that will solve all the issues except Russell coming home unless we request that Russell be given an envelope when he arrives, by Uncle Book."

"What do you think?" Maurice asked.

"That could make everyone suspicious and wonder why she changed the lock or it could simply state it is an expensive television that she is trying to protect from theft or anyone using her room," said Mr. Marshall.

"I vote to leave the door alone since she didn't mention the change to Louise when they spoke."

Robin said she agreed.

"Since any one as arrogant as Russell is, to bring a woman home before, he will probably not pass up the opportunity to do it again, she said, and the door needs to be the same as usual for tomorrow, at least."

"I agree, too," said Mr. McAfee.

"Make sure you pay that rent today, he said, and sign this paper, giving us your permission to bug your room and the common areas of the apartment as a paying tenant, whether on the lease or not. We can hope she doesn't have a lease with her brother, but if mail comes to the address with your name on it, and you can prove you resided there for more than six months, we're legal. The Traveler's Check will be your receipt. Put in the notation that you are taking over rent payments in lieu of Russell Watson who abandoned the premises two weeks prior. If she cashes or deposits it, she agrees to what it says."

"Write the number of the TC down, we won't make the move until everything is in place," he said.

"I know you want to trust the sisters," said Mr. Marshall. "But Robin, in real time, blood really is thicker than water and she is telling him everything you say and do."

"That's why I am certain, Russell will be home tonight, yes, they all knew he was bringing women home, long before that day, but remember, they knew you were in the city alone and had no idea you would advance beyond their control. If they kept you isolated, they were all you could turn to."

"They still think you're under their control, and that is good, they know you have a driver, but have no inkling he is your friend and confidant. They certainly don't know how close our family is to you or they would have ceased their game when they discovered it. I would like to give Uncle Book the benefit of the doubt, he said, but his sister is Russell's mother, so, reality check there too."

"I'm going to give you the advice I would give my own daughter, if she were caught up in a trap like this, expect the worse from Russell, he may even persuade you to call in tomorrow or do it for you, and that is to be expected, except he knows a delivery is coming and that maybe your saving grace, since you informed Louise you told them you had to work, he may save the worse for tomorrow; but in any case, think about this, to get justice, we have to make sacrifices, so try to enjoy it and do not let him see you cry or break down, he feeds off of fear. Be strong as the woman you are and it will be over as soon as we get enough on him to take to the officials."

"Okay, Robin?"

"Yes, sir."

"I want this scumbag," he said. "But the right way."

Robin listened to every word he said and was inspired. "You have me and Juliette for the rest of our lives," he added.

"Us, too," said Maurice and Mr. McAfee.

"It's getting late and what do you think Walter and Louise would like to eat tonight?" he asked. "Barbeque rib and coleslaw," she said.

"Then send it out and get it for them make it a little hotter than usual, he said, and give them a piece of pie. You have chicken, you'll need something on your stomach. Give her a couple of bottles of Chardonnay from my stock and a shot of Brandy."

"I'll take a shot of Brandy, too Marshall," said the lawyer.

"Bring the bottle and we'll all have some," he said. Maurice came back with everything on a tray. Mr. Marshall poured and gave a toast, "To Robin, the most courageous lady I know."

"To Robin," said everyone and drank.

Lawyer McAfee said, "I'll have another, it's not every day, you have a drink of, forty-year-old, Armagnac Brandy."

"One for the road," He drank the brandy and asked. "Did we turn off the recorder?"

"Yes," said Maurice.

"Delivery is here and I'll pay this," said Mr. Marshall, with joy. He brought the food in and separated it.

"Robin, yours has the wine in it," he said.

"But we'll mark them. Get a marker and put W/ L on this and R on this, now put them in a carry bag, the one they delivered in is large enough," said Maurice. "And more authentic."

"Did anyone want those donuts?" he asked.

"They're for Raymond," he replied. "And some of those sandwiches in the freezer."

"Okay, Maurice, where is he?" asked Mr. Marshall.

"He's been working on this case all day and tonight and tomorrow," answered Maurice.

"Good," said Mr. Marshall. "You prepared him?"

"Yes, sir," Maurice said, "they know me by sight, but not him and he'll make the delivery tomorrow, also. You were right about him, Robin, he made me proud."

"Then he made us proud," said Mr. Marshall. "When this is over, we'll talk with him."

"Give us a hug, Robin," and she gave everyone a hug and they all said, "be strong, it's day one of academy award time, but only one more to go, unless he seals his fate and discloses some nefarious plan, then we may be obliged to follow it to its conclusion."

"I'm taking her to the lions," said Maurice.

"But she has the same God with her that Daniel had in the lion's den," said Mr. Marshall.

"She's ready and we're ready," he said. "Let's get this night over, before my wife and I do something we'll regret."

"Leave your briefcase or take it?" he asked.

"It will look strange not to have it," she said, "but bring another bag."

She took everything out of her briefcase and placed it in the bag, took a stack of papers from the conference room and placed them in the briefcase with the keys to the office and code. She took a few Traveler's checks from her purse, placed them in her wallet in the bag, closed it up and asked that the bag be locked up until she returns.

"It is done," said Mr. McAfee and Marshall.

"Did we get everything on tape?" he asked

"Yes, sir," said Maurice.

"That's additional proof of fear," he said. "Go, Maurice, before I change my mind and I'll lock it up. She only has her house keys, lip gloss and compact in her purse she's taking home."

Maurice helped her with her coat, took her bags and they walked her to the car.

"We'll do everything as we always do," he said. "Including the part where I say pick you up at seven."

"Okay," Robin said.

They drove and he said, "Six minutes."

"Do you want anything, Robin?" he asked.

"Do you have anything to drink, my nerves are a little on edge?" she said.

"You have an entire bar back there, use it and I'll slow down a bit," he said. She was not used to utilizing the bar, as she never gave a thought to one being in the car until now, she located it and poured a mixture of things a twelve-year-old Scotch and a small bottle of Chardonnay. "It is not so easy to get drunk when you're trying so hard. A little tippy and a buzz and you are done."

"We're almost there," he said. "Take another one."

She did, and he said, "I'll empty all the trash, don't worry and help you upstairs, get your keys out and hand them to me."

He took everything out, took her by the arm and escorted her to the door, unlocked it and walked her up the stairs. "Straighten up a little, Robin. Wait."

He took her bag and opened it, took out a piece of chicken and gave it to her, hoping to disguise the smell of alcohol from Louise. She chewed and licked the sauce off her fingers and said, "That is good and hot."

"I must say it really smells delicious," then Robin closed the bag and asked for the keys, he handed them to her and she climbed the last stair and unlocked the door.

"See you at seven," he said.

"I'll be dressed and waiting," she replied, "three meetings before two, and please, be on time."

"Am I ever late?" he asked.

"No, you're not, I'm sorry."

"Seven," he said.

"Good night and thanks again."

"Good night, Mrs. Watson," she closed the door, locked it and walked to the room. She stopped in the kitchen and placed the bag with the initials W/L on the table, opened the door to the bedroom and went in. She placed her purse on the table next to the sofa facing the bed. Took the Chardonnay out and placed one bottle in the cabinet and opened the other. Pulled out the tray, opened the Barbeque chicken and took out a piece poured a glass of wine bit into the chicken and chewed, then sipped the wine. She pulled off her clothes and put on her gown and sat down on the sofa.

"It's very quiet in here," she said. Usually, the smell of food would draw Louise and Walter out of their bedroom, but there was not a stir. Robin went to the bathroom and turned on the water and placed the bugs under the medicine cabinet and thought about it and put them on top instead. She put her bath oil in and went to get her wine, sat it down and stepped into the tub. She thought she heard a sound then, she got out and opened the door and called to Louise, but there was no answer. She walked to the front and checked the door, it was still locked, she opened the door to the front bedroom, but didn't see a thing, she closed the door to the front bedroom and turned the key. She took the key out of the lock and took it with her, she wanted to place the chain on the front door, but decided not to, but placed the other bugs on the closet and returned to the bathroom. She locked the door, this time and climbed into the tub, sat down and lathered up and leaned back in the bathtub. Robin heard another sound, but said the house was old and it may be settling. She took another drink and lathered again. She leaned back with her glass in her hand and this time, she heard footsteps.

She yelled, "Who's out there and why are you hiding?"

She climbed out of the tub and dried off. She put on her gown and slippers, took the bottle of wine, glass and key and dirty gown and went to the door and unlocked it and opened it. She still didn't see anyone and the bag of food was still on the table. All that planning for Louise and Walter, and they are not home, she thought, what a waste of time, Robin placed her dirty gown in the hamper in the closet, and went into the room and looked around, placed the key to the front bedroom on the table beside the bottle of wine. She poured another drink, when she remembered she was supposed to help Regina take Celia for a new bedroom suite. She picked up the phone and called them.

"Hello," said Celia.

"Hello, Celia, this is Robin. I'm calling because I recently arrived home and remembered we were supposed to go shopping for the bedroom suite and give you your check. I was overwhelmed today and will do it tomorrow, if that is okay," she said.

"Yes, that will be fine," she said.

"So, we're on for tomorrow after work," Robin said.

"Thank you for calling, Robin," she said.

"It's not a problem, Celia, good night."

"Robin," she said. "Did the men find you today?"

"Who?" she asked.

"Two men came to the office today and asked for you, one was Russell but we didn't know the other one. They used the restroom and said to tell you they would not be home tonight.

"Really, anything else, Celia?" Robin asked.

"He took a diet Pepsi and tried to go into your office but the door was locked. We asked them to leave and Russell said he was there to see Mr. Marshall, too. Regina told him she would have Mr. Marshall call him and set up an appointment, if he would leave his number. He said never mind and don't mention they were there. I slipped a note under your door."

"What time was that, Celia?"

"Around three forth-five to four fifteen," she said.

"Thanks Celia. Listen, can you call me back in fifteen minutes and if I don't answer, send the police to my address second floor, then call Maurice and tell him what you told me, please. No disregard that, call Maurice now and tell him what you told me."

"Yes, I can," she said. "Fifteen minutes and I will call Maurice right now."

"And whatever he says to do, that's what you should do, and thank you, Celia," she hung up and Robin turned on all the lights and walked to the front door and turned on lights as she went with her cell phone in hand. She knocked on Louise's door and there was no answer. She locked the front door with the chain and went to the kitchen and checked the back porch, and left the porch light on.

She took a seat by the house and cell phones. Her cell phone rang, she answered it and was glad to hear the voice on the other end, it was Maurice. "I think I should come get you, Robin," he said.

"I don't know how they got by us, but they did," he said. "That was hubris. That was a warning of some kind."

"I know," she said. "I'm sitting here next to the front door besides the house phone and cell phone, with the chain on the door. Louise and Walter are gone. I took a bath a short time ago and had to get out of the tub, because I heard noises twice. Each time I checked the house, even called out and asked who it was and no reply. I was concerned earlier, but now, I'm mad, Maurice, the nerve of them!"

"There is a gun in here, hold on until I get it, please?"

"No," he said. "I am coming for you."

Robin looked at the clock and said, if it's someone who thinks I have money in the house, boy are they mistaken."

"I need to check the video's and ascertain whether we have evidence to sustain your experiences, real or imagined," said Maurice.

"Oh, it was real," she said.

"You're rambling," he said. "Listen to me, I want you to go lie down and sleep, nothing is happening tonight, it's his game and he's not working alone, they're all in it together. Go to sleep so you can be fresh and I'll be here to awaken you. I've been outside since I called you and nothing is stirring out here. The police are patrolling the area every half hour or more to make sure I'm safe, so there is back up. Go to sleep, if Louise and Walter return, I'll call you two rings and hang up or come up with them."

"Come up with them," she said.

"Okay, I'll have the police to stop and accompany me."

"Sounds good," she stated.

"That drinking did not work, I thought it would put me to sleep, but it didn't."

"Take another or is there a beer in the house?" he asked.

"Yes, Walter likes beer," she replied.

"Go get two and drink them both, you'll be out in no time. If you want to sleep in the car, you can do that too, just dress warmly with socks and shoes and come down with a blanket."

"You know, I think that is what I'll do," she decided. "Because if there is nothing moving outside, then, that can only mean that whoever is doing this, is inside the building since you can't see inside from outside, I think it would be good to be where you are. I'm coming out and not coming back ever. I'll stop the delivery tomorrow and do something different."

"Pack a bag or two with your best things and work clothes, you can buy whatever you need and let's go find you a place to stay. I'll be waiting," he resolved.

Robin went to the closet and took out her suitcases and went to the bathroom and took her bathing supplies. She went to the bedroom and packed five outfits for work, three-night gown sets, shoes briefcase and grabbed her purse and headed for the hallway. She opened the door and pulled her suitcases into the stairway when the phone rang two times and stopped. That was his signal informing her that Walter and Louise were home, but the outside door didn't open. Robin remembered the bugs and it was too late to retrieve them, so she locked the door and heard a voice say, "Robin, is that you?"

"Yes," she replied.

"Where are you going?" she asked.

"Where have you been?" she asked

"We spent the evening with Gerri and Charles."

"It was very scary here. Someone was here, trying to frighten me, I had to get the police to patrol the area and my driver to come over."

"So, everyone can remain safe, I'm leaving. Don't worry about the delivery, I'm cancelling it. I'll find a place and have it delivered there. I am not a lady easily frightened, but I don't like sleeping in a chair by the door. I don't know what you all and Russell have planned, but he needs to organize you all to do something constructive. Here are the keys to your house," she insisted.

"Robin, we're not working with Russell on anything against you and I'm sorry you feel that way. But since we're here now, why don't you come back in and go to bed and take a bath later to start your day fresh. By the time, you find a place tonight and get settled, it will be time for you to go to work, why not take that energy and time and go into your room and sleep and Maurice can go home and sleep, he'll be back for you at seven," Louise said.

Robin heard her say the exact same words she and Maurice had spoken earlier. That was her clue that something was going to happen. Robin called Maurice and said, "Go home I'm staying the night, so, pick me up at seven."

"Yes, ma'am, if you're sure. I'll be here at seven do you need me to help put your bags in?"

Walter said, "No man, I've got them." Walter picked up the bags and took them to the room. "I smell BBQ."

"No, you don't," Louise said. "I'll fix you a snack."

He said, "I do smell BBQ, as old as I am, I know the smell of BBQ." Robin didn't say a word, she put the Traveler's Check on the table besides the BBQ and went into the bedroom, said good night and closed the door. They went into their room and got ready for bed. Robin turned on the old television in her room and took off her coat, unpacked her suit for the morning and poured a drink of Hennessey, opened her bag of chicken and put it on the tray with her drinks and got into bed. She wanted a slice of bread; her bread was soaked in sauce, so she went to the kitchen and got two slices of fresh bread and returned to her room. She turned up the television and took several napkins and spread them on the bedspread and her gown, to keep from getting the sauce on anything, then took a bite of the chicken, and both it and the sauce were cold. She didn't want to see Walter and Louise, so she rejected the thought of warming it. She just took the napkins and folded them up, wrapped up the chicken and placed it in the bag. She wanted to leave it in the room to keep from going outside and bumping into them, but she decided to place it in the refrigerator and the napkins and soggy bread in the trash.

Robin got up, took them to the kitchen placed the food in the refrigerator, and the napkins in the trash grabbed a couple of kitchen wipes and hurried back to the room just as their door opened.

She took the wipes and cleaned off the tray and placed it back, wiped her hands and threw the wipes in the trash and went to bed.

The kitchen light was on and Louise was looking through the bag, she knocked on the door. Robin did not answer initially but she knocked again.

"The door is opened," Robin echoed.

"So, Walter did smell BBQ," Louise said, "this is pork and you don't eat it. Is it Maurice's?"

"No," Robin replied. "It was bought for you and Walter and I put everything on the table, thinking I would go to sleep and you would see the food when you returned home and eat, but someone decided to try to ruin my night and I forgot all about it."

"Thank you, we'll have it for lunch tomorrow," she said.

"My chicken was cold I put it in the refrigerator. Oh, I drank two cans of Walter's beer and left them by the seat I tried to sleep in, will you put them in the trash for me?"

"Sure, I did and moved the chair and the phone, too. I didn't know you drank beer," she said.

"Louise," answered Robin. "Before you and Walter went to Vegas, I didn't drink anything, but while you were gone, Russell tortured me so, he made me do and drink things I did not know existed before that week-end. Your brother caused me to be hospitalized with alcoholic poisoning, bruising and tearing. That's why I held on to that 'Tom Collins,' I was afraid until I sought help. Now, I'm no longer afraid. Thank you for throwing them away. Good night."

"Now, things make sense to me," she said. "I am so sorry, Russell abused you. So that's what removed the light from your eyes. Good night." she swallowed, and closed the door.

Robin listened as she walked back to their room and her footsteps sounded older as she walked. Robin turned off the television just in time to hear "What happened, why do you look like that, Louise?" The door closed.

Robin didn't want to imagine what went on behind that door or what she said to her husband. But Robin felt Walter knew some of what transpired with Russell, as he said, no one in that building can keep anything.

The knowledge of what Russell did have to be revealed. Satan keeps people bound by their own silence. It never ceases to amaze me how people can live together for years and not know one another or they claim to love one another, have everything going for them and still, choose not to honor their commitment because the grass looks greener on someone else's property.

Robin and Russell could never have a relationship after all that had transpired, for they had no trust, no respect and no love and Robin was good with that, for she had reached the last step.

Aretha Franklin sung a song entitled 'No Way' and it was applicable for them. Acceptance was the last step of grief, so Robin had arrived.

People really have a problem when they try to make someone love them, who doesn't want their love. She refused to join that club, 'No Way', and she dozed off to a welcome sleep.

Robin felt the bed shake and she thought she was dreaming, as she was rapidly being pulled out of the deep sleep. As her heart beat, rapidly increased, but unready to return to this dimension, she turned and a hand was over her mouth ushered her into a dark reality.

"Don't make any noise," he said. "If you do I'll smother your ass where you lay."

Robin's heart sank, as she fell back and nodded, okay.

"You bitch!" he said. "Where is the money?" I looked in your purse and in your briefcase and nothing but forty dollars in Traveler's Checks, what the hell is with you?" he asked. Focused only on the money, he shouted, "Answer me!"

She mumbled and he realized, it was his hand over her mouth that kept her from speaking.

"I'm going to take my hand away and don't make a sound," he repeated. She nodded again. He removed his hand and said, "I didn't intend to see you. Just scare you and come in, take your money and checks, that jewelry they gave you and leave, but you have nothing, as if you knew I was coming, but I know you and how you think, so it had to be a coincidence," he said. "But nothing? What can I do with a lousy forty dollars?" he asked.

"It's mine," she said, "you're not supposed to do anything with it."

"You're going to give me mouth?" he asked. "Well, you have talked enough about me."

"What do you want, Russell, I have no money," she said. "Why don't you go back where you were happy and leave me alone!" She turned over, demonstrating she was not intimidated by him, he had no control over her. He got up and walked to the door and she thought he was leaving.

Until she heard the door lock, then she sat up and looked for her purse with the camera and microphone. It was in place and she said to him, "There is nothing for you here, Russell, it's over. I've filed for a legal separation," she explained.

"What did you say, bitch, legal separation, 'hello'," he said. "Did you not get the memo through my absence, I'm already separated from you, but over?"

"Over," he repeated. "I'm the one who says when it's over."

"You did," she said. "And I have accepted it and am trying to move forward."

"With who, that Maurice?"

"That is not true, he is a gentleman," Robin recalled. "Something I have not spent time with in several years."

"Get up and take that gown off!"

"No, Russell, you're right about the separation, you certainly initiated it, but, in so doing, you have lost, no, you gave up your right to tell me what to do!"

"I'm going to say this one more time and that is all," he said. "Take that gown off!"

Robin didn't move, she laid right there and held her ground. He got in the bed, came close to her and said, "Do you really think I'm playing with you, bitch and he threw back the covers, grabbed her gown at the neckline and with one swift pull, he tore her gown off her, pushed her head under the covers and said you wanted to give me some mouth, then give it!" he said as he pushed her head into his crotch, she couldn't breathe and she bit him. "You bit me!" he said and threw her over on her stomach and penetrated her anally.

"It hurts, stop, please."

He took her gown and pushed it into her mouth and said, "Learn to like it."

She had never had that kind of sexual experience and he wanted her to hurt. She remembered what Mr. Marshall said to her and she began to smile, hearing his voice say, he's setting you free. Don't let him see you cry, be strong as you are. Robin stopped moving and just lay there.

"Move your bony ass," he said.

She just lay there and when he couldn't get her to move, he pulled out of her and turned her over and pushed her legs to the side and penetrated her vaginally, the gown still stuffed in her mouth, she shook her head, no. "You want me to stop?" he asked. She shook her head yes.

He said, "I want the money every cent you have, I want it!" She became quiet again. "Move that ass." he said. Robin just laid there quiet and still.

"What's wrong with you?" he asked. "Did you not hear me, I want the money and I'll leave."

She mumbled and he pulled the gown out of her mouth, "Are you going to give me the money?" he asked.

She said, "yes, but the bank is closed."

"I checked the accounts and they are closed one dollar balance, may as well be closed," he said.

"They wouldn't give you that information, she replied, unless you had someone pretending to be me, you suggested separate accounts, remember?"

"Right you are, but, either way, you closed the accounts so you must have the cash," he repeated.

"Do you really think I would carry that much cash around?" she asked. He thrust her harder but she didn't scream. "The money is in the bank," she said.

"Ok, we'll wait until morning and go get it," he stated. "We can't do that either, she said, it takes two signatures to get it and I'm only one."

"Who is the other signatory?"

"Mr. Marshall is the second and Maurice is the third."

"Why?" he asked.

"It is in the company fund, it will accrue more interest than a single account," she answered.

"How do you get it out?" he asked.

"It can't be touched, every ninety days it turns over so in ninety days," she said.

"What do you do in the meantime, for money?"

"I go to work every day and don't have any dependents, I have paid off my bills, no outstanding debts so my checks are clear," she said.

"Listen to me, he said, good you're so committed to your credit record, that makes it more for me; you're going to give me a check a month until the ninety days are up."

"You must be kidding!" she exclaimed. "Go to work and earn your own check, why would I want to give you a check I worked so hard for, while you're running around trying to play the man?" she asked.

"You'll do it to keep me from doing this to you every night or when I choose to, that's why!" he reiterated. "You, will never see me coming or going, never know when I'll strike or how, I might take half of the other check, he laughed, who or what is to prevent me?" "Who knows, I might bring a few of my buddies with me to have a little fun with you, too!" he heckled. "Do we have an understanding?" he asked.

"Yes, will you leave now?" she asked.

"No, I don't think you've had enough yet, he said. You know how bad it can get?" he asked. "You think this is bad, but think about this, five of my buddies and only us in the house and every one of them taking turns on you and some doing doubles and triples, filling every orifice in your body simultaneously for hours and hours maybe a couple of days, and they like to beat women, you'll beg them to stop and when they do, you'll be no good for another man as long as you live, if you live, he threatened. That will be fine, too, since I have insurance on your ass and one way or another, I'm collecting. I don't care if I must share it with the boys, they'll earn every dime of it, I promise you!"

"How much do you have on me?" she asked.

"Why?" he asked.

"I was wondering if I could manage to match it in ninety days, she said. Five Million, he said, and you took it out and signed it in the presence of witnesses, he said, to celebrate your new executive position".

"It never happened and the premiums must be high," she inquired.

"I have no idea," he said, "Mr. Marshall is paying them."

"What, he's in this with you?" she asked.

"It was beautiful," he said laughingly. "It was so busy in there that day, anything could have happened and no one would be the wiser, oh, anything did happen and no one is the wiser. While it was in full swing, Regina was in your office and a friend of mine happened to stop in, well dressed like everyone else. When Regina went to the little girl's room, my friend faxed the information to the insurance company and automatic payments are being made by your company for your insurance and mine and all I must do is abide my time to collect. I planned a little accident which means double, he said. Enough of that, can you double it in ninety days? he asked. I'm running out of cash!" "What is your accident plan?" she asked.

"Can you double it?" he asked.

"In ninety days, I can," she stated.

"Well you have a ninety-day reprieve," he said.

"When is payday?" he asked.

"Next week," she said.

"I'll be here to collect," he said.

"What did you do with all the money I helped you to earned?" she asked. "Surely you haven't spent it all?"

"I have bills to pay," he said.

"Where? I'm paying the bills here, so where?"

"All you need to know, is next week, your check belongs to me, are we clear?"

"Yes!"

He pulled out of her grabbed her head and shoved his penis inside, "If you bite it I'll kill you now and collect your life insurance. It won't be double, but it will do, for a while," he boasted. "Think of doing this with six men. He pulled out and pushed her away, you disgust me."

Robin wanted to die. He dressed and left, she took the bottle of Hennessey and gargled and spit into the trash can. She went to the bathroom and sat in hot water holding toothpaste in her mouth thinking, he had to be out of his mind if he thought she was going to continue to live there. He had to find her and that would not be easy to do, without access to her or someone they both knew. She would have her mail forwarded to the office, until she notified all pertinent people and companies, but she really didn't receive a lot of mail at Louise's house, then to a Post Office Box, she planned.

As she soaked, she prayed they had enough information to legally take the appropriate action. She washed her hair and blow dried it. Walked down the hall to the bedroom naked as a jaybird, walked into the room and pulled off the sheets, left them in a heap and fell on the bed. She turned her purse around and the other bugs were microphones only, to have a private moment. Then she got up and checked the doors, she looked at Louise and Walter's door and it was still intact, she went to the back door and it needed a key to exit, it was as if it had not been touched, Robin was perplexed indeed.

She was cold and took pajamas out and put them on then laid down on the bed to think.

Chapter Fourteen

Deliverance Delayed

Robin was filled with mixed emotions again. She had just completed the stages of grief only to find herself back to square one. How to overcome this horrendous experience and was there a possibility she could be whole again. She could lose herself in the work ethic she acquired and cultivated that she loved so dearly or she could just be lost forever. How could she hope to find genuine love or even date someone with the hope to find friendship not to mention marriage and family.

Once those tapes and audio were released to the justice system, she would be misconstrued as a whore or even a prostitute, branded for life even as the woman that was degraded, debased and destroyed; just as her life should be grand for her as she had reached a pentacle where struggling was no longer a necessity. She should be celebrating life, but instead, she was so ashamed. How could she look at her boss ever again without thinking he was thinking she was used, damaged goods, an inappropriate moral standard in character to lead the company and finally the day would come when he could not tolerate looking at her because seeing her reminded him of the degrading sights and horrible memories, of her, on tape memorialized forever.

Much like a man who met his wife and lived with her, got to know her and came to love her for the person she appeared to be and was until one day she's home alone, the doorbell rings and she opens the door to find a man standing there with a clipboard in his hand trying to get a petition signed but needs to meet the quota of signatures before he can take step two. He seems to be a person on a mission trying diligently to complete it. He was well dressed, well- spoken and looked like a respected citizen, so she drops her guard and takes the board to sign it; when suddenly out of the blue, the man gets the drop on her, grabs her, covers her mouth pushes inside the door, closes it, ties her up and rapes her over and over every way possible taping everything. Then finally he tires of her and leaves her in her husband's bed to be found, but before leaving, he reminds her he knows where she lives, the hours her husband works and where her child attends school and how she travels there.

She is warned if she reports it to the police, he would take the tapes he made of them and send them to their neighbors, their church, to her husband's job and finally that he would not just kill her, because to her, it would seem like a blessing, but he would kill the ones she loved. Then he leaves her to ponder a decision. What does she do? Does she go to the police, once she is externally delivered by being found but internally imprisoned, for justice or to keep someone else from going through the same trauma, or does she give in to his threats and remain silent, knowing he will strike again, making herself a vulnerable target and easy prey to be victimized perpetually? Things would never be the same again at home, her husband will never look at her the same as did a week ago, not to mention the fact that he would be reluctant to touch her again because he was blinded and consumed by the thought of his wife being with another man, abused by another man or wondering if she responded to him or whether he was better in bed and the list goes on. She struggled to free herself from the torment of the ropes on her hands and legs and a gag in her mouth. If only she could get free, she wouldn't have to watch her life changed and shattered into a million pieces or her husband trying to be brave as he faces his co-workers embarrassed because they know his wife has been taped while being raped or enters a barber shop and suddenly the room becomes silent or in a checkout lane in the grocery store and everyone is staring at him, how much of that can he take, she questions, for people have a tendency to blame the victim and eventually, they blame themselves. Yet, of one thing she is sure, she will not put him nor her child in harm's way. However, without professional help, it will eat at an individual, like a cancer, until it consumes him or her until even suicide looks like the only way out. Coming forth can only ruin her life not redeem it by catching the perpetrator. If only she had not opened the door, if only she had not been willing to sign a petition, if only.

For Robin, it was too late, too many people had seen the tape, even though she knew of possibly four, that was four too many to face on a day to day basis until retirement. She was having second thoughts. She had just begun to reclaim her life, now the struggle to regain it had to begin again. Maurice could never look at her with the same respect he once had, lawyer McAfee, although she had just met him, could not see her as the woman who saved a business when she could not save herself, Mr. Marshall to whom she looked upon as a father, could never look at her as a leader again, and if Raymond was really a part of this team, even he, could not look at her with the eyes of hope for a better future for he and his mother; when Robin was hopeless, was diminished, because they all had a new visual, the tape. And no matter how she cleansed or dressed up in expensive clothing, they would only see a ripped night gown or even change her hair coloring and style, her hair would always look wet, messed up. The visual would always over- ride the debate within ourselves and others with rational words. We all are primed with the euphemism that a picture is worth a thousand words.

Robin was faced with a dilemma and she had no one with whom she could discuss her problem. She looked at the situation and decided it was important to make a doctor's appointment. Russell was reckless and careless, she had to find out if she received anything from him. Secondly, she would be fitted for a diaphragm in the event he managed to locate her and last, to ascertain if she were already pregnant. Robin made a note to speak with a person with the gay/lesbian community.

Robin was stepping into her skin and making progress, it would come in stages but she was certain she would not be bound by Russell's chains of bondage. She would be delivered. She needed an ear to hear her out.

Robin thought about Celia and decided after she met with the team, she would approach Celia regarding two things: The issue she was dealing with and next, the issue Celia was dealing with. Celia was dependent upon Regina because she took her in when she had no place to go and she was willing to be bound by misguided gratitude rather than suffer the same experiences of the streets and nowhere to lay her head. Robin had taken on the responsibility and was very committed to her consequently. She was beginning to think they could purchase an apartment or townhouse together, which would solve both their problems.

Chapter Fifteen

The Evidentiary Disposition

Maurice was on time, he had a poker face and said very little, so Robin knew instinctively that the material had been reviewed but not by whom. She was quiet, had regressed as well. The drive was uneventful and extremely short, she thought. But they had arrived and there were more cars there than usual.

"Maurice, did you know all these cars would be here?" she asked.

"No, Robin, I was instructed to bring you in now to my office," he said. "Please, I know it is the wrong time and place to ask this of you, but I must. Do not go paranoid on us or with us today. We are the good guys. It's alright to be a skeptic, but make sure your timing and the sources are key factors."

"Thank you, Maurice," she said.

He took her hand and helped her out of the car and escorted her into the building, as usual. When she entered, she was ushered into the Security Office and seated. She looked around and there was a television monitor up, a recorder a duplicator a stenographer and steno machine a notary other than the one utilized by the company. A detective and a patrolman, the Deputy Commissioner of police, Mr. Marshall and the lawyer, Mr. McAfee. It was astonishing how many people were accommodated in that room, not to mention Robin, Maurice and Raymond. Robin was originally concerned about four people, but there were far more than four.

Mr. McAfee made a brief statement that the evidence had been reviewed by the Chief of Police and he found there was more than sufficient evidence for arrest, should Mrs. Watson pressed charges, they would pick Russell up immediately. There is an issue of husband and wife privilege, however since she filed for a legal separation and a restraining order two days ago, as the record shows it was granted. "Privilege does not apply," he said.

"He did not show and they were granted by default. He admitted to several major felonies and he will need an excellent attorney to get around that evidence. The only problem we foresee," said the Deputy, "is the landlord, who can argue that she did not give permission for surveillance of the common areas of the apartment, however, we're waiting to see if she cashed the Traveler's Check for rent. We notified the bank to inform us immediately after the transfer of money takes place," he said.

"How do we get around the fact that he has a key to the door?" asked Raymond.

The Detective answered, "We would have a problem if he had used the key, however, he did us a great favor. He committed unlawful entry. The camera caught him entering through a secret passage that leads from the Pantry. There is a secret passage that leads from the downstairs closet and exits through two apartments. Vera's is one and the second is the sister, Louise. We do not believe she is aware it exits in her apartment. So, the noises Robin heard while in the bathroom, were made by Russell to frighten her and to make her question her sanity."

"We have a sworn statement from Mr. Merry and Mr. Hawkins, that no one was outside the house or entered the house from the outside of the house, yet. The camera with date and time stamp, clearly shows that Russell was there and what he did while he was there. When Robin left the bathroom to check the front bedroom, locked the door and removed the key, she also checked the front door. If he had used his key, he may have had standing, provided he had paid his rent and was not evicted, however, that point is moot. He was not invited in, nor was he expected. He was an intruder and if he had been shot or killed in the process of committing his horrendous crimes, it would have been ruled justified."

"Are there any other questions?" he asked.

"The death threats he made and the extortion are they punishable?" asked Mr. Marshall.

"They are, for he used force and the imminent threat of life was repeated over and over along with the rapes and future threats of rape and abuse by his buddies, are all punishable. If we could wait until he takes the check, that proof could not be argued as hypothetical. Under the circumstances, with the torture he applied during his horrendous sexual production, he left no room for reasonable doubt; he is serious, desperate and lethal. He is escalating! We are looking at charges totaling forty years to life, but without a trial, we can plea him down to twenty-five years, without the possibility of patrol.

He continued, "We will not dwell now on the 'if' thing, but if a woman is abused, she should always file a report so there will be something tangible on file so if something happens to commit a criminal act, he will not come across as wrongfully accused, no prior offenses reported and be eliminated or given the benefit of the doubt, because nothing was reported. It makes it difficult to differentiate between innocent and no report for some cops, so they error on the side of caution and go with innocent rather than go with the he said she said, especially when there is no witness nor video of the alleged crime. We have the statement from a Celia Davis that Russell had been here earlier inquiring about Robin's whereabouts and the message he left was threatening. He was clearly stalking her as well."

"We have the complaint about the honeymoon horror and confirmation from the hospital regarding the alcohol poisoning for which he brought her in and admitted her. She was a non -drinker with alcohol poisoning made the doctor's uneasy and reported it, as attempted murder with the visuals of the bruises between her legs, whelps and scars on her abdomen and thighs, legs and the torn vaginal trauma. There should have been a follow up, but someone dropped the ball or we might not be here today. We're waiting," he said.

There was a beep and Maurice answered the phone. "Security Office, Maurice speaking," he said. He listened and said, "Thank you, I'll inform them. Louise cashed the Traveler's Check. She wrote for deposit only to her personal account for rent of Robin Watson, is how she endorsed it. The money is in her account. Robin paid six months, with five months in advance, for her sole use as stipulated in the memo section. That was an interesting move and crucial wording."

"Okay, we have that piece of the puzzle, what would you suggest now counselor?" he asked.

"The case is tight but we want a noose around his neck. The only way to do that, is arrange for Robin to have a payday, bug the Pantry, get Louise on board and set him up for the climax. He wants the big bucks from the company's account, if planned right, we can get him for grand theft of company funds, which adds time," he said. "The down side is Robin must remain there until payday and get instructions. The Plasma television should be delivered today as planned and perhaps the room should be updated and bathroom with half the hallway painted to make it brighter in there. All this is predicated on the decision Robin makes. If Louise agrees to work with us, it will be worth it."

"Hell, I'll pay for the renovations to get that bastard behind bars," said Mr. McAfee. "Are you game Robin?" "We'll take my fee and do her top floor and I'll get my brother in law to draw up the specs and start work tomorrow."

"What if I buy the building?" asked Mr. Marshall. "And let everyone stay, charge them rent and they cannot sell the building then nor leave for five years. If the structure is good and foundation is solid, then we could purchase the land to the corner and merge the building to make the building modern and roomy with a patio on the first and second floor and backyard for the basement with inside garages and storage areas and sign it over to Robin. Louise will pay a hundred dollar increase in rent and the other tenants a hundred fifty increases for the five-year period to be re-evaluated after that time and rent increased on the anniversary date.

"They must provide a security deposit which will be placed in escrow," Robin said. "That should be an incentive for all. Russell and his heir's will be banned from the building, however. Unfortunately, retaliation is a human reflex, so it is possible they would seek to destroy the property and that must be considered before purchase, if the likelihood of total loss is acceptable."

"Well, said Mr. McAfee, if the property is insured, there can be no loss. As far as Russell being banned, he will automatically be, due to incarceration".

Robin reminded them that if the work can begin tomorrow, Russell will still be on the streets, because you are waiting for the big crime. "A restraining order is in effect for you now, but if we can get Louise to take out one, that will be just as good in multiple ways," he said.

"I think that will win everyone over, we'll save the secret pantry renovations for after his arrest," she said.

"We are on board," said Mr. Marshall and Mr. McAfee. "Maurice take care of that, please, the property next to the building to the corner."

"Yes sir, as soon as I hear Robin's decision."

Robin said, "I thought you would be repulsed and disappointed in me after last night, I was ready for all of you to reject me; are you saying you're not embarrassed by me and still willing to call me friend even though I brought this misery into your lives?"

"What are you talking about, Robin Watson?" asked the Detective and Deputy Commissioner. "You are not the blame for what Russell did to you."

"Oh, no," said Mr. McAfee. "If we did anything to give you that impression, please forgive us. I want to go on record as saying, I think you are one of the bravest women I know, not one of, but the bravest; and it is a pleasure and privilege to call you friend, you inspire me."

"That is why I am willing to do whatever is needed to get that low life scum behind bars for the rest of his miserable life. He has no business out among human beings. We are all in agreement about this, Robin, can't you tell we're serious?" asked Mr. Marshall.

"I did all that worrying for nothing, if I knew I was not alone, I can do it. Yes, let us put Russell in his rightful cage, like the animal he is."

"That's a go," said the Detective.

"Let's get Louise on board, how soon can you have those specs for the renovated building, Mr. McAfee?"

"Tomorrow, with plans to begin the following day," he said.

"How do you know your brother in law will agree to that?" the Detective asked.

"I didn't make myself clear, he runs the business, but I own it."

"I'll give him the layout of the building today and he'll give us his improvements for the entire building and we can show them to Louise, tomorrow," he said.

"After she is aboard, make the deal with Mr. Book to buy the building from him. If he wants to move, that will be acceptable."

"Once she and Book are in place, we'll have her leak the word that Robin is getting paid and will have bearer bonds for one night until the bank opens and we'll wait for him to make his move then we'll make ours," he said. "Did we leave out anything?" he asked. "He may want to kill her so we'll be ready to make the move as soon as we detect she's in danger."

"We'll give her a safe word, like 'popcorn'. If she says she has a craving for popcorn, we'll know it's urgent to move."

"And we'll come in through the pantry and back door; they're the closet to the bedroom. Block off the pantry exit while the front door is being opened, we'll have a key to the front door, we'll get it from Louise to keep from breaking it down," he said.

"But when we leave that house, we will not be leaving without Russell Watson. You know I thought about his plan to kill her in her apartment and receive the straight payout for wrongful death, and you know, it works. It works because of the secret entrance through the pantry. If the person wearing gloves does it, it is doubtful that the crime would ever be solved. It would play out like an inside job and if everyone had an alibi, it would play out like a paranormal mysterious death, since all the doors and windows would be closed and locked from the inside with a chain on the door and deadbolt inside key locked with the key still in. They would get away with murder, no one knows about the secret entrance and exit. Masterpiece!"
"Let's put him away before he conceives a plan to make someone fall down the stairs, that could bring in the double indemnity."

The plan was in place and everyone expected to emerge as victors after the sacrifice, which they knew, would be substantial. Yet, they were in this together, as one and nothing could tear that apart. They were operating from the biblical precept, that no greater love is this, than a man who lay down his life for his friend. A true friend is a priceless jewel and Robin had discovered that she was rich beyond measure, for she had friends. Money doesn't make nor can it buy friends, to have friends one must be one!

The question to be decided is can Louise become a friend?

Chapter Sixteen

Phase One

Maurice stopped by the house to talk with Mr. Book and found that they had much in common. The two worked hard to keep their parents happy and strived to make their lives better and God provided by blessing them to meet the right people at the right time. They had come far and now, Maurice was sitting there ready to ask a question that would either result in his leaving the house without a deal or he would remain to celebrate having made a deal.

"Mr. Book," he said. "I have a proposition which I wish to submit to you for your consideration please take your time to seriously ponder it and give me your answer ASAP."

"What would that be?" he asked. "Would you consider selling this apartment building and remaining as a tenant with a newly renovated building, or would you like to start over in a different location, knowing that the family was still residing in this building with more space and a new and improved look and feel. The plan would be to purchase the property from here to the corner and add balcony/patio to the second floor and a patio to the first floor and a patio to the backyard for the basement. That way, everyone can do their own thing for entertainment or tranquility without infringing on the other families' time and activities. A garage to the building and an outside storage area in the back, increase the size of the, kitchens and modernize them with new equipment, remodel the bathrooms, increase the bedrooms and add closet space, add a balcony to the second floor, patio to the first floor and patio to the back yard for the basement.

"How much are you willing to offer?"

"How much will you take?" asked Maurice.

"One hundred thousand dollars in cash," he stated.

"I will get back to you tomorrow," he said.

Maurice got up to leave and he thanked uncle Book for listening and considering his proposition and extended his hand to shake it, when uncle Book placed the other hand on top of Maurice hand and asked, "How soon could I have the money, if I said yes, now?"

Maurice asked him if everything was okay.

"Yes," said uncle book. "Why is it okay for a woman to change her mind and when a man does, it is questioned as if he took sick?"

"I asked you a reasonable question. It would only be sensible and polite to answer it."

"I am so sorry if I offended you, Uncle Book, you have always treated me fairly and I want it to be said of me that I was and am a straight shooter when it comes to people in general," said Maurice.

"Well, Maurice," said uncle Book. "There comes a time in every man's life when opportunity knocks twice, but that only happens in rare situations; the trick is to recognize the knock from the wind and open the door. I recognized it for a second there, I thought it was the wind, but then I recalled the sound was the same as it was when He knocked before. I will take your offer, son."

"May I ask what made you decide?"

"He did," said uncle Book. "He asked me what I was waiting for, I had done my job as a son, a brother and husband and father now it was time for me, he said, I can't teach them any more than I have and it's a different generation that doesn't want to follow the ways of God, either you draw or be drawn and my foundation is firmly rooted, now it is time to move on while I can do for my wife a few more tricks. "I have a good wife and honestly, Maurice, what I see out there every day is unreal. I want to show her how much she means to me while I can. Not every man can say he has the right wife and she is a good wife but if you are blessed to find both in the same body, you should not hesitate to let her know and do not take her for granted because there is someone out there waiting to take your place. I have a nephew, you met him, Russell, I used to think he was a smart young man until he showed everyone just what kind of fool he really is. I told him he had a good woman and she has proven that she is strong and smart, and faithful. But that nephew pulled a dumb stunt that is so ridiculous I washed my hands of him.

"May I ask what he did?"

"He played around on that beautiful wife of his and he brought his woman to this house and had sex in their bed and the wife got sick at work came home early and caught them in bed together. She would have been in her rights to shoot them both and I doubt she would have spent one night in jail. If she did, I would have bailed her out myself and brought her home with me and my wife took care of her until she got on her feet and told us what she wanted to do and help her to do it."

"That woman he is with, cheated on her man to be with him, don't he know it is just a matter of time before she cheats on Russell to be with someone else. In the meantime, she will break him, he won't have a dime and I want to get away before he tries to take what I have, to make her stay with him, she doesn't care about him, it is the Benjamin's she wants. It broke our hearts to see how he broke Robin's heart. Oh, he'll never get another dime from me and I don't want to see what is going to happen to him because he has caused too much heartbreak to get by or away.," he said. "So, this is the knock that will take us away from here. You haven't heard his wife sing and play that piano, what a treat," he said. "We just want her to be alright, now and maybe she will sing again. Now I told you why, do you still think I'm crazy?" he asked.

Maurice said, "I never thought you were crazy and still don't. I think you care about people."

"Young man, never forget this, every other person says he is a humanitarian but as much hate as there is in the world, that cannot be a true statement, it is impossible to be a humanitarian and hate humans," he said. "Do you agree?"

"I agree," said Maurice

"And so, do I," said Mr. McAfee.

"This is the owner of the building, I believe, Mr. Book meet Mr. McAfee, the lawyer."

"I am the owner, sir," said uncle Book.

"Go do your chores, and I will handle this," he said. Just as they sat down, the delivery truck came up.

"I guess Robin didn't cancel and I should help the young man out. Is there something you need, before I go, uncle Book?"

"Maurice, take these keys and open the apartment and go all the way to the room outside the kitchen and open that door so he can hook up the television. He shouldn't be long, but when he finishes lock up for me, please?" he asked.

"Of course, uncle Book, my pleasure to help you."

Maurice helped the young man take the television out, it was a large one and they took it up the stairs and he unlocked the door, they picked it up and carried it into the bedroom, and marked an area on the wall, and began placing the parts for the television to rest. The man slipped him some items and he found all the places to provide the necessary coverage and especially in front of the passage way, inside the room and behind and under the bed.

"Help me lift it," he said.

Maurice said, "Let me cough first." he coughed and picked up his end and they put all in place. It really looked nice.

On the way out, they both added the items in strategic places as they were exiting the bedroom. Maurice locked the door and slipped him a folded bill for uncle Book and they walked down the stairs and Maurice told uncle it was beautiful and he handed him the keys and said all locked up.

"Thank you," said uncle Book.

Maurice waved bye. The deliveryman told Uncle Book to sign where the x is stating it was delivered and setup. Uncle signed without a glance and the young man shook his hand as he left with the bill placed in uncle Books hand and Mr. McAfee asked him to step outside with him to smoke a cigar. He did as the trunk of his car opened and he reached in and handed him an iron case with a black handle. Uncle Book handed him the deeds and they both smiled and said fifteen minutes and Maurice took off.

Mr. McAfee called Mr. Marshall and they talked and then he was given a phone number. The lawyer left, as he headed to the office, he made one stop at the courthouse then proceeded to the home office.

The construction company arrived at the building and spoke with Uncle Book. Fred, the man who ran the company, informed Mr. Book that they were installing debris portals on the right side of the building and would have three crews working simultaneously on all three floors to complete the work by Saturday. Uncle Book said he doubted they could complete the work in three days but gave them total access to the property. He said he wanted to see the completed job.

They installed the first large circular tubing on the second floor placing the open mouth cycle in Robin's bedroom that led to the dumpster. The first-floor tubing was placed from the kitchen window to the dumpster and the basement had to be manually handled, so they reversed the tubing and placed one into the bathroom and the other in the bedroom. They were to replace everything and remodel with new appliances throughout the house stylish and contemporary including the faucets. There were three portable toilets on the grounds for the families and two for the employees. Uncle Book was both excited and anxious; he sat fascinated as he watched.

Maurice returned to the office to find out if there was any word from Louise, when he was asked to come into the conference room.

He went in to find Mr. McAfee, Robin, and Mr. Marshall, talking and he took a seat.

"No, just the active players; everything we anticipated Louise doing, will now be done by Uncle Book. He's wants justice for Robin, so, he's going to file the complaint, give us the key to the door, and leak the news that Robin's payday has been moved up and she has bearer bonds in her possession for one night. He will make his move, he can't resist, that's a done deal." Mr. McAfee proclaimed.

"We can stick with our original plan for Russell."

"Robin called inform us Celia's bedroom was ready for us to view." "We'll stop to surprise Celia with our gifts for her bedroom." Mr. Marshall said.

"Maurice, get her a blue throw rug for the door or runner." he said. "She can use a small desk and lamp. We will remember that. Let's go, so we can check her check book and savings."

Robin requested that be done in Regina's presence.

"Make sure it's done just as she requested." he said.

They closed, went to their cars and headed for Regina's home. When they arrived, Celia was so pleased to see everyone, she offered them tea and they all drank and briefly chatted.

"Is the bedroom ready for viewing?"

"Yes," she said dying with pride. "Well, you better show it to us, Celia before we all decide to sleep on it tonight and disappoint you."

"Oh," she said. "I'd love the company, please."

"No since this is your first night, we'll let you have first sleep in your beautiful new bed." Mr. Marshal said with a smile. He found Celia's company refreshing as he stated on numerous occasions.

She took them into her room and her bedroom suite was lovely.

"Now, the room needs painting," Maurice said. "We'll set aside a day and come over and paint the house, Regina, if that's ok with you."

"Certainly," she said.

"It looks so inviting, Celia," he said. "Let me see your checkbook and savings please, do you mind?"

"No, I'm thrilled you care enough to ask," she said.

"Good because one of us will check weekly. I like how you did this, Celia," he said.

"That was Robin's idea," she said, "she takes such good care of me."

They finished their tea and said good night, see you tomorrow and left. When they were in the car, Robin thanked them for making Celia's night.

"It meant so much to her," Robin said.

"I know it did Robin, thanks for playing the family card. Now it's your time, you go home and here is your briefcase, with your faux bearer's bonds. Go home, go to bed get the rest you need and your house is under remodeling now. You have no bathroom and shower, no bathroom floor; there are portable ones outside for the entire house. We'll feed you and let you use a bathroom, maybe, before we take you home."

"Thank you, gentlemen," she said. "You're too kind, show me the Bonds so I can be familiar with them."

They showed them to her and she said, "This is excellent work, I would be convinced."

"If she would be convinced, they are perfect," Maurice said.

"Your television is up and running, keep it on, even if it goes dark, don't be concerned," said Maurice. "But the lighter, the clearer; too dark, the flash kicks in. Turn it on the second you get in. We don't know what the kitchen is like, so, what do you want to eat?"

"Chinese and take some to uncle Book and Louise and Walter just as if nothing is going on." Bill said.

"Fortune cookies, too, I like the taste, they're not too sweet."

"Was that Chicken and Beef or Shrimp?" he asked.

"One of each and no one else gets a fortune cookie though. We have fried rice and white rice with EFY.

Thanks, and no alcohol, tonight. What a difference, from all the days before, but I may be slightly addicted now, a beer or two is appropriate." Robin commented

"We are taking you home now, Robin." Bill stated.

"Good night family," she said. "You're wonderful."

"Good night Robin, so are you," they replied.

Maurice announced, "Three minutes and do you need anything special?"

"You've been so good," she said.

"We're here. Let me take that," he said. "I have a tray."

He took her with his free hand and helped her out. "Where are your keys?" Maurice asked.

"I have them out, they are in my mouth, now," she said.

"If the light isn't on when we arrive, don't turn it on, use the television all night," he advised.

"See you at seven and I'll knock on uncle's door and give him his box," he said.

He knocked and he was at the door in a flash. "Chinese, exactly what I had in mind; goodnight, Robin."

"Goodnight uncle book, but are they home?" she asked.

"Just came in. I told them the work has begun and will be over in three days. Portable toilets are in the yard," he said. "Go eat sweetie."

"I will," she said.

They went up the steps and unlocked the door and everyone came to the door, the lights were on.

"What do you have there?" Walter asked.

"Chinese."

"That sounds good, do you have enough to share?"

"I can spare a serving or two, Walter," Robin replied.

"Good, do you want to eat up front?" he asked.

"Not really, Walter; but, I'll have a few of your beers."

"'A few, she said,'" Walter exclaimed.

"Do you have a problem with that?" she asked.

"No, just surprised," he said.

"You'll get over it, Walter."

"I'm going to the kitchen, is there a kitchen?"

"Yes, there's a kitchen," they replied.

"Let me turn on the television," she said.

"And we can spread everything out on the table while I put my briefcase in the bedroom."

"Right behind you," Walter said.

"Did you cook or you bought something?" Robin asked.

"Honestly, we waited for you, we just knew you had something delicious," she shared.

"Supposed I only bought enough for me, since I never know when you're going to be home, wouldn't I be justified?" she asked.

"That's fair and you're right," they said.

"Louise, why don't you fix the plates while I go to the bedroom," Robin remarked.

"Sure, and what do you want on your plate?" she asked.

"Half a teaspoon of everything, Louise."

"Okay, can we have a taste of everything?"

"Except the fortune cookies, they are mine."

"I don't see them Robin," she said.

"You must have left them in the car," she said.

"Sorry," they said.

Robin returned and they were seriously eating.

"So, you really were hungry, huh?" Robin asked.

"Yes," they said. "Chinese never tasted so good."

"It is good, but, where is the beer, Walter?"

"Walter doesn't want to share," she said.

"Excuse me," Robin said. "He's eating like a horse and doesn't want me to have a few of his beers?"

"Walter, you are so disappointing!"

"I wish I had known earlier," Robin said, "He's done for good, right?"

"I'm sure he didn't mean it," Louise said.

"I'm just as sure he did, Louise," Robin said. "When I said a few, he showed his hand.

Louise was a large woman, six feet two inches tall, very burley broad shoulders, that gave a visual example of a man, so most people including her Walter, just did what she said, no exchange of words. She could be scary.

Louise went out and returned with a six pack of Walter's beer. It obviously had been hidden in their bedroom.

"Help yourself, Robin, and I'll have a few too." Louise said.

"Good, I'm not going to dwell on that; I'm done eating and going to watch television," Robin replied.

Robin knew something was happening, because common sense dictates that a smart person doesn't argue over beers when they're starving for food. That was about something else. Robin took Shrimp, Chicken and Beef and mixed them and ate the meat with pickles and beer and looked for a slice of pie. She didn't see any, so she went to bed. She slept in her pajamas and drifted off. She was in deep sleep and enjoying it when she heard her name being called. "Robin, do you have my money?"

"I told you, Russell, next week is payday," she said.

"Well, I heard it through the grapevine it was today, and you have a bonus of bearer bonds," he said.

"Only a few people knew that, Russell," she said. "You really don't want to bother those bonds!"

"I really, really do," Walter said.

"So, that was your problem, you 'Judas goat', you eat my food, and have diarrhea of the mouth to Russell and steal from me," Robin said. There was a knock on the door and it opened and there stood Louise, you're in on this, too?" Robin asked. "They want the Bonds you told Walter."

"Oh, no," Louise said. "Walter get out of here and go to our room.

"No, Russell and I are taking the Bonds!" he exclaimed.

"Then what's your plan, genius?"

You're going to kill her, too, because you can't let her live, she knows who did it!"

"Did Russell tell you to do that Walter?"

"No, Russell said we had to take the Bonds, and beat her up and I had to rape her."

"Go to bed, Walter."

She went over to Russell and slapped him upside his head several times and said, "You tried to send my husband to jail with this bull or did you plan to kill him, too, after all, he would be the first one to crack to the police, I know he's not much, but I love him and we've been together for twenty-five years, you would take that from me, your sister, do you have purple piss running through your veins for blood?"

And she hit him again and again, with her huge fist. "Now I don't know how you got in here, but you need to leave the same way, you do not live here nor are you welcome here. To do me like this and Walter, knowing he is on the short bus, you are dead to me, worse than a traitor," she said passionately.

"I can't believe you," she continued. "I have watched you with your selfish ass, use women and think nothing of it, but I never thought you would think so little of me and Walter to place us in a position like this, and I was wrestling over betraying you, because you're my brother, and blood doesn't mean a thing to you."

She hit him again, like a man, and said, "Get out now before I kill you, take all these thugs and that female dog of yours with you and leave."

Russell's woman came into the room.

"What's the hold up, Walter and Russell?" she asked.

"So, you're behind this," Louise said. "I am not surprised, it would take a mind as sick as yours to think that this half-baked scheme would work. I knew time his money left so would you, now you're both trying to get my husband arrested, brother!" she exclaimed.

"Get her and get out; the bible says thou shalt not kill, but it doesn't say I can't beat the hell out of all you, making you wish you were dead."

"Where are the Bonds?" she asked.

"Wherever her briefcase is," Russell answered.

"Find it, Russell," she said.

"Louise is right, we're in trouble," Russell repeated.

"This means we must kill Louise, too."

She took the gun and walked up to Louise and said, "It's your husband or his wife, choose!"

"Find that dam briefcase, I didn't do all this to go home empty handed," she said.

"Walter, you know what it looks like, find it and it will be me and you, honey," she said.

Oh, that was the wrong statement to make in front of Louise.

Louise knocked the gun out of that woman's hand and knocked her out.

"You're messing with the wrong woman's husband, now," she said.

"Russell, you gave your woman to my husband?"

He didn't say anything, she walked over to him and knocked him out with one punch and called the police.

"You're like a mad dog," she rejoined. "Russell, I am going to help you, I'm going to put your low-down self out of your misery, I am personally going to see to it that you rot in jail."

When the police came, she pressed charges against both for breaking and entering with a deadly weapon, attempted robbery and threat to kill Robin and her until they made her mad. They were arrested for those charges and the other charges and given more years to contemplate the unexpected, i.e. Louise, plus for each offence and no possibility of parole. His woman had two other offenses, which made her a three-time loser so she doesn't have to worry about money anymore nor a place to stay for she's a guest of the state and her children will become wards of the state.

Russell would never bother any of them again.

Robin was relieved, on one level but she felt a stirring from the things of the past and she felt she was in a loop watching the same bad movie over and over until she was a participant a player in that movie but it wasn't a movie, it was and is the circle of life!

Chapter Seventeen

The Circle of Life

When predators perfect their crafts, they develop a sixth sense that helps to identify their prey. This statement is not borne out of an in-depth study of psychology but of experience. Although Robin used to have an aversion to the word victim, that was no longer true because it took her numerous years of torment, suffering and abuse at the hands of those taught to trust. During the formative years, children are encouraged to automatically trust those in authority, uniform, our elders, relatives and friends of the family, but statistics prove that more people are molested, abused, raped and even killed by the same.

She believes the word victim does not hold the stigma that people are purported to believe is politically correct.

Yes, Robin is a victim and the thing that makes her appreciate the word with a positive connotation, is the fact that she is a survivor, a fighter and an overcomer. The truth accepted, everyone is someone's victim, hence, there are no victimless crimes, it is part of the cycle of life. If you are not the predator then you're the victim and if not the victim, then the predator or perpetrator.

For almost fifty years, she has lived with the knowledge of what she experienced, but the part of the experiences that are most disheartening and devastating, is the emotion deemed as fear. Fear is the thing that eats at the very soul of an individual, like a cancer and consumes the flesh, from within, until life is ended. Fear will keep you inside to the extent you become austere, a hermit, a prisoner behind a maze of steel bars within one's mind, while safety is not in exclusion but the inclusion of Christ, whose perfect love casts out fear.

Is it all allusion? she asked. How can one be safe when the one's sworn to protect and serve are the very ones she fears? Robin's mind raced as she had a flash back.

Robin was not the first and she knew she would not be the last, but there was nothing she could do if she wanted those she loved to remain safe. Verbal threats are one thing but to have a loaded gun put to your head with the promise to blow your brains out, by a deadly serious trained law enforcement official, with finger on the trigger, is no joking matter. She was still afraid, because he was still alive, and all the drama and experiences with Russell triggered something in her that she thought was buried. However, she was learning that fear begets fear and even though it is buried, until it is resurrected and faced, it is only covered up. The secrets had been kept far too long.

They caused added distress and illness after illness, and before it kills her, she must unearth the cover and face it! If he comes for retribution, she will not die from fear, but in freedom, for breaking the silence.

Her real name is unimportant and rightly so, for the time is rapidly approaching that she may end up in one of those places or gunned down in her modest and still standing home, because she is daring to speak up and out.

The landmarks of yesterday's past are almost gone, due to the machines utilized to tear down the houses that once stood in the neighborhood when a well-known super cop, reigned in the city. The mention of his name, caused pause to those in the know, but for those, who never committed a crime, because of his rank and name, he was respected.

He had siblings and relatives who taught school in the district and had homes in the more prominent areas of the city, so few if any, would have thought that he was capable of the acts that he pulled under the covers of darkness, but it was her misfortune to be another victim.

Nothing bad happened in her area of town, it was mostly inhabited by family oriented, working class people who believed and taught their children, with pride, to respect one another and their property. Every week, you either spoke with the members of the neighborhood at the grocery store, church or home-based barbershop or beauty shop. Most of the children had a paper route that they did before school and one afterschool; her brother developed a strong work ethic at an early age and all the children helped him either in the morning hour of delivery or the afterschool delivery for he had two paper routes and family was everything, then church and then school.

Talent was recognized and developed from these three and a lot of famous people came out of and to, this small town like Miles Davis, Jackie Joyner and Tina Turner who sang at the club on Seventeenth and Piggott, called Jimmy Bell's and stayed on the corner of Nineteenth and Baker Avenue right at Twenty Street, across from John Head's tavern in East Saint Louis. Robin was too young, then, to go out, but she loved hearing her uncles and cousins talk about the places, the music and dancing that took place on the weekends and sometimes in mid- week.

There was a tavern on every corner and just about a church on one, too, but there was a respect given to the black church then, even though the area was racially mixed, that was an era that will never return. Robin played the piano for the church and after Sunday night service, she would walk the four blocks home from the opposite East end of her street on odd weekends and the five blocks from the West end of the neighborhood on even weekends. She would sing and reminisce as she walked. To the pure, all things are pure.

She was a college student and planned to study for a test that night, so she hurried home from church, instead of carefully pacing herself. It was the second Sunday night and the weather was wonderful and the service was inspiring which made her walk home, less tiring. Now, she was crouched in the corner of her room rocking back and forth just shaking and murmuring to herself but without understanding. We looked at her and asked if she were okay and she responded, with a forward rock, not that she was communicating with us. Trying to get through to her was like trying to enter an electric gate with a popsicle. It was a cousin that suggested that we consider it to be fear of the test, she was supposed to take. We agreed it was a form of fear of something, but never a test. We left her alone in the room, but checked on her every hour, and she was still sitting in the corner on the floor, rocking back and forth. The following morning, she was up and dressed, and headed out the door, to take her test, when she collapsed.

She was taken to the emergency room. After several hours, a doctor came and reported that Robin had experienced some severe trauma, bruising and asked if she had complained of being attacked for her symptoms were consistent with those of rape victims. Ruby told him about the previous night, how she found her in her room sitting in the corner rocking back and forth unable or refusing to communicate with us. She tried everything, thinking it was fear of the test she was scheduled to take today, so she left her, but checked on her every hour, with no change.

"Then, this morning, we checked and she was up and dressed, so we thought she appeared over whatever it was, she walked to the door with her books and collapsed, I brought her here. She never spoke a word during the trip here," Ruby said. "What can I do to help?"

"We want to report this to the police," he said. "But when we mentioned that to her, we had to sedate her; her reaction was consistent with fear and it wasn't until she stated nothing happened we promised not to contact the police, she quieted down. I am recommending that she be placed on a seventy-two hour hold for psych evaluation."

Ruby, quickly responded, "Did she threaten to harm herself or someone else?"

"No," he said. "It's just a gut feeling based on years of experience."

"Well, until you can give us more than a gut feeling, we refuse to comply, so we'll be taking her home."

"Yes ma'am," he said. "She's in room four, you can get her dressed and I have a prescription for her to keep her calm, but I strongly recommend that she see her doctor tomorrow and give him the papers you receive when the nurse discharges her."

"Ok," said Ruby. "And thank you doctor. It's not that we don't respect your diagnosis, but it's difficult enough for a black person to make it with an education, but having a psychiatric notation attached to your file, eliminates any possibility of making it."

"I understand," replied the doctor. "Make sure she sees her doctor as soon as possible and I've attached a note for her class recommending she be given the test at the teacher's discretion. Hope it helps. Please get her help or she'll be back here or in some place like it."

Ruby called the college and spoke with her professor and informed him she was calling from the ER and had a note to that effect, and asked if he would consider giving Robin a make-up examination, but she had to see her doctor and she had not made an appointment yet. He, stated he would give her a make-up examine, if she has a note from a physician confirming she is ill, that she was a good student, and "tell her to get well soon and return to class," he said.

Ruby then called the doctor and asked if she could make an appointment for Robin, and was told she could come in as soon as they left the ER

He was her family doctor and she was known to them, so they permitted her to come. Ruby told him what happened and he asked her to wait in the waiting room, while he had a chat with Robin. The appointments for individuals never lasted longer than thirty minutes, unless it was something pre-arranged or an emergency and then everyone had to wait until he concluded the office visit, but this lasted for over an hour and he rang for the nurse, she went into his office and came out about ten minutes later, then Robin came out and the Doctor asked Ruby to come in. He told her Robin had experienced a trauma of a serious nature and he wanted specific tests done, that his office was unequipped to handle, so he was sending her back to the hospital for the tests and he would call with the results. He recommended that Robin be on bed rest for three days then she could return to class, but he wanted to see her in a week.

She asked him, "What was Robin's diagnosis?"

He responded, "She should tell you, she is of age."

"I understand," she said.

She took her back to the hospital for the lab work, and it didn't take long, the ER doctor saw Robin and spoke with her briefly and left, as a code was called over the PA system about a GSW to the abdomen. The ambulance was bringing in the patient as we were leaving.

Ruby asked Robin if she wanted to go talk, while they waited for her medication and she said she had talked enough for one day. She wanted to go to sleep.

"Soon Robin," Ruby said. "Just let me get what you need and we'll be home shortly."

"Thank you," she said. Robin was permitted to take her test and she saw her doctor once a week for three months and then she seemed herself, again, she was coping well and began to socialize and returned to playing the piano for the choir. She formed her own group and was doing very well.

They had a service one night on the south end of town and Robin went with the group to sing, the driver did not inform Robin he was not taking them home, and left the service before it was over. On their own, they decided to walk with each other as far as they could. Robin was the last person of the group who lived farther than the rest, so she had to walk the two blocks home alone.

She didn't mind, so she said goodnight to her singing partner on Gay Avenue and walked the long winding road of Twentieth Street, she noticed a car parked in the field on the left side of the street, under the bridge and wondered why it there, so far off the road? She had not seen it there earlier as they left in route to the service, so she hurried to get out from under that bridge; she always felt it would collapse one day and she didn't want it to be while she was walking under it. She hurried to pass the iron and granite pole supporting the bridge, to her right.

As she passed it, she was grabbed and pushed into the weeds, by some man.

"No," she said. "No please stop."

He hit her across the face. She heard a car and struggled to get free to get the attention of the driver, when she realized the car starting was the car that was parked in the field.

Robin tried to scream, hoping someone would come to the door, but the way the street was, due to the railroad owned the property on that side of the street, she had just passed the last cross street and there were no houses on that side, so she struggled and the car pulled up and stopped, a man got out and helped the other one put her in the back seat, as they took turns with her. They had something over their faces like a woman's stocking, that disfigured their facial structure and their breaths smelled of alcohol, she didn't know what they planned to do with her when they were done.

She tore the sleeve of one and scratched him, but he didn't stop, she just couldn't fight anymore, suddenly they stopped and opened her purse, she dropped it when she was grabbed, one took her I.D. and said, "We know where you live, if you call the cops, we'll know and come back. You don't know when we might stop and party with your sister and nieces, keep your mouth closed."

They opened the door and pushed her out into that open field like she was trash thrown by the side of the road.

She tried to fix her clothes the best she could, she didn't know how she was going to get into the house unseen or how she would explain her appearance, but she got up and went home. Unaware how she made it to the house, she found herself on the back porch. Since locking doors was still a future event, she tried the door and it opened, she was in the back bedroom and she took off her clothes, put on a robe and went to the bathroom, she took a hot bath, so hot until it almost scalded her. Afraid of contracting some disease, she looked for something to clean her body out, she made a poultice to help keep from catching anything. She didn't know what else to do, she got dressed for bed and went out and there was Ruby.

"What's wrong, Robin?"

"I'm tired," she said. "Do you remember where we put those medicines the doctor gave me for stress?"

"Are you feeling depressed or want to talk?" asked Ruby

"A little, I thought I would take one before I hyperventilate," she said.

"Oh, that sounds like a good plan to catch it early," Ruby said. "Try the second shelf in the back. I started to throw them away, but had not gotten to it yet, good thing."

Robin looked and found them exactly where she said they would be.

She took the medicine and placed it in her room. She was trying to keep it together, but the silence was screaming inside of her, she took another pill and she awoke shaking, she went to the bathroom and pulled out the poultice and wrapped it in newspaper and put it in the trash can and took the trash can outside to empty it, for she knew that if her sister saw it, she would recognize what it was and what it was for. Grandmother had taught them many things about herbs that she learned from her mother who was Cherokee and when the occasion required it, that information was utilized. This was one of those times.

She opened the door and stepped outside and walked to the trash can, opened the top and put the trash inside when a horn blew, Robin replaced the top, turned and looked, it was the same car, the lights blinked on and off then on again and they drove off. Robin ran inside and locked the door, put down the trash can and went to her room. She got in bed and couldn't think, she wondered if she were doing the right thing, but she knew she could not put her sister and nieces in harm's way, so she took another pill and remained silent. The following day, she made an appointment to see the doctor after class, but was told he would only be in that morning and she could come in at nine o'clock.

Robin was there and waiting when he arrived. The doctor saw her and asked her to go in and he would be in in two minutes. She saw the nurse and she pulled her file, took it into his office and placed it on his desk, Robin took a seat. Doctor came in, and took one look at her and said, "You're going to call the police and file a report, this time."

"I can't," she said. "They came by the house late while I was putting the poultice in the trash, blinked their headlights several times then drove away. They threatened my sister and her daughters. I can't have that on my conscience, too."

"You said a poultice? What for?" he asked.

"There were two of them, Doctor," she said. "And they smelled awful, I was afraid I would catch something, so I fixed a poultice and inserted it, I awoke shaking, so I removed it and wrapped it in newspaper to keep my sister from seeing it, and took it outside to the trash can, that's when I saw them."

"Oh," he said. "Let's look Robin."

He examined her and took a sample then he said, "I'm giving you two shots, and some cream and ointment for those bruises. My nurse will clean them up with Beta-dine and give you gloves to use insert the cream at night before bedtime. I'm going to discuss your case with a colleague of mine. So, come back in one week. Predators are like magnets with radar; they zero in to the frequency of their prey and draw or feed on the prey's fears. One time, it could happen to anyone, he said, but twice in less than six months, with two predators simultaneously, makes me uneasy, I signed your birth certificate, Robin, I don't want to sign your death certificate."

He continued, "Go to class, and stay with groups of people, not with just one person, but several and make sure it is coed, study, no Sunday evening or night services, as everyone knows, church is your passion, and return early Monday. I'll give you a statement for today, and I hope to have a statement for you, next week, he said. I have an idea, but I want to confirm it with an expert."

Robin followed his instructions and returned the following Monday morning. Doctor knew she had class, so he arrived early and was waiting for her. She felt better in her body but he examined her and said he received the test results and will treat her with large doses of Penicillin and she should be fine, she did good with the poultice.

"But better by coming in," he said. "One more dose of Penicillin on Wednesday."

"I spoke with my colleague and he concurs that something is amiss. We think you're being profiled," he said. "And since your routine is so well known, let's mix it up. I want you to return on Wednesday and Saturday."

"When you leave here, I want you to be paranoid and assume everything you do, is being watched or recorded," he said. "Don't tell anyone in advance what your plans are, but Ruby, if she asks. I know it is difficult to reschedule rehearsals, so we will not go there, except to say, change the routes by which you travel. If you normally go south, then take the long way around, get a reliable ride to and from, your events with a stable older adult, who will not drive off and leave you stranded. I cannot stress this enough."

"Stop being so independent that you think you don't have to rely on anyone else, because you do, I do, we all rely on someone, that's why I have a nurse," he said. "These are common sense things, but when you live where doors are not locked, one tends to be too trusting. Everyone cannot be trusted and I know you know that. I just don't want you caught in a loop or devastated for life by the horrendous acts of a few deviants. We can't recognize all of them, but there are some signs that signal us that things are not what they appear and we need to trust those instincts."

"Yes, sir," she said. "And thank you."

"Remember to get your note from the nurse, I left it on her desk if she isn't there." he said. "See you Wednesday morning, evening. And my friend will be here on Saturday, if he doesn't have an emergency."

"Yes, doctor," she said. She picked up the envelope and left remembering everything he said.

She kept her appointments, but her health began to decline rapidly, she was diagnosed with Multiple Sclerosis and it wasn't long before she needed in home care. A young woman named Martha was hired to help her. Like most of her workers that followed, Martha worked well if Robin could sit up and watch, but she became weaker and unable to be watchful, she had to trust. One day after Martha had been in her employ for over five years, she had company and it was a niece who found a check on the floor, in the bathroom. Her niece took the check to Robin and asked if that was her signature.

Robin looked at the signature and said, "No, it's not mine, it looks like Martha's. Let me see that again?" She was shown the check and she saw it was made out to the Electric company for several hundreds of dollars, but the address was not hers, it was Martha's grandmother's house. While the niece was there, she answered a phone call regarding a charge card and payment due from a bank Robin had no account with.

"Where is Martha," asked the niece.

"She took my clothes to be washed and is picking up my medicine and groceries," Robin said. "In my car."

Robin's niece called the bank and gave Robin the phone, "Tell them you want copies of your statements for the past six months and you need to freeze your account until you are physically able to come in."

Robin identified herself to the lady and was put on hold; a cashier spoke with Robin and asked, "Did something happened since you left here?"

"Left there," Robin repeated.

"What do you mean?" she asked. "You just made a substantial withdrawal, I did the transaction personally."

Robin said, "It wasn't with me, I'm in bed and my niece has been here for over an hour and found a check on the floor I did not authorize and brought it to my attention, that is why we called. Another bank called stating a payment was due on a charge account I have no knowledge about. My niece dialed and gave me the phone."

"The person had your Driver's License," she said.

"Well, she hasn't returned, but she doesn't look anything like me nor my license," Robin said. "I need copies of my statements, and I want to stop or freeze my present accounts."

"I will put an alert on your accounts, but there will be checks that will bounce NSF, however, that can be cleared up after you make a police report," she said.

Robin called the police and reported it and they said they would send a Detective to take the Report.

The Detective came and took the report and left a file number and stated that, "Should anything else come up, call and have it added to this report number."

Robin's niece gathered all the information and discovered she had opened several accounts in her name, had found her brother's name and opened accounts in his name and practically cleaned out her accounts. Martha returned and the niece asked her for all the keys to the house and car, Martha gave them to her and asked, "What's going on?"

Robin's niece walked her to the door, opened it and said, "You're leaving, that's what's happening and don't leave town."

Martha's grandmother called Robin asked her not to press charges. Robin asked her how will she be reimbursed if she doesn't press charges what about her credit record? She didn't say anything.

Robin said, "I must do what I must do and Martha took a lot of money and did a lot of damage to family members financially."

Robin hung up. She called a friend of hers, the Dean of Students, at an area college and informed her what had transpired and she agreed to take her to the bank to see about the matter.

The following day, there was a knock at the door, then the doorbell rang, and it was another Detective, who said he would be handling the case with Martha. She recognized him but said nothing, she was alone in the house, then the doorbell rang, again, "I'll get that," he said, he left his card, opened the door.

Ruth spoke with him briefly, then came in and said, "I see Detective Randle is on the case."

Robin didn't say a word. She went with Ruth to the bank and they spoke with the President. Robin was still silent. She received a police report and wanted to scream when she read it, he wrote it up as Deceptive Practices. Robin later discovered that the Detective was Martha's cousin and her grandmother's nephew, whom she asked to take the case for no other reason than, to keep Martha from going to jail.

Robin had been raped again by the same man this time in daylight and on the job and there was nothing she could do about it. "It was the circle of life," she thought.

Robin knew she was blessed, because when he came, he knew who she was and what he had done to her, if Ruth had not arrived when she did, she would have been at his mercy, and perhaps with the same gun at her head, again, or worse. It took a lot of nerve for him to show up to the house of a woman he had rape to help another woman to whom he was related, so it would not be difficult to imagine him carrying out his promise to kill her! Protect and Serve?

Ruth and Robin took the case to the States Attorney Office and he refuse to prosecute because the case was written up and changed by him to Deceptive Practices. Who polices the Police? Robin asked.

Detective Randle knew what he was doing always and he was sanctioned by the State.

The silence is broken, for Robin, now the healing can begin in the mind first before it flows to the rest of the body. Robin chose to believe that memories, in the form of flash backs, serve more than one purpose, they also help to purge us of the impurities that hinder us from moving forward with wholeness and sanity, should we accept it as such. She took a card and wrote the word 'Life' in all capital letters, she held that card up to the mirror, then turned it towards herself and she saw the word within the word was IF, she circled it and thought to herself, LIFE is IF-E at worse, when we fail to learn from our trials and become paralyzed with our overwhelming experiences of fear, to the point we feel there is nothing else to accomplish, on this planet, we succumb to hopelessness; at best, IF (In Faith) we can deal with the unpleasantness that comes with, the circle of life, learn and grow from it, pick up the pieces and unite them as one within to form a useful tool or gift, to pay it forward, we are conquerors, as fear is swallowed up in victory. Which can only be achieved through a right relationship with Jesus, the Christ.

Chapter Eighteen

Picking Up the Pieces

Robin was a fighter, wherever there was a challenge, she wanted to find the solution, and she had numerous challenges to face, and she welcomed the flash backs, for within them, she found renewed strength, rekindled fire and a restored joy that arose from the torment as the phoenix rises from the ashes. She could now pick up the pieces and move forward to the lives awaiting her touch.

There is a difference between good friends and true friends and there are times when it is difficult to discern the difference, but time has a way of revealing the truth, while accepting or rejecting it is exercising man's free will.

The Marshall's, Juliette and William, took Robin to their home for an extended weekend that was designated to last until the apartment complex was completed. She went to work from there, learned to laugh again and socialize there, made a new friend for life there, in Johanna. Johanna became a different person; the frequency of the episodes she once experienced began to decrease after her second night there. Robin spent the first night observing, not participating, her first day of the week-end, which Robin spent there, kept the Marshalls in Johanna's room all day, with a period of four hours, not consecutively, when they were not in her room. Observing them, Robin concluded, she understood why the Marshalls had so many horrific days with Johanna.

The second day, Robin spoke with the Marshalls and suggested they go out for lunch and she would have lunch with Johnna and they could turn their monitor's on in Johanna's room and leave and not to worry about her, she would be fine. Somewhat apprehensive, they stated they could not allow Johanna to be a burden to Robin on top of what she was experiencing. Robin persuaded them, her request would trickle down as beneficial to them, but it was for Johanna. That is when they agreed to go.

Robin asked Juliette if she could speak to her cook and she was told, "Whatever you need done, Robin, the staff has been informed to do. You never have to ask for permission for anything, you're at home."

"Thank you, Juliette," Robin said.

"Robin, why are you thanking me, you're at home, enjoy yourself not as a visitor, but as a resident," she shared.

"Yes, Juliette," she replied.

"Now, Robin, I haven't been anywhere in such a long time, I'm a little uncomfortable," she said.

"Well we cannot have that," Robin replied. "Let's go to your closet and find a nice dress or pant outfit for a nice luncheon."

She took her by the arm and they walked into her closet, "Wow," Robin said. "We're in a department store."

Juliette laughed and said, "Navy blue or royal blue, Robin?"

"Neither," she responded. "Let's wear something colorful like that lovely orange and black with yellow two-piece with the matching shoes and bag."

"You have great taste, Robin," she said.

"Once he sees you in that, you two may end up at the apartment," Robin said.

"That would be a novelty," she said. "Robin, I haven't felt attractive and desirable since our darling Johanna came, I love her so much, I've devoted my life to her and haven't thought about the sexual needs."

"Juliette, I think it is commendable what the two of you have sacrificed to help improve Johanna's quality of life, but the quality of your lives isn't supposed to suffer as a result. You have needs and your husband has needs, and please do not forget that, or you may find yourself in the shoes of a thousand other women, who neglected their husbands. Remember how easy it is for a woman to play on a man's weakness, remember Russell?" she asked. "There are women who will do anything, fifty percent of which we have never heard before, twenty-five percent of which we haven't tried and the balance of which we do not want to try, so we are beat before we get into bed. So, I'm beginning to think that should I be given a second chance to find love, once I know it is mutual, I am going to compromise to some extent."

"A good man is difficult to find and if you have one, do not drive him into the arms of the first woman who pays him a compliment. I didn't think about that, Robin," she said.

"Yes, I know," Robin revealed. "But now that you have thought about it, what do you plain to do about it?"

"I have no idea," Juliette said.

"Juliette, make the time and you'll remember," Robin said. "Have a flash back and when the dust settles, it will be as if you recaptured time and you two deserve it."

"Let's have a look at you, Juliette? My, you look gorgeous," she said.

"Thank you, Robin, I do look different and feel differently than I have in many months," she said.

"Let's go out and greet your date and do not worry about Johanna, if I have a problem I cannot handle, I will contact you," Robin reasoned. They stepped out and he was pacing, the floor.

Robin picked up her camera and took their picture after he turned and said, "Juliette, you look radiant and perfect for where we are going. Maurice is outside waiting for us, shall we?"

She walked and he whistled, he was flirting, already.

"Mr. Marshall still had fire," thought Robin. "I pray he uses every spark and flame on making themselves happy, tonight."

She went to the door and waved to Maurice as he helped Juliette into the car, he waved and winked, Robin knew she was not the only one sending positive thoughts the Marshall's way. Robin closed the door and spoke with the cook and went into Johanna's room.

Robin looked upon it as a privilege and thanked God for the opportunity to serve Him through serving her. She talked with Johanna and put on music she could identify with while waiting for the cook.

She handed the picture she had taken of the Marshalls' to Johanna to get her response. Johanna stared at the picture and said beautiful and handed it back to Robin and that answered one question for Robin, as she put the picture away as the cook came in and set up with a few of the staff.

While they were there, Robin asked Johanna to accompany her to the rest room. While they were there, Robin told Johanna they were preparing for lunch and had to clean up. Johanna went to the face bowl and turned on the facet, lathered her hands well and rinsed them and dried them off as she asked, for a happy meal and soda. Robin stepped to the door and whispered to the cook, "Cheeseburgers and fries it is with milk shakes and cherry on top, as discussed."

"But add broccoli florets," she added.

Robin returned and lathered her hands, just as Johanna had and knowing she was watching, asked. "Am I doing this correctly, Johanna?"

"Yes," she said, as she motioned for her to pick up the towel to dry her hands.

"Thank you, Johanna," Robin said. "I am starving."

"So am I," she said. They went out into Johanna's very large suite and they were seated as the cook and two helpers waited on them.

They placed a McDonald's bag on the table and asked if they should plate the food and Johanna said, "No thank you, I want to eat from the bag."

"Why don't we do that," Robin said. "And I'll have a strawberry milkshake."

Johanna said, "Chocolate, please."

And they were placed in front of them, as ordered. Johanna smiled and said. "This is fun, Robin."

Robin replied, "Yes, it is, Johanna."

She asked if they could have fish for their next meal and Robin said. "Only if you eat your broccoli, Johanna."

"I will," she said.

She ate her half cup of broccoli florets and completed her happy meal with chocolate shake. (Johanna's meds were placed in her shake as Robin requested). Robin asked her if she would like the prize in the bag and she said yes. After they ate, they moved to the sofa and Robin asked Johanna to read to her and Johanna went to her books. Robin told the cook Johanna wanted fish for dinner and she said, "Oh, yes ma'am."

"That is wonderful, you may go and thank you for the special service," she said.

"Johanna, have you found your favorite book?" Robin asked.

"No, but I'm still looking," she said.

"I heard you thank cook, but I don't understand why," she said. "Wasn't she doing her job that my grandparents pay her to do?"

"Yes, she was doing her job, but even though a person is paid to a job, it is always a good thing to let them know you appreciate the fact that they did their job well. It is called common courtesy, a part of etiquette, while it encourages the doer to aspire to do better not taking them for granted, it also keeps the speaker, hopefully, humble and considerate," she said. "Words and phrases change during decades, it may be called something else in five or ten years."

"Thank you, Robin, for explaining that," she said. "I found my book, it's my favorite."

"What is it?" Robin asked.

"The Song of Bernadette," she said.

"Oh, I love that book," Robin said. "It is slightly different in the French version."

"Do you speak French?" Johanna asked.

"Yes," she said.

"Perhaps you will teach me," she said.

"I would love to," Robin replied.

"Can we read it later?" she asked.

"We can begin reading it tonight, but I must prepare for work tomorrow," she said.

"Thank you, Robin. We've had a great day," Johanna said. "And I didn't have one episode, it's amazing."

"Yes, we praise God for His Mercy," Robin said.

"God?"

"Yes," Robin said, "God!"

"Will you tell me about Him?" she asked.

"Certainly," she said.

"In lieu of reading the book," she added. "We can begin the book this week, sometime." Robin looked at the clock and it was almost five o'clock, but, Johanna was in good form and spirit. Robin smiled and thought, it seems Johanna isn't the only one in good form and spirit.

Robin picked up the phone and buzzed cook,

"Yes ma'am, dinner will be ready in fifteen minutes, are you two coming down or would you rather be served in Ms. Johanna's rooms?" she asked.

"We'll be down to the kitchen," she said.

"You mean the dining room Ms. Robin?"

"No," Robin said. "The kitchen."

"Yes, ma'am," she said.

"Johanna, why don't we try something new," Robin said. "Let's go down to eat."

"Should we dress for dinner?" she asked.

"Not this time, since cook said fifteen minutes, it would be inappropriate to have them wait, and dinner would be dry," Robin said.

"Okay, let's wash our hands and we can go down," she said.

They went into the bathroom and washed their hands and face dried them and walked together to the dining room, when Robin said, "We're eating in the kitchen, tonight Johanna, the dining room is too large for the two of us, besides, we're becoming friends and should not sit at opposite ends of that large table."

"I didn't think about that, but I'm glad we're becoming friends," she said, kitchen it is."

They entered the kitchen and they were seated and served. The fish was lovely, it was Salmon and Johanna had the same sides as her new friend.

She surprised the staff, by stating the three of them were welcome to sit and eat, too.

They thanked her and explained they only prepared enough Salmon for two and their meal would be prepared afterwards. Johanna said, "Thank you, again." when they were done, she commented "it was so gracious for them to allow us to have a grass roots meal in their personal space."

The head cook stated it was a pleasure to see her up and about and they were happy to serve her outside her room, they gave them a cupcake with berries, which they ate and Robin hugged them and Johanna followed suit. They left the kitchen with a huge smile and were headed back to Johanna's room, when the door opened and in walked the Marshalls with a look of disbelief on their faces.

Juliette ran to Johanna and asked. "Did you have a good time?"

But before Johanna answered, Mr. Marshall said, "Juliette, do you see her standing next to Robin smiling and talking and you asked that question, of course, they had a wonderful time, it is in the air. The atmosphere has changed."

He closed the door and sat Juliette in a seat and nodded to them and he sat down.

"Tell us where you are coming from and what you did today," he said.

Johanna looked at Robin and asked, "May I please tell them Ms. Robin?

"Yes, you may," she replied.

"Thank you," said Johanna. They sat there in awe as Johanna began her statement.

"We had dinner in the kitchen," she said. "Salmon, I wanted fish. And the staff served us and surprised me with a special cupcake they prepared for us because they were so pleased I ate outside my room. It was delicious."

She continued, "We had a happy meal for lunch and chocolate milkshake for me and strawberry for Robin, who gave me her prize. she said. Robin taught me a little etiquette and common courtesy, we talked about different things, she is going to read me my favorite book and teach me to speak French, after she tells me about God, who helped me today."

"Did I forget anything Robin?" she asked.

"Oh," she said. "I forgot the most important thing, Ms. Robin is becoming my friend and I am becoming hers. Thank you for bringing her here grandpa and grandma. I love you, both."

She got up went over to them and hugged them, tears began to flow and Robin, eased out to prepare for work and left them to their special quality time. She cried on the way to her rooms and while there, she fell on her knees to talk to God in prayer. Robin didn't time her prayer time, but when she arose, felt revived. She prepared herself a to do list and she laid out her clothes for work for she knew she had to check on Raymond and on Celia, for there were unresolved issues with them that required immediate assistance.

There was a knock on the door and she said,

"It's unlocked, come in, please," It was Juliette, she said she had to stop by, before going to bed. "

"Have a seat, Juliette," Robin said.

Robin took note she had changed that beautiful outfit and now she was dressed for bed.

"Juliette, please tell me what has caused that glow to fall upon your face?" she asked.

She leaned back on the sofa and said.

"It was a blessing this day in so many ways," she said. "I am happy to have someone I trust to talk to. I know you have work in the morning and when you need me to go, just say so, and we'll pick up where we left off, as friends do," said Johanna. "We were at lunch, and had surf n turf, we talked and listened to each other. We were at a very nice club."

"I think I'm acquainted with it," Robin said.

"We danced and a very nice gentleman came over and asked my husband for permission to dance with me, he said 'yes'."

"The man, the ambiance, the occasion, the outfit had me convinced that I was desirable," she said. "We had a magnum of champagne and drank it all and you had not called to be rescued. We went to the office, to the apartment and relaxed. It is so comfortable there and neat, we laid down and you thought of everything, so we didn't need a thing. We had each other and I had a flash back, everything came back to me, and him and we had a wild sexual experience or should I say experiences. We didn't have to worry about the help over hearing us or even the neighbors, not that we worry about them at home, but there are times when we have company and can hear what is going on in the next room."

"Did you have fun?" Robin asked. "And is there anything that would make your next visit there even better?"

"No, if we do what we did, it can't get any better," she said.

"I am so glad to hear it," Robin expressed.

"But I was right about the apartment, but wrong about not getting better."

"When we walked in the house and saw you and Johanna talking and smiling, we couldn't believe it was our baby, the same one who kept us up all night screaming and crying not looking human, but deformed in face and body, we haven't heard her voice in so long, we thought we were hallucinating," she said. "Or you were playing tricks on us, but we knew you wouldn't do that to us, so the longer we stood there, the more certain we were that it was our baby, Johanna."

"When she asked for permission to speak, it blew us away and she was so eloquent, we were proud parents and still are. We dared to hope, Robin, when we heard what you did with that boy who had Autism, we dared to hope," she said. "But we never really thought we had it right when everything pointed to the growth of the company."

"Then we were scared when Russell started to plan to get rid of you, we almost lost hope, but we were reminded that the greatest victory comes after the greatest attack and you were really being attacked and when it drew my husband in, we were told that meant you were really sent to deliver our Johanna, so we were willing to fight to the finish for you and you showed us what love was regarding people, we learned so much now we've received so much, you're priceless and you've only been here two and a half days really, it's God."

She got up and hugged Robin and said. "We know you must go to work tomorrow, the business suffered while you were away and my husband was at the Helm, but he just could not swing it. We brought in two top people, who cost us an arm and a leg, if one had been able to stick it out for over three and a half years; one could not make nineteen months, it was bad. Regina even thought she could do it, six months after we let her try, money disappeared, the company went into a slump, oversea investors pulled out, things were charged to the company accounts and no one could explain how or why."

Robin just let her talk and she tried to remember as much as possible but especially those things which directly affected the company, her and the employees. She had Regina's number so she would start there then the renovations and uncle Book, Celia, Raymond and Maurice, and we'll find the mysterious someone.

Robin hugged her back and suggested she go to sleep, tomorrow would be a big day, Johanna was returning to school, after an extended time away and she had to be the one to take her, since her husband had to be at work, at least make sure Robin was there and she needed to find a movie for Johanna and Robin and they were to have three hours together. She had to make the plans.

"Maurice will pick you up, Robin," she said. "Don't worry about transportation. I'll make sure you have the time you need with Johanna."

"You two can rest tonight," Robin said. "Johanna will be good. I want to see all the books."

"Marshall will have them for you, Robin," Juliette said.

"See you in the morning, Juliette, the Lord willing. I'll look in on Johanna before I fall asleep," Robin said.

"Good night, tomorrow is the beginning; we shall see what it brings!"

Chapter Nineteen

The Return of Robin

Robin was up early and dressed, she hurried to Johanna's room to say good morning to her new friend and give her a pep talk for school, to find her in bed.
She turned and opened the draperies and asked.
"Good morning my friend, why do you get to stay in bed and I go to work?"
She sat up and said, "Good morning my friend, do I have to go to school, today?"
Robin took a seat and asked, "Johanna, is there a reason you don't want to go to school, please talk to me? You know I'll do anything for you, and if there is someone bothering you, I'll get them for you."
Johanna said, "They make fun of me, Robin, they say I don't have a mother or friend they make fun of my clothes, throw spit balls at me, call me fatty put pictures of a pig on my seat and it is so embarrassing there is no one I can talk to, even the teachers won't listen, so I stopped telling them and I stopped going to school."
"Ok, my friend and family, you're my little sister, get up and get a shower; by the way, did you mention this to your grandparents?" she asked.
"Once, they said to give them a chance to know you and they'll love you, but they were wrong," she said.
Robin went to Johanna's closet and looked around, she went to an elite school and her wardrobe looked appropriate to Robin, but it didn't look like the young girl she had come to know who was in transformation. Robin picked a pair of jeans, a colored top and a jacket with a scarf for her

neck and put them on her bed; matching tennis shoes, a backpack, a body bag to go around her waist for her change and I.D., a pen and pencil and a small phone book, with Robin's, Juliette's and Maurice's phone number, lip balm and mints. Robin found two hair ties that matched and Johanna came out of the shower.

"What is this, Robin?" she asked.

"This is your new look for today," she replied.

"But there is a dress code," she said.

"We'll Johanna, let's get their attention and if they listen to you, and stop these children who are giving you a rough time, then we'll listen to them and wear their dress code. You have my phone number in your address book, if anyone gives you a problem, give them my number, not your book, so memorize it, and ask them to call your sister, Robin. If you're close to a phone, there is change in your body bag, to call me, grandma and Uncle Maurice. Let me do your hair this morning," Robin said.

She did two pony tails, one as usual, braided, and the second in top of her head with hair ties, and side kisses, when she finished, she asked.

"How do you feel as you look in the mirror, Johanna?"

"Like I'm seeing someone for the first time," she said.

"Very good, Johanna, that's how everyone will feel when they see you. Just be yourself, but always respectful and gracious very polite common courtesy, remember. Do not try to please everyone who speaks to you as a matter of fact, explore today, and discover who this bright, beautiful young person is. I'll ask Juliette to check in with the school on you and so will I. Enjoy your day, Johanna."

Robin hugged her and put the purse around her waist and said, "Enjoy being you, Johanna."

"Thank you, Robin, and you enjoy your day, as well," she replied. Robin nodded and smiled and walked her out and into Juliette's room.

"Juliette, Johanna is exploring today, she's tired of being ignored by the school when she complains about the students conduct, making fun of her, calling her names like fatty, telling her she has no friends or parents, her clothes, everything. Hopefully, she will get their attention, today, and we'll all play it by ear, today. She has your number, my private number and her uncle Maurice's in case of emergency, to give to the proper authorities, if needed. How do you feel about this?" Robin asked.

Juliette looked at Johanna and said, "You have all our support, Johanna, you have a lot of love: Look at you, lovely and poised, confident, like your sister and friend, Robin. I'm taking you to school, today, and talking to everyone. We'll have a great day."

Johanna smiled and said, "I feel loved!"

With that said, Robin went outside where Maurice was waiting, he helped her into the car and she said, "You should see your niece, Johanna, she is so different."

"I see," he said. As he waved and got out of the car and walked towards her. Robin did not hear what he or she said to each other, but she saw the response as he picked her up and swung her around, then put her down and shook her hand. She said.

"Thank you, uncle Maurice, I love you, too."

Juliette came out and asked Maurice to take them to the school and return to pick her up later.

"No, I spoke with my husband, and he instructed me not to drive, but to take my time and talk to everyone and you will return for me when I call."

"I have a car full of beautiful ladies," he said. "How lucky can one man be? Five."

"What does that mean?" asked Johanna.

"That means I will have you where you're going in five minutes," he said.

"Oh, she said, you say that all the time and I wanted to ask about it, but didn't until now."

"Good, you're discovering who you are, that's why it's important not to join in with the first people who talk to you, today; they don't know who they are, yet, and it is so easy to be misguided, Johanna."

Maurice announced arrived. Juliette turned to Robin and said. "Thank you, Robin, I never would have thought of all this, nor put the pieces together, so quickly, if at all, I call you later."

"Johanna has my private number in her address book, I gave her, use it as often as you need," Robin said, "and you would have figured it out."

"Thanks for the confidence, Robin, I'll make you proud this morning," said Juliette.

"I'm already proud of you both," Robin replied.

"Me too, Robin," Johanna said, "see you and uncle Maurice later."

"Yes, dear, you will," they replied simultaneously.

Juliette, took Johanna's hand and they walked together to the entrance of the school, they smiled proudly, and drove away.

Robin felt a sense of hope, as she watched Juliette and Johanna openly bond, and thought, sometimes all people need is a nudge, to point them in the right direction.

Maurice said, "Robin, only you could get me a niece, where I have no siblings."

"You should consider yourself blessed, Maurice, that a lovely young girl accepts you and loves you without judgment of all your faults, that's genuine love, cherish it. Johanna didn't do so badly either, she gained a crazy uncle who will battle the minions of hell, to protect her, that's a win, win in every language I know."

"Well," said Maurice, "I think we all were blessed the moment you entered our lives, for you have changed us all, for the better, maybe one is unchanged," he added. "But speaking for the rest of the family, we tried it without you, and no one came remotely close. And the Marshalls would still be hostages in their own private palatial hell along with lovely Johanna, if you had not returned and the business would be closing, we all know this."

"Thanks for the accolades," she said. "But we thank God, and we will be speaking with Regina, today; I promise to give her every mercy, however, I have my own private grievances with her for how she treated or mistreated Celia."

"It is not my policy to talk about the family, but Regina, doesn't have the family's interest at heart."

"That is nothing the rest of us don't know, we just can't do anything about it, because she has us over a barrel," he said. "There is no one to take her place and she knows that, but you and you can't do both jobs full-time, so she doesn't feel threatened."

"Yes, thanks for sharing, Maurice, but there might be a solution no one has considered," she said.

"Let's see if we can make that happen," he said.

"What is that Maurice?" she asked.

"What you have in mind, I have missed the sound of your mind turning, but I hear it loud and clear, Robin has returned!"

"Three," he said. "I must prepare you, I have updated security and no old codes are active. I'll let you in and set you up for entry as soon as Mr. Marshall gives us the J. D."

"Would that be Job Description?"

"It would," he said. "He's been waiting for us, but, his wife called and explained you were taking care of Johanna and he was good, gave us instructions to support you in every way, and we have and will."

"That's good information," she said.

"The building has suffered," he said.

"Those who were in power, sought things for themselves and didn't care, but I was given a separate funding they were unable to touch, so I maintained the security or there would not be a building with contents, such as they are."

"That is sad, Maurice, I'll need all the books, privacy, to choose a team I can trust and put in place in a minimum of two days and are employee records up-to-date?"

"Yes, that came to me when Regina was in command and I never got around to returning them," he said.

"Good, but people change, you have and I like it, but what about Celia?"

"Celia, is the same Celia we all grew to love and know, she's still the teacher's pet, but is genuine and faithful to the family."

"She had several opportunities to go over to the wild side with Regina, but she remained steadfast and faithful even at the expense of her freedom and her bedroom suite."

"She pays for everything at Regina's," he said.

"Well, you'll see her soon and you'll need this diet Pepsi, drink up, they sure help you think."

"I'll take that."

Mr. Marshall came in and said, "Welcome home, Robin, sorry we didn't keep it up to your standards. Do you remember Mr. McAfee?"

"Of course, is he here?"

"He was, but he had to leave, since we had a family emergency, but he drew up the papers just as I asked and all is needed is for you to read and sign them and you're in control retro-active five days ago, when we contacted you, as promised," he said.

"Make copies of these for me Maurice."

Robin signed the papers.

"I gave you complete control, Robin."

"Maurice, welcome the new CEO," he said.

"There was a new office made twice by the top men who were here briefly, look at them and choose one or both or remodel on a small scale, to begin, I'm just suggesting."

"Mr. Marshall, please feel free to suggest to me anytime you like."

He smiled and said, "Thank you Robin, you're the only one who has said that, but it is in the contract, I can offer suggestions, if asked."

"Besides, no one knows the people better than you and I need your input," she said.

"I'm at your disposal, Robin."

"Thank you, Mr. Marshall."

"What will you have us do, Robin?"

"Will you and Maurice make sure I have the Codes and any other security requirements I need and the employee files? I will check out the offices, do you have a recommendation?"

"The larger one has always been my favorite," Maurice said. "It has more security than the other."

"Alright," she said. "Let's put a little paint on it and fix the mandatory things, is there room for an executive assistant and phones in place?"

"Room for two plus two and phones will only take a second to activate, after painting and I recall your color."

"I'll work in the conference room until it is complete," she said.

"And when will that be, Maurice?"

"Tomorrow, Robin, you'll be moved in to begin the day."

"Touch up Mr. Marshall's apartment, for security, update the system, issue new codes and keys," she insisted.

"Where is Raymond?" Robin asked.

"I thought you were informed."

"I think I should sit down, have another diet Pepsi and take a deep breath," she said.

She leaned back in her chair and prepared for the worse. "Tell me, please."

"The first top executive liked Raymond and he tried to keep what you began intact, but, he couldn't handle it, he threw his Ivy League hat out the window before he jumped," said Maurice. "The second ivy leaguer liked Raymond a little too much and tried to blackmail him for sexual favors."

"Was he successful?" Robin asked.

"Yes, a few times he entrapped him until he came to me for help and I confronted him with his contract on the moral's clause and his performance was poor, it was difficult to believe he held his MBA and he built a new office when there was a very nice one with everything one could want built by the one who preceded him, just to hide his sexual persuasion, and paid top dollar for construction quality and haste, without the security surveillance. He resigned after thirty-two days on the job."

"Then, there was Regina, who just couldn't find the money to continue Raymond's employment and education fund, so she fired him to save money. The company finances took a dive then the books mysteriously were watered in the second office and no one could do an audit, forensic or manual. She got away with plenty, but she spent it as quickly as she stole it, and that is why she is still working and Celia is paying all the bills," he said.

"Okay, someone please tell me one of you kept in touch with him."

"One of us kept in touch with him, Robin," Mr. Marshall said.

"How is he?" Robin smilingly inquired.

"He is confused and unemployed. I dropped the ball," Maurice said. "I should have talked with him after it happened, but there was always something I could use as an excuse for not seeing him."

"Then, fix it, go get him and bring him to the office! Has Mrs. Marshall called?"

"No, not yet," he said.

"Then you can pick her up and make the arrangements for the office repairs and security, but leave me the files in a plain covered envelope, clear?"

"I'll get them, now."

"Thank you, Maurice."

"What time are the employees arriving?"

"The plan is for him to pick up, Celia and Mr. Gulley at eleven and Regina will come in at one o'clock."

"Mr. Marshall, will you interview Regina first for me?"

"Of course, you're the boss," he said.

"Is there a reason you should not interview Regina?"

"No, Robin."

"I'll go through the files and the next two people I find with the X factor, I'll give to you for first interview," she said. "I want all your notes and comments also tapes."

"Yes, ma'am," he said.

"I think you should call me Bill, since I'm working for you."

"No, working with me, Bill, hopefully," she exclaimed.

"That's good," he said.

"Since you have an office upstairs, you can feel free to use the facilities as you like, to be comfortable."

"Thank you, Robin."

"Let me know when you're taking lunch, we need to know where you are when Juliette calls."

"Sure thing, Robin," he said.

"Bill, do you know what the disposition of the apartment building is to date?"

"Yes, Robin. The renovations went very well; Louise and Walter are on the second floor. She tried to get the first floor, but I blocked that, because she agreed to the second floor. Uncle Book moved, but returns to check out the first floor weekly, at my request. He found a lovely home in a quiet area and he and his wife are very content."

"That's good. Tell me more about the apartment."

"The first floor has three bedrooms and two baths, living room and dining room, spacious kitchen, with all the modern appliances, washroom and the only floor to have an office/den family room with half bath. There is a very nice patio covered sitting area and Uncle Book left his patio furniture, which is covered and of course the garage that houses two cars on the back with entrance into the den/family room. There is a privacy fence and basketball goal and baseball diamond with a short cut leading to CTA enclosed," he said.

"The basement is beautiful with three bedrooms, two baths, kitchen dining and living rooms. It is vacant too. When Vera passed, the children could not handle being there with the reminders so they were released from the contract."

"How much is the rent?

"You're the owner of the building, you can charge whatever you want for any new tenants, Louise and Walter are locked in to their price, for the life of their tenancy. However, they pay their own utilities, maintenance on the building and full upkeep since there are no other tenants."

"Well, for a building such as the one they live in, with an up to date utility room, washer and drier, central air and heating, instead of steam heat, they would pay condominium prices."

"There are laundry rooms on every floor," he said.

"Can the appliances be removed?"

"They built everything into the walls, but given enough time and the desire to do it, it is doable. You own the block, so you can put up surveillance wherever you desire," he informed her.

"That is something to research," she noted.

"You don't remember, arranging to buy up the property that was vacant, for taxes and you had the foresight to put funds aside for and that is why you own the block on both sides of the street," he said. "You hired Mr. McAfee to handle your business and he's done an excellent job. He was looking forward to giving you a report, this morning, but you can arrange to see him anytime, you're a good client.

"Forgive me for not having total recall; I am blessed to say I have forgotten more than some have learned. Bill, I look forward to hearing from Mr. McAfee."

Robin had an idea or two or three. Since she knew where she stood, financially, she knew how she could help. A bright light appeared and she asked, "What was that?"

Bill said, "Someone is approaching the building, probably Celia and Raymond."

"Do you want to speak to them alone?"

"No," she said. "If I feel the need to speak to one I'll ask that person if he/she wants popcorn."

"Oh, the safe word we agreed on," he said.

"Yes, Bill, you remembered."

"Robin, it's hard not to remember those days, they were the most infuriating, disappointing, disgusting and horrendous days I have experienced, but I learned a lot from them and grew. What you endured, words cannot express and how you made a come-back is even more remarkable. Whatever you're made of should be bottled and sold for the price of gold per ounce. I think about it all the time. I don't know another person who would be brave enough to do what you did for the sake of others and justice," he added. "The team work that we had was unbelievable; no wonder we were unbeatable and prospered, we were selfless and considerate and we genuinely cared about each other. If we can recapture that oneness again, with the same fierce leader, there are no limits to what we can accomplish. The most difficult thing we must overcome is distrust. The employees have seen and experienced so much deceit and treachery with the last three leaders, I don't know if they can overcome it," he said. "But if anyone can get a breakthrough with them, it is Robin; she's the only one who has proven by example her abilities and moral, ethical and biblical standards. I know my credibility is shot. And I would not waste their time trying to persuade them of something I don't believe, to choose me, but I will stand firm for Robin for she has the heart and soul and the army of the Lord needed to bring us back a second time. I will tell the world Robin is the man with the plan."

"I'll second that," Mr. McAfee said. "Good to see you, Robin! If ever anyone is looking to participate in a real fight, Robin is the right General to lead the charge. I've never seen anything like the strength, character and determination that I personally experienced during an all- out warfare. The team work, I even worked with my brother-in-law in peace and it was mutual, and unbelievable that it took place, but it did and we've worked together periodically since that time, but not with the intensity as those days, before, during and after, it was awesome. Now, the Return of Robin has shaken the very core of humanity and begs the question, what justice will be wrought at the hands of this capable woman this time who will go down and who will remain standing? Robin, a lot has transpired since we were all together, but the business has rejected, what educational institutions deem highly qualified candidates abiding time waiting for your return and I, too, have waited, please know whatever you need to accomplish your plan, and I know you have several, count me in, I will gladly stand beside you. I will return after you conclude your talks. Wait for me."

"I'll be here," she said. "Come around two-thirty."

"I will," he said, he hugged her and said, "Together again."

Bill said, "That is one happy man, Robin."

Robin looked in the corner for the refrigerator Celia placed in the room for her Pepsi, and it was gone, she got up and went to the kitchen and opened a diet Pepsi and returned to the conference room. She smelled paint and asked, "Does anyone smell paint?"

"Yes, I saw Maurice and someone going to the office over an hour ago," he said.

"Well where are Celia and Raymond?"

"Raymond and Celia are in the waiting area."

"Please, call Celia in," she said.

"Mr. Gully is out front in his cubicle on the job and Celia is on her way in."

"Should Regina arrive, someone keep her in the waiting area so we will not be disturbed," she stated reluctantly.

"May we use Maurice's office?" she asked.

"You're the CEO, you tell him," said Mr. Marshall.

"I would like to hear his comments, if he has any," she stated.

"Sure, the door is unlocked," Maurice replied.

"Thank you," she said. "Let's go to a sound proof room."

She picked up her papers, purse and someone picked up a case of Diet Pepsi and carried them into Maurice's office. They took seats and Celia came in, she saw Robin, ran to her and hugged her.

"You have no idea how I PRAYED GOD would send you back to us. 'The Return of Robin,'" she said. "Just in time to save the life of the company and the lives of the family."

"Amen," Mr. Marshall said.

"Celia, since you prayed for my return, you know I need the truth from you, so how are things with you and Regina?"

"Robin, you returned in time to save me!"

"We want you to know that everyone in this room is on your side and in your corner. We are concerned about you and what you're going through, Celia."

"Do you have a lease or contract with Regina?"

"No, remember what you told her, she was not to make any changes without going through you or Mr. Marshall, well, she found a way around that. It has been loan me Celia," she uttered excitedly.

"Do you have anything written down like cancelled checks with the word loan in the memo section?"

"Yes, ma'am, I had her to sign everything and I always wrote checks even when she wanted a loan for twenty dollars. My number of checks has increased amazingly, but I kept every check and have them with me."

"Hand them to me, Celia," responded Robin. "Take these checks to Raymond and ask him to add them and determine when the payback dates are. See if she is late repaying any; find any discrepancies, like loans close to her own payday, shortly before or afterwards. Tell him to use his imagination, put himself in the mind of Regina and try to think as she thought, but not to hurt himself."

"Ask him to avoid her should she come in and do not answer any questions just get up and come to the Security Office. Celia, would it be fair to state that you are grateful you are not on the streets, but you are not happy living with Regina?"

"That is more than a fair statement, it is an accurate statement. If I can get out of this trap, I would not hesitate to move," she confirmed.

"Well Celia, how is that bedroom suite you bought, it should be paid for by now, right?"

"I slept fine for two weeks, then Regina said she slipped and hurt her back and asked if she could sleep with me in my bed until her back was better. After two more weeks and she didn't see a doctor or file a claim with insurance, she would have to go through me to do it, I called her on it. She told me that she filed the claim and she needed more room to rest, so she suggested that since she took me in out of the cold weather, I should let her sleep in my bed. I told her she could sleep with me and she said that the mattress needed to be queen size for us to sleep in the same bed and since it was just a full-size bed, I needed to sleep in her bed and give her mine. I said she could buy herself a bed and she said she would look for another roommate. I didn't have anywhere to go and she knew it, so she sleeps in my bed. When I stated she should make the payments, the next day she had a sign in her window, room for rent! I just make the payments." she said.

"How do you buy the food and did she give you the eight hundred dollars and security deposit she's holding?"

"No, Robin, I pay for all the food and she tells me what I can eat and what I can't, she has gained the weight," said Celia. "No, she has not given me a dime nor said anything about the money she's holding. I don't know what she does with her money, but she lives off mine."

"Celia, pay day is this week, right?"

"Yes, it is," she said.

"I have a building and you can move in with me on the first floor and we'll pay half on everything, what do you say?"

"I'll have my own room?" she asked.

"Yes, and bathroom, a large kitchen, patio and large yard and garage also a laundry room of our own. You can purchase your own food and I'll purchase mine, it doesn't matter, there is a large new refrigerator freezer and we will have plenty of room to store our food. I'll buy furniture for my bedroom and we'll get Regina to either pay for your bedroom suite or return it to you. I think she should pay for it, though and you get another one. If you want, we can pay together for the living room and dining room and family room furniture but I will buy my desk and computer you can buy yours. You can see the apartment when you want. All the appliances are in the house. I won't be there all the time, I have a little sister and I must spend time with her every week or every other week, I don't want to wear out my welcome, so you will have a lot of time to yourself, is that okay?"

"Yes, I have not had that type of freedom," she said.

"Well, you will," Robin insisted. "But you will need to take the train or buy a car. Louise takes the train maybe you two can ride together, it is the getting home that may be a problem unless Raymond...Just see the apartment and let me know before Friday and if you complete the lease, get your permit you can move in. Today is Monday so you have today and tomorrow but we need to know by tomorrow to have everything turned on, which can only be done with your occupancy permit. Send Raymond in Celia and Bill, you take Regina, I want to hurt her!"

"Thank you, Robin again," Celia chanted.

"A content worker is a productive worker and we are family," Robin remarked.

Raymond came in and said, "Celia loaned Regina a lot of money and she can get most of it legally, but she's going to lose a lot, because of wording."

"Bill, did you hear that, it will take someone as smart and slick as her to get all of Celia's money back. You're up!"

"What is the total she received in loans, Raymond?"

"Regina owes Celia twenty-two thousand five-hundred and sixty dollars," he said. "That is a lot and without interest, too."

"She is going to pay back every dime. That is just ridiculous what she has done, she needs to go to jail. When she comes in and I take her into the conference room, call the police and ask them to send out a detective to make a report," Bill said. He was or seemed as angry as Robin.

"Ask Celia to come back in. Celia, we added up the loans you did with Regina and they total thousands of dollars, how much do you have in your checking and savings?"

"I have fifty-two dollars and thirty-seven cents in my checking and two-hundred dollars in my savings," she said.

"Celia, that is a long way from what we last saw," said Mr. Marshall. "Are you willing to file a report against her to retrieve your money?"

"Yes, sir, I am," she said. "I need to move or I'll be back on the streets."

"How much did you pay for the bed?"

"Two-thousand and seventy-five dollars for the bed and Nineteen hundred for accessories," she said.

"So, that is a nice neighborhood, Celia."

Celia was in a precarious situation. She needed to move away from Regina, which seemed impossible because of her dire financial situation. She was embarrassed that she had been taken so many times by the same person. Now, Regina had shown her hand, that she was not the altruistic individual she portrayed herself to be, but a seasoned con artist who preyed on the down trodden, with no one to pursue their plight, to be used and thrown away.

Regina was thinking Celia should have been gone months ago, but Celia's friends, prevented her from taking her usual course of action, of destroying the person responsible for her livelihood; which kept Celia remaining seemingly untouched.

To accomplish that, she avoided the outward visual signs and utilized verbal and mental abuse to make her feel worthless and undeserving of a hand up leaving death as an only option.

If she could trigger a suicidal spirit or action, she would be in the clear.

Although tinkering on the borders of self-destruction, Celia continued to rebound as friends and loved ones encouraged her to take a stand. Now, with the return of Robin, Regina knew she had waited too long to implement her plan and underestimated the bond between Robin and Celia. But people will go to extraordinary lengths to protect the façade they have labored to the publicly portray and to keep their dirty little secrets when leading the double life of Walter Mitty and Celia knew all Regina's secrets.

Chapter Twenty

REVELATIONS

Robin asked Raymond to return to the Security Office and for Celia to go the office and help Maurice to keep her out of sight while Bill spoke with Regina. Regina and Bill went into the conference room and Raymond into the Security Office. Robin asked Raymond how he and his mother were getting along and he spoke candidly with her.

"Robin," he said. "After you left, everything fell apart here, there was no one speaking for the subordinates. The bosses only cared about their image and status not caring that without the business, they had no status nor security. They brought in the people who were supposed to get the business out of trouble and ended up placing the business in more jeopardy than it was in. When you left, the business was not in trouble. I was paying attention because I was learning from you. I can pinpoint when the company began to go under, but no one wants to hear it, yet, it began when the first MBA arrived. And went downhill from that point. Ms. Regina and Mr. Marshall were very close."

"Raymond, what would you say about them being in that room talking now about her reimbursing Celia?"

"She will never do it," he said. "They don't know that I know but if it is reimbursed, he'll pay it."

"Listen Raymond, don't give it away, go ask Maurice to call Juliette and find out if she needs a ride, yet?"

"Yes, ma'am," he said.

Robin got up and went to find Bill and Regina. She opened the door and walked in and found them in an embrace. Robin asked Bill to go see about Juliette and Johanna, she was worried about them.

"Okay Robin," he said.

"Thank you, Regina, for helping to get that stain off my tie."

"You're welcome," Regina uttered.

"Regina, come with me to the Security Office, please, go in while I get a diet Pepsi," she instructed.

"Ok," she said.

Robin contacted Maurice and asked if he could record the conversation from his office remotely and not to mention it to Bill.

"Yes, and I'll pick up a case, or two, Robin."

She knew Bill was with him. She had a bigger problem than anticipated. She got a diet Pepsi and returned to the office, sat down.

"Regina, how are things going?"

"Good," she said.

Robin slowly raised her Pepsi to her lips and took a sip from her straw, then asked.

"Are you and Celia okay?"

"As far as I know," she said.

"I have your loans from the cancelled checks Celia wrote to you totaling over thirty-thousand dollars," she said. "I want you to write me a check right now for that amount to reimburse her."

"What are you talking about?"

"I'm sorry, Regina, if I didn't make myself clear, just one more time, write the check to reimburse Celia for the money you grifted from her as loans you never intended to repay as well as, the money I left in your care to hold for Celia until she opened her own account and payment for the bed and accessories she purchased for the bed, and before I ask again, I'm calling the police."

Robin began to dial 911, when Regina said, "You don't have to do that, hang up and we can do this."

"I don't see you taking out your checkbook," Robin said, as she talks to the operator, this is Robin Watson, CEO of

Marshall's Inc, I need an officer at—" and the phone went dead.

Robin looked up, and there she stood with her finger on the dial.

"What are you doing, Regina, they'll only call back, since they have my name or send an officer here, what do you want to do, you have about five minutes to decide?" Robin asked.

She went into her purse and took out her check book and wrote a check for the amount requested and Robin said, "Put in the memo section, 'Reimbursement for loans from Celia Davis'." She did and the police arrived. Robin asked them to come in and she explained the situation, they had a solution.

"Call the bank and confirm she has that amount in the bank on speaker phone - and page Celia," he said. He spoke with the officer of the bank, who spoke with Regina to confirm she wrote the check and the police said they were personally escorting Celia to the bank to cash that check and if he could expedite the transaction, it would be appreciated. The other officer had Celia, with her check in hand, in the car and were on the way to the bank.

Robin asked the President if there were any other signatories on that account or if the account was linked with another account? He said hold a moment…the officer took a seat and Robin waited.

The President returned and said, "There is a William Marshall associated with this account."

"From what period?" she asked,

He told her.

"When you say associated, what exactly does that mean?" Robin inquired.

"He initiated the deposit and deposits monthly on the fifth of every month."

"For what amount?"

"One thousand a month."

The officer identified himself again and asked for the number of the account from the monthly deposits. That number was given and he asked one last thing:

"Is that an individual or corporate account?" he asked, "Corporate, he followed with and your name?"

"Martin Chase," he said.

We thanked him and he stated the check was just presented, and I initialed it, and the balance is, you are requesting it Regina?" he asked.

The policeman looked at her and she said.

"Yes, I am."

"Two-hundred seventy-nine dollars and five cents. Can I help with the additional account?"

He looked at her again.

"Yes," Regina murmured

"Transactions or balances?"

"Both," she replied going with the flow.

"I can only give the last five transactions," he said. He named them and gave the balance of, "Seven hundred thousand nine hundred and eighty-seven dollars and twenty cents."

"Confirm the number," said the police, and he did.

"Isn't there another account?" Robin asked.

"Let me cross check," he said.

"Yes, William and Juliette Marshall's accounts ending in 0979 and 0634, Celia Davis and the officer are in route with the cash," he said.

"Thank you, Mr. Chase, while I have you on the phone, Regina, your credit card payments are due, would you like to make payments?" he asked.

"Now how many cards are due?"

"Five now and five delinquents, only because you are such a good customer," he said.

"How many of those are corporate cards, and their totals?"

"Just a moment please," he returned and said, "Seven are corporate totaling six hundred twenty thousand dollars."

"Pay them from the seven hundred thousand account balance and close those accounts, please."

"Just a minute," he said.

"Yes, they are paid in full and closed not to be reopened," she said. "As of this date without contacting the police department officer Sam Winters badge number 5879."

"What about the remaining three?" he asked.

"The total balance please?"

"One hundred seven thousand dollars," he replied.

"Pay off the balance from the balance of the Ninety- nine thousand and five cents and close that account and cancel the cards confiscate and destroy them when presented for use, please," she requested. And the other account we will take care of tomorrow."

"Is there anything else, we need to resolve?" asked Regina.

"No, the bonds will automatically rotate," he said. "But since you closed the account of collateral, the CD's and Money Market accounts cannot be touched for a year without penalty."

"Thank you."

"It was a pleasure serving you, and we appreciate your business. Have a great day," he said.

"You, as well," she replied and hung up.

Celia came in at that time and asked Robin if she could take the money, she asked the police, they asked if she were related.

Celia said, "She is my guardian who helped me out of this."

"Of course, but just to avoid further conflict, I'll make a note," he said.

"Your name and position here?"

"Robin Watson, CEO," she said.

"Will there be anything else?"

"Yes, will you go with her to Mr. Gulley in the front and have her turn over all her keys, I. D. code will be changed immediately and her last check will be mailed, she is not allowed on these premises from the moment she walks out the door. I am requesting a restraining order and order of protection for Celia Davis."

"I'll fast track that, for I do foresee a threat, as soon as, you or a representative petition and I will write up a complete report and personally bring you your copy and file the Orders for you, but you and Celia must appear in court. I am blown away, too," he said.

"Where is your Security Officer?"

"Maurice, please report to your office."

"The other officer has escorted her, Regina, off the property and an alert has been placed on her license plate to be reported if in this area," he stated.

"Where is Maurice?"

"I'm here," he said.

"Where is Mr. Marshall, is he in the office where you were working, Maurice? And I would be careful how I answered from this point, Maurice. It seems there is going to be a big mess and you're going to have to choose sides, I hope you choose wisely, because he has committed serious crimes and his wife and Regina are going to cause a huge drop in stocks, if not close the company," he said. "How long have you known about Mr. Marshall and Regina?"

"Approximately two months after Robin left, but I thought it had just happened when I found out."

"Please, Maurice, tell me you didn't plot and scheme with them against me," she asked.

"No, Robin," he said. "He never went against you, as a fact, he was genuinely excited about your return, I even thought there was something between you two, because he thought so highly of you and was so excited at the mention of your name."

The officer said, "You said you thought, what happened to change your mind?

"I have equipment everywhere and I overheard he and Mr. McAfee talking one evening and he said you need to get rid of these rookies with their MBA's and get Robin back to save this company while there is something to save, she's the only one who can do it."

"Now who said that?" asked the officer.

"Mr. McAfee."

"The attorney, McAfee?" he asked.

"Yes, sir."

"Why do you think he made that statement?" he asked.

"Because he knew it was true," he said. "Everyone, knew it, even the CEO's in Europe, asked Mr. Marshall to bring her home. They threatened to cancel their contracts and investments, if he didn't promise to bring Robin home. Mr. Gulley speaks foreign languages, but they felt comfortable speaking their languages with her it was the bonding experience, if she said something to them, they could take that to the bank, it would be done, they had confidence in her. Their wives loved her, their daughters claimed her as their sister. RESPECT."

"When it was made known she was ill, flowers were sent from around the country, we had to continue to send them to a Nursing Homes to empty out the offices and make space," he said. "It was difficult for everyone and companies tried to hold on and investors tried to wait, but their profits were no longer coming in, so even with the new bosses, they just didn't have her touch to unite. The business declined, but Mrs. Marshall, Johanna, Mr. McAfee would not give up on getting her back. He was here early this morning waiting to see her, but she had an emergency with Johanna and she dealt with her and didn't make it but he was happy just knowing she was in town and returning to work here. He left and said he would return to see her before the day ended. He did return but she was busy organizing, but he saw her and she asked him to return after five this evening and he'll be here!" Maurice said.

"It sure sounds like this man and you have something going on," he said.

Robin spoke up and said, "You don't know me, he's married. I would not consider a married man for anything but a friend."

"Well, Robin, it seems you don't know him."

"I'm sure you're right," she said. "I would never say I know a man, not after my experiences, a woman never knows a man. There are secret compartments in the minds of men that never are opened and there are those that can be triggered by a smell, touch or sight of a strange woman or man. No, it would be hubris, to say I know a man. I think a woman must be comfortable and content with her perception of who he is."

"No, what I mean is Mr. McAfee isn't married."

"Since when and how do you know?" she asked.

"Since, two years before we met in this room," Mr. McAfee said.

"Now, why am I the subject of a conversation among all of you? What happened?" Mr. McAfee asked.

Robin said, "Please excuse me, will you fill him in, please, and I apologize for talking about you behind your back." and she left.

"Wait, Robin," he said.

She turned and said, "I'll be here, you need to listen to them."

She left the room and got a Pepsi and sat in the kitchen when Raymond appeared.

"Did you know about them, of course, you did," she said.

"I think he was lonely and she took advantage of his needs," he said. "Look at her, he has a beautiful wife, the only reason this happened, is he was vulnerable. She zeroed in on his inner pain over his grandchild and she made herself available to him on one of those occasions he stayed here to rest. She planned it, but he could have said no."

"You're so right, Raymond, it's hard to trust, but I'm praying to meet someone who will be patient with me and love me for who I am, not who he wants me to be," she said.

"Now tell me about your mother and how you've made it."

"It has been a real struggle, Robin, especially when I was molested by the leader," he said. "He asked me to fix the light in the bathroom in his office and rigged the light switch, I was later told. He used chloroform and came upon me from behind, in the dark and it knocked me out. I came to and he was massaging my penis and sodomizing me, I didn't realize that a person's body would respond during a rape. It took counseling for me to get to the point I can discuss it and you're the first person I've felt comfortable with to talk to. I blamed myself and couldn't go out the house, for a week, then the counselor helped me with information. Knowledge is powerful. I would have blamed myself forever."

"Raymond, I am so sorry that happened to you. No, it wasn't your fault, he was a sick young man who was attracted to you and because he felt he didn't deserve a nice young man like you, he felt it necessary to force himself on you. It is sad that he didn't have the courage to talk to you to determine if you were inclined to favor the same sex, but he was unstable and insecure as well as dangerous. I am grateful that I am not talking to a headstone in a cemetery," Robin shared. "I hope his actions do not hinder you from being open to finding love, Raymond. Don't let him take that from you and don't you relinquish it to him, just give yourself time to heal, stay confident, positive and mingle, promise me."

"I promise, Robin."

Robin waited to see if he had expressed his thoughts.

"How are you and your mother doing?"

"We're holding on. The landlord gave us a week to become current or we have to move."

"How much do you pay there, for how many bedrooms?"

"We were paying five hundred a month, utilities included for one and a half bedrooms and a bath?"

"Raymond, did you pay last month's rent and security deposit?"

"Yes, but we used the last month's rent three months ago, so we're behind two months and nowhere to go."

"Raymond, how much does your mother receive a month?"

"Eight hundred," he said.

"Well, Raymond, after you receive your first check, fill out a lease, you must be checked out and need references and a down payment of a minimum of a Thousand, with a set time for the balance to be paid. Get your occupancy permit and you'll have a place. Rent payments should be on time," she said. "Or it is grounds for eviction. It will probably take that week or two to finalize everything, but we can try. Honestly, will your history withstand an investigation for tenancy?"

"Yes," he said.

"Then don't lose faith."

"No, ma'am," he said. "Never."

"How much furniture do you have?"

"Not much, you saw it."

"Yes," she recalled. "When you go home, talk to your mother to get her permission to have the background check. So, it can begin in time to have things completed as soon as possible to get that permit to move. It would prudent to talk with your current landlord about your arrears now that you are working. It is in the basement but it has new appliances, in the kitchen, three bedrooms and two bathrooms a living and dining room and a garage attachment a nice big fenced in yard central air and heat and a laundry room of your own a patio, a basketball court and baseball diamond and access to CTA from your yard. I know you cannot afford the regular price, that an agency would ask, but after the information comes in on you and your mother, we can sit down and discuss it. Then we would try to set you up for a small credit at the furniture store to purchase and payoff a piece at a time until it is completely furnished. You can even cut the grass and keep the lawn beautiful and she can plant a flower garden, does that sound like a plan?" she asked.

"Are you sure?"

"Yes, I'm sure," she said.

"How many people or families are in this building?"

"It is a three-family building, much like a condominium. Go through your old furniture, see what pieces are viable and clean them up, so if the information returns quickly, you will have something to take in once the permit is received. What you are uncomfortable with, sell it or leave it your landlord may take it as partial payment."

"Who else is in the building?"

"On the top floor is Louise and Walter and on the first floor, is Celia and I. Celia will need company getting to and from work. I leave too early so you two will take the train unless I work at the same time you two do and I can give you a ride. Celia and I will be furniture shopping this weekend if she obtains an occupancy permit. The Law is very clear, with no exceptions, a person cannot move into an apartment without a lease and an occupancy permit and there is no way around that without a person being fined or worse. I am not going down for someone who will not do his or her part," she said.

"There are rules in life as in love that just should not be broken. If a person would ask that of a landlord, then that person will not pay his or her rent and the landlord should rethink their occupancy, I would.

It is a quiet area, except for the train, and that is how the residence will remain. The noise is to be limited, and I will put anyone out who fails to obey the rules. So, as soon as the information has been processed, that you submit, then we will discuss lease and terms and price, to be taken to the city for the permit to have the utilities turned on in your name," she said.

"I know I could get three or four times the amount I'm charging but I want people around who will appreciate what they have and protect it, Raymond," she said.

"Mr. McAfee is waiting to see you."

"Please show him in and bring two Pepsi, he may not like Pepsi."

"He'll be polite and drink it," said Raymond.

"Thank you, Raymond, show him in, please."

"Mr. McAfee, I am so sorry to keep you waiting, so much has transpired, but I am all yours, now," she said.

"I wish that were true!" he exclaimed.

"Have a seat, and talk to me," she whispered.

Chapter Twenty-One

Robin and Robert

"We were never properly introduced," he said.
"I am Robert Edward McAfee, Esq. and I am an Attorney, pretty good they say. I am divorced, with two adult children, both young men who live out of my house: Robert, Jr. is a lawyer and Michael is a doctor, both single.
May I shake your hand?" he asked.

"No, you may not, but my old friend, better give me a hug," she said.

He walked up to her and she held out her arms and he walked into them and embraced her.

"Thank you, Bob, Robert Edward, Sr., Mr. McAfee, whom ever you are, I sure do need this," she said. (as she held on for an extra minute and laid her head on his shoulder.)

"It has been a confusing and disillusioning day," she said softly.

He took her by the arms, looked her in the eyes and said.
"Let's talk about it, Robin."

"May I call you Bob?" she asked.

"Absolutely," he said.

"I thought I was making a difference, but discovered I was being played for a fool, by someone I love and admire as a father and if I had to give my life for him, Johanna or Juliette, I would not have hesitated that included you, as well," she echoed.

"I know, Robin, when I heard, today, I could have been bought for a penny!" he said.

"No, before you ask, I did not know and never would have guessed that one, I'm still surprised!"

"I do not believe it happened because he was vulnerable or she took advantage of him, as suggested, he could have said 'no'."

But I tried to keep him safe from other women so he would not cheat on Juliette and I failed. It is impossible to look her in the face now. We were forming a great relationship with Johanna, now it's gone."

"I suppose I lose you, too, was it all an illusion? Just Celia and Raymond are real? Please tell me it isn't so," she pleaded.

"Robin, it isn't so and you will never, never lose me, I promise you that," he firmly stated.

"Maurice left, too and I cannot return to their home, I'm going to the apartment building and stay on the first floor; Celia and I will be moving in soon, but I am not good company, I'm rambling," she said.

"Can I trouble you to take me, Celia may show up, she can't go to Regina's, she's in danger! This is a difficult thing to comprehend, Bob," she said.

"What is Robin?"

"You are," she said. "Have you ever seen me in a state like this, Robert?"

"No, I can't say that I have, but you haven't seen that side of me, either," he said.

"Why do *you* think it is?" she asked.

"I guess because you never felt the way you do, now?"

"You are 'good'," she said.

"I don't have to go anywhere, there is an apartment upstairs and I have the keys, do you have a code to lock up?"

"No, he replied, why?"

"I hate to break this to you, Bob, but I don't have a code either."

"Maurice was supposed to give me one today, but after the police arrived, everything went off schedule, he disappeared without giving me a way out, so I'm locked in! I hope you don't have an emergency or have a date, because I have news. You are good, so, I know you have figured it out, you tell me."

"I am locked in, too?"

"Your answer sounded like a question, Bob, but you're locked in with me," she said.

"Turn off the lights and let's go upstairs and get comfortable," she said.

"Don't worry, I would never take advantage of you, there is nothing else we can do, but sit and talk or watch television or dance and there is food and drink, should you be so inclined, Robert."

"I have no previous engagements, nor anyone who will miss me," he said.

"I cannot believe that, an attractive man, such as yourself, so well-spoken and sensuous, those blue eyes, I never paid attention to before, does not have a previous engagement."

"Yes and no, Robin. I do have a date tonight, but it was not pre-arranged. Why didn't you notice me before?"

"I am your date, right?"

"Right, you're good, too, Robin!"

"Now, Robert, I have not forgotten part B of your question, I will answer it after you comment. You are in a precarious situation, as we speak, unlike a blind or natural date, in those instances if the company or chemistry is not right, you can always find an excuse to leave. Not tonight and I apologize. I did not notice you because my mind is fixed that if a man is married, it automatically shuts down. I have seen those eyes before, somewhere, it will come to me. I know you have someone. I believe you are good company, too, Robert."

"Well, I can cook," he said.

"I have not had time to do any shopping for Mr. Marshall."

"I have not checked the refrigerator, so there is no food, maybe cans, let's check, Robert."

I talked Juliette into making love with her husband here last night, she'll probably blame me for that when this mess is revealed. She may or may not have fixed the bed, I did not check, today, so if the place is unkempt, please overlook it, let's see what is here. I think she said they had sandwiches last night and she placed some in the freezer. What part do you want to check, Robert?"

"Let's do it together, Robin."

"Ok. Let's explore, Robert."

They looked in the fridge and there were leftovers, but he didn't take anything out. He looked in the pantry and she stood back as he began to take out can goods.

"Do we have an opener and pans, Robin?"

Robin took out pots and pans and plates and silverware and napkins glasses for water and wine.

"What else do you need, Robert?"

"You can have a drink and sit," he said.

"Maybe you'll ask me that question again later, Robin?"

"If you're sure you don't want help, I'll go put on some soothing music and take a warm bath."

"When I finish cooking, I'll call you, Robin."

She went into the bedroom and Juliette had fixed the bed. She turned on the Sinatra album, slightly raised the volume. She looked in the bottom drawer, where she had emergency clothes and took out a gown set, she opened Mr. Marshall's drawer and took out a pair of pajamas, placed them on the bed and pulled back the covers. She turned on the faucet and put in a scented jasmine and oil that filled the apartment with an aroma that set the atmosphere for magic. She took down her hair and washed it and the fragrance of it was stimulating and begged to be smelled, stepped into the bathtub and relaxed. There was a knock on the door, she said, "Come in, Bob is that you?"

"Yes, I have a glass of wine for you."

"Thank you, Robert, how is the food?"

"The sauce is simmering, Robin."

"Are we still talking food, Bob?"

He was quiet and she said, "I'm not coming on to you, Bob, relax, but there is something in play here."

She took a sip of wine and asked.

"Have you noticed that all things seem to be calling us together? I haven't been with anyone since you know, I have deliberately avoided situations that remotely hinted in this direction. Now, you knock on the door while I am taking a bath and I am still in the same place with Sinatra, wine and you scared to death, it is unbelievable to me, Robert."

"I'm not scared, Robin, I came through the door with a glass of wine no one forced me."

"Exactly, Bob, a glass, where is yours?"

He got up and went out of the room as Robin listened to that Old Black Magic. The door opens and Bob re-enters with his own glass, and asked.

"You were saying, Robin?"

"We're having Pasta, Robert?"

"Yes, Robin, is that alright?"

"Absolutely," Robin replied.

"How long before it is ready, Bob?"

"Twenty minutes, Robin."

"Do you plan to sit and watch me bathe, Robert?"

"We'll I don't want to be alone so watching you bathe is less lonely than sitting in the kitchen with that sauce."

"Bob, would you like to sit in the water with me?"

"I would love to sit in the water with you, Robin. Let me turn down the heat, Robin."

"Only on the stove, Robert."

He returned to where she was waiting, and the sauce smelled delicious from the opened door, he took off his clothes and stepped into the bathtub and said. "The water is getting cool, Robin."

"Well, you should come closer and together we will warm it up, Bob."

He came closer to her and took her face in his hands and raised her chin and drew it closer to his until their lips met.

"Oh, Robin, I have dreamed of kissing those beautiful lips of yours."

She leaned in and kissed him back.

"We should try that again outside the tub, Robin."

He stood up and gently raised her up and they gazed at one another and she asked.

"Robert, how long have you felt this way?"
"Since the first time I met you and lost myself in those big beautiful eyes of yours, I lost my heart to you."
"When did you know, Robin?"
"When I was at the Marshall's home observing them with Johanna and you kept appearing before my face and the sight of you made me tingle all over, my body perspired from heat. Are you sure we just met through the Marshalls, Robert?

"That is the second time you've asked me that, Robin. Why, when did you meet me?"

"This morning when I was told you were here to see me, I felt my body stir when you showed up but had to leave, I didn't want you to go, but after you hugged me, it was alright, I remember saying to you after two o'clock, you left and as you were leaving we said two o'clock. But I heard someone say, five o'clock and I heard that lawyer is married and my heart sank; I thought 'that figures'. I was talking to someone about opening his heart up to love and mine was wide open but slowly began to close. When the policeman spoke to me about not knowing you, the man and something between us, I was so angry that you were married and you came in at that moment and I couldn't look at you but when I heard you say that you were single two years before meeting me, I hoped again and had to leave the room for fear I would lose restraint, grab and embarrass us. Now, here we are accidentally locked in the building together it seems too coincidental to be one. Yet here we are and I'm satisfied, just being with you."

She took out towels and gave him one and dried off. She went to the drawer and took out two robes and gave him one, "She kissed him and said, "It's a dream".

He said, "Please don't awaken me."

"The sauce is smelling good," Robin said.

"Oh, I've never burned sauce before," said Robert.

"Don't start now, Robert, I have an appetite."

He tied his robe and went into the kitchen and Robin found slippers and took him a pair.

"Don't catch a cold on us, Robert."

"Don't worry, Robin."

She went into the kitchen and asked, "Robert, did you plan this, I know I didn't, but it's hard to believe that this happened, did you?"

"I think we had help, Robin."

"Thanks for being honest with me. I really want to have an honest relationship, after all this time, to meet a man who cares about the truth, respect faithfulness and love. What more can one ask for?" she thought.

They ate the pasta and washed the dishes and she put them away, turned out the light and snuggled up close to him, she took his hand and walked to the sofa and they sat down, she turned to him and asked, "Robert how long is the help to last?"

"We are locked in for the night, Robin."

"You have a very good friend, Robert. Under different circumstances, I would be irate, but your friend chose the right day, when all hell broke loose!"

"Our friend, Robin, our friend!"

She moved closer and said, "It has been a long time for me and I haven't been able to trust anyone until now, and I really want to trust you Robert."

As she leaned closer and her robe fell open revealing her unblemished breast, he reached up and gently rubbed her chest and said, "Robin," as his voice that was so confident, now trembles as he spoke, she laid her wet head on his chest.

"Robin, I want you to trust and love me, I know the woman you are and you have my respect my love and every fiber of me. I don't want to possess you or control you, I just want to be with you, take care of you and show you that loving someone is so special and although I want to make love to you, loving is more than that.

No, I don't have a problem with an erection; I just want you to be ready, healed of the pain. I can wait for you. I've been waiting for you for years, now."

"Robert, I'm not the kind of woman to sleep around, I'm a one-man woman and it is marriage or nothing. I need to know if I were healing, that is why I asked you into the water, I apologize for using you, but if I had not done it that way, we would not know that I really can be open to love. My mind wants you and my body wants you, but God has been too good to me to do it anyway, but his way."

"Robin, you don't owe me an apology."

He pulled her robe together.

"You're a beautiful lady and I look forward to seeing where we can go."

"So, do I, Robert, and you make me feel beautiful."

"That's because you are, Robin!"

"But you're dangerous, mesmerizing, I forgot how easily I catch cold, being with you!"

"I forgot to purchase a hair dryer, Robert I need to dry my hair with a towel."

"Do you want to help me, Robert?"

"Name it, Robin, for you to become ill, now, is not an option!"

"Why don't you just rest, while I get a towel to dry it?"

He went out of the room and returned with a towel. "Some women are tender headed, but not, Robin, right?"

"Right, spoken like a man who has turned a few heads! You don't have to be gentle, Robert."

He took the towel and massaged her head then dried it to the ends.

"My, that is so nice," she said. "I can tell you have had practice. It must be nice to be good with your hands in so many areas or are you just a perfectionist?"

"A little of both, Robin, but speaking of being good with your hands, Robin, you're the very best."

"As you get to know me, and I hope you have made up your mind, you'll discover, I don't just use words to get what I want, I love to find the right words for the right woman!"

"Shake it or comb it? Which would be the right word and action for this woman, Robert?"

"Shake, Robin, I like the curly look, Robin."
She shook her head and he said.
"There is a dryer."
Robin had never seen that dryer. Robert picked it up, plugged it in and took the comb and it dried her hair, he combed it out and when he finished, he said.
"That was exciting."
Robin took the hair dryer from his hands, unplugged it, and said.
"You think that was exciting, grade this from one to ten."
She took the robe she had on and opened it slowly, as he looked at her naked body and said.
"You need to put that back on, Robin."
He walked backwards as she approached him, he agreed. "But I'll call it as I see it, Robin."
"Please do Bob, be candid, precise. Bob's turn."
She advanced towards him, he walked backwards.
"Skin: beautiful and light creamy bronze, nine."
"Bust: thirty- four, still perky and full, nine."
"Waist: twenty-two perfect contours, nine. hips: thirty-four, curvaceous, nine. highs: slim and petite, nine."
"Legs: slim and two scars, nine."
She noticed, he stopped moving backwards, she advanced.
"Mole on the right hip, I've never seen that before," She advanced thinking he can only do one more step.
"Grade it," she said.
"Mole, placement, size, very dark, but unique, I've seen them on faces, close to the end of lips, on cheekbones, in the cleft of the chin, grade."
She advanced- "Mole, ten."
"He stepped backwards, fell on the bed, his robe opened.
"My turn," she said. "Legs, hairy, eight; skin tone, Robert needs a wax, hard to see clearly, five;"
He untied his belt, and opened it.
"Body tone, he works out periodically, good, firm, seven; facial expression puzzled, anticipating, beguiled, mixed

emotions nine; eyes, deep, dreamy, revealing the blue is inviting, emotion."

She puts her knee on the bed.

"Tempting, ten;" she pushed on the bed, and he said.

"You forgot one."

"We both did, we'll grade each other together, kiss me," she said.

He kissed her and he moved upon the bed, she moved with him, they made it to the head of the bed, she takes a pillow and places under his head, looks at him and says.

"Robert, I want you, but I don't want just part of you, I want as much of you as I am going to give. I ask you, to get up and walk away, before you hurt me. I don't want a man, I have to follow around and keep up with, to keep him faithful, I am faithful; if you find someone you want instead of me, tell me, don't let me find out from someone else or later from you, promise me."

"Robin, I'm not going anywhere, I've waited for you to return and you returned to me. I could have played around while you were away, but no one I saw or knew before, erased the memory of you and I had no desire for anyone else, I'm afraid you're stuck with me," he said.

She kissed him and rekindled the mood and this time, they climbed Mt. Everest together. Robert held her and said, "Robin, I dreamed of us together and though my dreams were as good as a dream gets, being with you surpassed all my dreams. I have had sex with other women and for a short time, deceived myself into believing my wife and I were in love, and although we have two children, I finally accepted the fact that we were not in love, as she informed me, but inside I knew and the proof is, we never experienced love making as you and me, only sex without intimacy. I have never had an experience of the sensitivity, the sweetness and thrill of making love that have soared me to heights that only eagles travel taking a panoramic view of the great loves of the world knowing we have unlocked mysteries that few have dared to dream of and emerge fulfilled. In every sense of the word!"

Robin cried, he held her and said.

"Don't cry Robin, I love you."

"I love you, too, Robert. I know what we experienced was real and I've never felt that before, never. You've made me so happy, those were tears of joy."

"Robert, if we don't see each other again, I will never regret being with you, this night. I am realistic, most of the time, but, I want to dream with you one last time."

He turned to her and asked, "What do you mean, one last time?"

"In a perfect world, we would be accepted as a couple, by friends and family, but in this imperfect world, we will not," she said.

"Your business will suffer, your children will practically disown you and as a result, our relationship will decline to the point, we will resent one another, I cannot profess to love you and knowingly hurt you."

"Robin, in this imperfect world, you have climbed your own Everest and become a woman revered and respected a CEO, a multimillionaire, accepted by all ethnicities, why would you give up on us before we've begun?"

"'If you love someone, set him free', I love you, Robert, every morning you awaken, you'll know there is a specific woman, out here, who lives for no other thought than to love you, as she is loved by you. I can live with this, not the hiding and lying. So, love me, Robert, love me," she said.

He kissed her and caressed her soft silky skin and she kissed him with a passion that took their breaths away. Robin made love to him, as it were the last time, the thrill of his touch, the squeeze of her vagina on his penis, the pulsating, their hearts beating in sync and the ecstasy of their climax, hurt so good, that she gasped and they called their names, together.

"Robert, I would not have known making love could be so wonderful, if it were not for you and taking a chance."

"Yes, time and chance comes to us all, but we should siege the moment in time and caress the chance, for they may never pass our way again."

"Thank you," she said.

"Tell me, how large a part did you play in our lock in, dear?"

"Because it is us, and truth is essential, I will be totally honest. Maurice and Bill have known I love you, since before you left. They were my confidants and my exhorters," he said. "I never would have maintained my sanity, if it were not for them checking and reporting to me about your setbacks and improvements, they almost stalked you, but by cyberspace. My friends have already accepted you, and those who will not, have never been my friends," he said. "But I digress. When Juliette called with the emergency, he suggested that I return and talk to you tell you how I feel and go from there. Maurice informed me that he felt you were ready to receive the information and I should make it soon before someone else beat me to the punch. When you said to return after five, his mind went into over-drive and he spoke with me after I left talking to the police, Maurice said, 'man if you feel bad, can you imagine how Robin must feel, her hero caught and maligned, as it were, you should be there for each other.' he said. 'She still has trust issues,' he said, 'but, you can be patient with her and console each other'. I asked him how will the opportunity present itself? He said, 'man, are you sleeping? The opportunity has presented itself, she said after five. Everyone will be gone after five, long before five,' he said, 'I know I will. There are some things she wanted to have done, Celia needs a few things and so does Raymond and his mother need furniture, I'm taking them to make the purchases and have it taken and delivered to the apartment.' You gave him the money with a note to keep for yourself and he took it upon himself to do that for you, so we could have this time together. If there is an emergency, he'll be here, security will inform him first, but he didn't give me anything like a key or code, he just said a brick would let me in. I removed the brick and closed the door within five minutes as instructed and we are locked in. He's bringing us clean clothes in the morning. Bill and Juliette know we're together, they are so happy about Johanna and how you've transformed her, they were delighted for us. Now, to add my final two cents, Robin, I work because I want to, not because I need or must. It would not impact my way of life, at all, if I never have another client; but to try to live without you is unthinkable!" Please, reconsider?" he asked.

"Robert, that was the most romantic story," she said. "Does Juliette know about Regina?"

"Robin, it was my hope we could avoid this discussion," he said.

"Robert, we are going to have this discussion before the week is over, and probably under stressful circumstances leading to hostile feelings even the choosing of sides, why not avoid it and have the discussion under intimate circumstances, after all, neither of us can get up and walk away."

"You are right about the latter part of that statement for certain. No, as far as I know, she is unaware of Bill and Regina's affair as we were," he said. "Now, love of my life, back to us."

"I give you a grade of nine," Robin said. "Gotcha, right?"

"Got me," he said. "That is one of things I love about you, no one can rightly call you predictable. I give you a ten."

"Thank you and for that grade, I want to reward you with a hug," she said.

"That's all?" he asked.

"Let's start with the hug," she said. "Ready?"

"Ready," he said.

Robin reached over and touched his hips then his underarms and finally his groin and she remained quiet. After lying there for a while, in anticipation of his hug, he said.

"How long do I have to wait for my hug, dear?"

"Where you been?" she asked.

"I gave you your hug over ten minutes ago."

"I must have missed that, it must have been the briefest hug in history, honey, can we do it again?"

"Anything for you," she said.

She touched his hip, then his underarm and finally his groin and was quiet. She turned over and looked him in the eye and asked.

"Was that good for you, honey?"

"Robin, am I becoming narcoleptic?"

"Why did you ask that, Robert?"

"Because you are behaving as if you hugged me, but unless I am dropping off to sleep and missing the hug, I am not receiving it."

Robin turned over and kissed him and said to him.

"I didn't think you missed a thing."

"I never said I don't miss anything, honey, because obviously, I have missed two hugs, and not just any hug, but, your hug," he said.

Robin looked at Robert and asked him.

"Do you play?"

"Yes, I play ball, golf—"

"Stop honey, that isn't the kind of playing I mean. We live lives that demand we remain focused and strict as well as mature and you made me realize that what we do daily isn't all there is to life. I like to grow and in my experiences, good or bad, I try to learn something that will make me say, that experience was good for me because I now see or feel something that wasn't there before. It may not be a big something, but a simple something, that isn't visible to anyone else and cannot be shared with everyone, but just someone, and that is how I feel, like playing. I've played the same game with you twice and you didn't get it, but I am compelled to share it with you, for I plan to utilize it in different ways to alleviate stress and just to make me smile if I should feel like crying. I'm calling it 'Bob's game'. I said your reward would be a hug. While the person is looking for a hug, turn the word into an acronym and give them the unexpected. I did this, touched your hips, like this," she touched his hips; "Not bad."

She touched his underarms, like this and this time she tickled him, he laughed and said, "No one has tickled me in years."

"It brought pleasant memories, laughter, right?"

He replied, "Yes, Robin."

Then, she touched his groin, "Like this."

"You can do that twice," he said.

"Aw," she said.

"The man is playing and having fun and he doesn't know it. Now, think about what I just did with that brilliant mind of yours and tell me the results."

"You gave me three hugs," he said.

"I told you, that you are unpredictable."

"Who would think you would make up a game based on the intimate experiences between us and name it after me," he said. "That, is a nice game that adults can play as fore play or after play. I like it. Robin, if I can inspire you to make up a game in the short span of time we've been here, think about what our love could inspire for future events?"

"Robert, that was sexual inspiration, there is a difference between love and sex, so do you agree?"

"I'm just saying, baby, if sex can inspire you, love can inspire you more, is that a nice save?"

"Oh, yes, it is a nice save," she said. They kissed and fell asleep in each other's arms.

They awoke and took their bath together and played Bob's game in the water and they were young at heart. Robin was much younger than Robert, but together, it was difficult to tell there was a difference for they both behaved as youngsters. They dispelled the poet's stand that youth is wasted on the young! They had coffee and toast and Robert had four eggs for breakfast. They heard a noise in the stairway and Robert went out in his pant and shirt and re-entered with fresh clothes and personal effects. They dressed and played Bob's game and decided they had a secret that should they choose, they could use the acronym hug when alone. She decided to wear a braid and bangs with her dress and Robert stated, "You look like a little girl. You are far too young for a man my age. I think you are safe today, miss. I'll stop by at noon to see if you have a second for lunch or a hug, if that is acceptable with you?"

"That is acceptable," she said.

"Do you need me to stop by the apartment or the furniture store?"

"I don't know how Maurice left things," she said. "However, you have keys to the building and the vacant apartments and I have not been shopping for my bedroom or den and office/ family room. If you're out looking and see something nice, give me a call."

"Gladly," he said. Smile. (A new word in Bob's game.)

Robert was a changed man. His outward appearance was miraculous, he felt alive and his mind was open and expanded, he had a fresh outlook on old situations and an open mind for new situations. There was a strut to his step, a defiance to the numbers which comprised his age.

He held Robin and they kissed, he said he would leave before the employees arrived so there would not be another conversation regarding relationships. She agreed as they held hands to the door and he said smile as he tickled her hand, they laughed as he opened the door and she listened as he went down the stairs, she smiled, closed the door and finished dressing. She cleaned up the bed, Robert did the dishes, picked up her belongings, looked around for anything Robert left behind, and locked the door and went down the stairs to get a Pepsi. Robin opened the door for her Pepsi and there were none. She looked for the small refrigerator found it and there were two remaining, she took one and drank it as she thanked God and took the other and went to view her new office.

Maurice was installing the phone system and gave her a tour of the front and she said, "This is a complete apartment office.

He said, "It is enormous, Robin, you should see that bedroom and bath, to die for when you have time."

"This is my last Pepsi," she said.

"Please pick up a few cases for the office here. Is there a refrigerator in here?"

"There is a complete kitchen and pantry," he said.

I could go broke furnishing places," she commented. "Please tell me he purchased furniture, Maurice."

"He did, it is in the other office," he said. "I've got it, it will be in place before noon, cleaned and ready for use."

"Did Regina use it?" she asked?

"No, she didn't," he said.

"Thank you, Maurice for everything."

He smiled and asked, "We're good?"

"Better than good, Maurice," she said. "Were any of those credit cards that were cancelled one you utilize, if so, I'll have one issued to you."

"No, all of those were hers," he said.

"Let me know when you plan to have the furniture moved in here and I'll be in the conference room until it is finished," she said.

"What time is Raymond due?"

"He and his mother and Celia are going to the courthouse for occupancy permits and Restraining Orders."

"I'll work the cubicle with Mr. Gulley and I need those applications for employment. Did Celia purchase or lay-a-way her furniture, if so, when will it arrive and what bedroom did she choose?"

"Ok on the furniture. Celia purchased hers and delivery is scheduled for tonight. I thought you wanted the Master bedroom suite with the Jacuzzi and bathroom and she chose the one she wanted."

"It is my hope that she received her occupancy permit, if delivery is tonight," Robin stated.

"Because I have no idea who would be there to receive it. Very good, we'll furnish the third bedroom after mine. Robert is looking and I will, too, unless something changes then I will have to implement plan B. How did she like the apartment?"

"She thought she had 'died and gone to heaven,' she said, she had nothing like this and was paying more than you proposed."

"Did Raymond and his mother like their apartment?"

"They felt the same as Celia. They were pleasantly surprised Raymond went a little wild with the furniture choices, I had to limit them."

"I need to hear more about that Maurice. How much did they spend on furniture?" she asked.

"He wanted to furnish the entire place and they have expensive tastes," he said.

"For someone who hasn't made a day's work yet, that makes me nervous," she said. "I think I need references and need to speak with the landlord, before you give them the keys. They must have their permit, but they cannot get that without a lease, which I know they do not have. They are all making the incorrect moves. I need you to do surveillance up all around the apartments, someone is always looking to take advantage of the weak and unsuspecting, with the area somewhat uninhabited, it would be easy to step into harm's way going or coming from the train. It would be wise to cover the doors and windows, please, across the street, in the rear and cover the fence by the CTA. These jobs are separate from those at work, these are personal jobs, so I will pay you personally for working for me, what you charge. Don't let them abuse the privileges, Maurice. If they request anything, tell them you are not authorized and they must speak with me. The courthouse is the only authorized transportation for them and that is for Raymond and Celia only, but not during working hours. Their personal business must be done on their personal time. They do not have access to the bar and travel is allowed from the courthouse to the job only, in case I did not make myself clear. They must make their way to the courthouse. You know, this has too much potential for overlapping, I am rescinding that way from the courthouse to work, it should not be done during working hours, inform them, if you see them before I do, refer them to me," she said. "Employee's only without the boss. Call them to give them an update, take the CTA to courthouse, cannot justify the travel for personal use."

Where are they living now? What has Raymond done since his termination? Robin was informed she would be penalized if the apartment is occupied by anyone but the owner before occupancy permit is issued. "Inform Raymond that they are to stay at their apartment until the occupancy permit is issued."

Robin called the furniture store and inquired about the purchases and date of delivery. The Hawkins purchases totaled over three thousand dollars and they had completed application for lease and not paid anything towards rent, but making a purchase of that magnitude, at this point, is absurd, she thought. She requested that the furniture order be placed on hold until the occupancy permit has been issued. She would call back and inform them when to release it with a code. Games, Bob. Robin was paranoid, but just because a person is paranoid, does not mean no one is out to harm them, even if it is misdirected. Robin asked to confirm their source of payment. Ask them to apply for store credit. The corporate credit card could not be used for new employees. That was to be determined, they said.

Robin went down to the cubicle and took the applications with her. She was working Regina's station when an incoming call came; she answered the call and discovered it was Regina.

"Yes," she said.

"Robin, this is Regina."

"I know," she said.

"Robin, I need my job," she said.

"This is a business line, Regina you should know that and if you want to talk about personal matters, you must call the office line between 2 and 4 PM" and hung up.

"Robin, please don't hang up," the voice said.

Robin said, "Regina, you cannot come to this building, there is a restraining order on you for five-hundred feet. So, even if we could talk, other than now, where would you suggest that it take place?"

Regina replied, "I'll call you back."

"No don't," Robin said.

She talked with Mr. Gulley and asked him if he recalled the day of the celebration and the day after?

"Yes," he said.

"What made those days so memorable?" she asked.

"I had to do everything by myself," he said.

"You mean the kitchen?" she asked.

"That was during the celebration," he said.

"But before the celebration, I had to work every station in the cubicles."

"Where was Regina?" she asked.

"She was upstairs taking care of Mr. Marshall, 'he was very sick,' she said and had to stay with him for hours, and some strange lady, I have never seen, went into your office and went through your papers and used your fax machine," he said.

She remembered what Russell said about his lady friend. "Why did you not mention it before?" she asked.

"I was certain you had to know, she just walked around doing things and how would she know where things were if she was not working for you?" he asked.

"I see," Robin replied. "What day was that Mr. Gulley?"

"The day he was too sick to go to the meetings, too. Regina, went upstairs while you were taping the meetings and they were very good, Ms. Robin, I heard you and you were good."

"Thank you, Mr. Gulley."

"Regina said Mr. Marshall called from upstairs and said he was too sick to get out of bed and could she help him?"

"She went upstairs and stayed until I could not hold down hers, mine and unassigned and I went upstairs and knocked on the door and she came to the door with a robe on. I asked why she no dressed? She said, 'he upchucked on her and she had to wash her clothes and would be right down'. I told her I would tell you to help and she said, 'he didn't want your help, he wanted her help and not to tell, I get fired'. She still no come down. I knocked again, and she still no dressed, I look for you and no find," he said. "You were in the Security Office, I know. Went back upstairs she came down right before you go up."

"Did Regina go anywhere else to help Mr. Marshall after that day?"

"Yes, she goes to old office. We took furniture out today and put in your office, hope you like it," he said.

"I will because you did it from your heart," she said. "Did they go to the old office before I returned?"

"Yes, before you returned, is how she run company into ground, almost got company closed, you keep open, I know."

"Thank you, Mr. Gulley," and she patted him on his back. Robin knew she had a bigger problem than she realized. The only people who can help are Juliette and Bob and neither will be pleased about it. Juliette will be in denial for a long time, if she is innocent, Robin thought. She knew something was off there, because if it were her, she would have called to find out when she would return, if only to see Johanna, something is off. Robin thought it would be good to talk with Bob for advice.

Robin went to her new office and called Maurice, he said he was at the courthouse. She asked if he understood the talk they had, and if he received her message that work had to take priority over absentee workers? She asked him to return to base and let them figure it out. Everyone disregarded her instructions, they must be taking them from someone else, that is why the company is failing, she said, undermining and failing to receive instructions from the proper authorities. She was angry and disappointed.

Maurice came in and explained he could not leave them with no way home and she asked him if he were assigned to work for them or this company? Robin was furious. She asked him to tell them no work, no pay. They should have done this on their own time. As she was reprimanding him, Bob came in and she asked Maurice not to be a taxi for people not on the job.

"Thank you for fixing my office. I can go to work with a vengeance."

"Hello Bob, may I have a hug?"

He came over and gave her a hug. "I think I know where we first met, on girl's night out with my two sisters-in-laws, at the exclusive lounge, Maurice took us to. It was a lounge unlike any I have visited which would total two. You were the man who came over to our table and asked me to dance. I don't dance and tried to explain that when you said, 'we only have something to gain by dancing, if only for a few moments of tenderness we may never experience again.' I went with you to the dance floor and everyone thought we were secret lovers because we captivated the audience we were described as chemistry, fit together, one of my sisters in laws told you. After kissing my hand, you said you didn't want to know the name of this lovely lady but we were destined to be together and you were a determine man who would find me no matter where, one day."

"That was not me," he said.

"They told me to call him back and ask his name and if I wanted to go out with him they would not blame me, but I could not."

"It was not me," he said.

"Bob, I know, it wasn't. We lost an entire day's work with three employees down. They were taken to the courthouse to get permits for occupancy and missed the day. My wrath has over spilled to everyone including you, I am so sorry, are we good?" she asked.

"Robin, we're better than good, we are amazing," he said. "Let us see how can we fix the problem. Can the workers come in and work the night and double the morning?"

"No," she replied. "The overseas work schedule is fixed to minimize pay, you know how that goes. Our one day pay, is equivalent to three of their days, so, I can't justify it. Besides, we don't know when Maurice's staff will discover they are chasing their tails at the courthouse and leave and where they plan to go next. Makes it impossible to set a schedule for them to work, if we don't have a working schedule here. Today, they were paid for no work, overseas, only their presence. Mr. Gulley was the only worker, today, and he is disillusioned with both Regina and Bill. Speaking of whom, Regina called while I covered the cubicle this morning, stating she needs to talk to me, she needs her job. I told her to call back between two and four, this is an overseas connection. She knew where she was calling, she was checking to see, if the area was covered, to determine how much leverage she had and how much she could milk it for. Now I do not know whose idea that was, hers or Bills. Have you heard from him, today?"

"No, Robin, I have not," he said. "Should he contact me, is there a message you would like relayed?"

"Yes, he needs to talk to me, thank you. Is there a conflict of interest here?"

"No, I am your attorney, until you replace me," he said.

"Well, my attorney, is there a personal conflict of interest?"

"There are some grey areas," he said. "But I will bring in or recommend an attorney for you or the company, your choice. Until then, I need you to respect the boundaries, that have been created because of Bill's indiscretion. Since you may not be aware of them all, I will say boundary as a stop word. How does that work for you?"

"I'm trying to snatch a company back from the bowels of hell, Bob, you tell me how that works?" she asked.

"Stay with me Robin," he said. "There are things that can put the company in even more jeopardy, that I am trying to protect legally, to avoid a takeover, and I don't want to put the company in new hands, that don't care what has transpired and worry about what they may do with that information, which could easily be leaked. Are you with me?"

"I see," she said. "Well, we have another internal problem, close the doors."

She motioned to the restroom, he followed her, she turned on the water and whispered into his ear, "Mr. Gulley knows about Regina and Bill, the intimate details before I left, dates, times and places, he was so reckless. He is Chinese, never absent from work, always listening, even when he is communicating with them on our check, he claims he is concerned about his job, the company closing, but something is off, Bob; we get our equipment for surveillance from them and Maurice has it everywhere. If he is a sleeper, then the company is already in trouble. Information is power and Bill and Regina were so careless, and indiscreet that too many people have information, including the police. How do we fix it? Is it fixable?"

He asked her a question after telling Robin that 'Bill is the reason Regina received the position to run the company into the ground,' unquote; "You will save it, Ms. Robin, right?" I think it was a question open to far too many questions and interpretations.

"I understand your concerns, I will check it out immediately," he said. "Now, let's go back out and follow my lead."

"Yes, Bob. You go out first," she said. "And ask if I am alright from out there."

"In one," he said. She looked in the mirror and turned off the water and Bob called, "Robin, are you alright in there?"

"Will be out in a second, Bill," she said.

"Just checking," he said. "Can I get you a Pepsi?"

"Yes, thank you," she said. She walked back into the room.

"How do you really feel," he asked, he put his hand to his head.

"I am a little tired, let me take my meds and check on everyone and call you tomorrow?" she asked.

"I will check on you later."

"If you don't mind, please," she said. "I would appreciate that."

"By the way, you said you wanted to go to church with Mr. Gulley, did you get the address and times of service, I think you miss church and need to go," he said. "Find out the information and I will go with you."

"Will you?" she asked.

"Absolutely," he said. "Let me know."

"Thank you, Bob, you don't know how much it would mean to me to be in service surrounded by friends," she said.

"Get a little rest, if you can, and I will check on you later. Eat something, that may be one of your problems, too."

"Thanks for the advice."

"No problem. Take care," he walked out of the office and went to the cubicles. "Mr. Gulley, you're about to clock out, right?"

"Right," he said. "Can I help you?"

"I'm a little concerned about Robin, she needs spiritual uplifting; she had shared with me that she wanted to attend services with you and I thought I could cheer her up and surprise her by going with her, will you give me the location and service times?" he asked.

"My pleasure, Mr. McAfee, here is the card with the times and days, we will be glad to have you both," he said. "If you let me know when, then I will make sure my whole family is present to meet you both."

"Mr. Gulley, that would mean so much to not only her, but me, as well. We are family and have never met your side, it is past time," Robert said. "We will see you, soon. Now do you have a code to get out?" asked Robert.

"No. not yet, I just leave before five, when the locks click and come when the boss Maurice comes," he said.

"Who gave you those instructions?" asked Bob.

"Ms. Regina," he said.

"Well, we shall see, do you need anything from the kitchen or something?" asked Bob.

"If not too much trouble, I can use a few things," he said.

"You go in there and get whatever you need and I will block the door," he said.

"Ok, I will hurry," he said. Bob went to the door and held it open, Mr. Gulley knew where everything he wanted was and he returned as he said, "I took two bottles of wine, no?"

"Fine, I said anything, Mr. Gulley."

"I put back," he said.

Bob, took him to the door and asked, "Did you check out?"

"No, not yet," he said.

"Where is your time card?" asked Bob.

"Over here," he said. "I have over and Ms. Regina will not pay."

"What is your first name? asked Bob.

"I am Raul," he said.

"May I call you Raul?"

"Yes, yes," he said.

"Well Raul, Regina is not here to make decisions anymore, from now on, talk to Ms. Robin, okay?"

"Okay," he said.

"I will let you clock out now and I will put my initials here, and you'll be fine."

"Thank you, Mr. McAfee."

"Call me Bob," he said.

"Thank you, Bob," he said. He put his card in que and they walked out together. Bob got into his car and waved goodbye. Raul waved goodbye and watched Bob leave, then he got into his car as Maurice was driving up and stopped to see what he would say to him. Maurice got out and walked over to Raul's car and asked if he was okay?

"Yes," he said. "I was talking with Bob."

"Bob?" said Maurice.

"Oh, Mr. McAfee."

"Was there a problem, with him?" he asked.

"No, he wants to take Ms. Robin to my church to make her feel better and I gave him a card with the days and times of service," he said.

"I see, Mr. Gulley, may I have one?" he asked.

"Yes, yes," he said.

Raul reached up and took one from the visor and handed it to him. "I hope she feels better, I think Bob likes her, she could do worse. I think they would make a good couple."

"Why don't you share that with them, they need to know that," Maurice said.

"I will. I will let you know when they plan to visit so all can be together, no?"

"Yes," said Maurice. "I'll be waiting to hear. Thank you, Mr. Gulley, did you clock out?"

"Yes, Bob signed for me," he said.

"Okay, I will see you in the morning and have a great night say hello to the family and look forward to seeing you all soon."

"Thank you, Maurice, you too and check on Ms. Robin help make her better everyone," he said. "She is inside. Goodnight."

Maurice waved as he drove away.

He hurried inside and checked Mr. Gulley's card and saw that Bob had signed and okayed his overage. He replaced the card and went upstairs to see Robin. She was lying on the sofa, he asked if she were alright? She said she would be better, soon, and thanked him for his concern. She asked how he knew she wasn't feeling well and he told her Mr. Gulley told him that Bob said it and Bob signed his time card for the overage and made a note to review his pay under Regina to present and suggests an evaluation.

"Thanks for that information and will you bring me that information as soon as possible, Maurice?"

"Yes, and I have your code here and keys, as he placed them on the desk should I leave Bob's as well?" he asked.

"You may," she said. "How are Celia and Raymond?"

"They spent all that time at city hall and discovered they had not filled out an application for a lease to submit."

"I'm not touching that, the company lost a lot of money today with no one here but Mr. Gulley and I had to run things, I should have them here working through the night and until tomorrow night nonstop, if I could make the connection with overseas. I am sure it would be refused since they paid people there for just being present since they did no actual work performance. I am going to catch it from every side," she said. "There is no way I can justify the loss and the travel expense for non- workers, today taking personal time on unauthorized corporate time. In addition to all that, Regina called on the overseas line while I was covering the cubicles and asked to speak to me while she was speaking to me! The nerve, is everyone crazy or is this a bad scene from Groundhog Day?" she asked.

Maurice said, "It sounds like all the above, but don't make yourself sick over it, we will get everything sorted out if you stay well. I'm going to get those files you requested. You have Pepsi here; I will check in case you drank them all and make the necessary adjustments."

"Thank you, Maurice," she picked up her pad and wrote, *are you sure the room is safe to talk?*

I will make a sweep, he wrote, *when I return do not speak to me just let me do my thing and I will give the nod if all is well. Rest* he wrote. "Be back in a while," he said.

"Ok," she replied and placed the pad down. She laid there and began to think.

Chapter Twenty-Two

Cleaning House

Robin laid there and considered her options, realizing that she must have the facts before she could develop a plan, but the first order of business, would be to make sure the office was a safe place to conduct business. She picked up her pad and began to make notes and as she reviewed them she saw a plan developing but second, she had to clean house even if it meant breaking bonds.

The door opened quietly, and she remained calm and still. She continued to write as Maurice did his thing. She was caught up in her plans and before she knew it, he was trying to get her attention. She turned the page on her notepad and handed it to him with her pen and held her breath as he wrote; then handed her the pad. *I found two but I need to check where you are, when you're ready to move, take off your shoes and walk out the door and be quiet no calls, just quiet, I have a sound track that will continue to say I'm still looking from the kitchen it will speak when I push the remote don't answer just be quiet until I return to the door to let you in.* She took off her shoes placed one in each pocket and stood up and tipped out and left him in the office. There was a loveseat outside the door she sat down and put on her shoes and sat quietly. She waited patiently she wanted him to do a thorough job. She sat back and relaxed. She heard his voice faintly several times from the kitchen as he had said. Then she looked up, he was in the door beaconing for her to return to the office. He closed the door and wrote. *I'm going to sweep the private areas very carefully and especially the supposedly locked areas, the files you requested are on the desk, go over them while I'm doing this, we may need a meeting asap,* he wrote, *from what I have found and I have checked your office. There is more than enough work to keep you busy I'll sweep the hallway before I leave this area but I need the key to the bedroom that is on the desk,* she motioned for him to take it, he did and went to the bedroom in the rear of the office and she knew he was inside. Robin had not been to the bedroom, to even see what it was like, she had not been to the restroom before Bob came. She considered the conversation she had with him and if there were anything that could be misconstrued or used against the company, she wasn't sure. That was a conversation she would have to have with him a later date. She turned her attention to the files that were before her and began to check Mr. Gulley's time cards. What she discovered made her embarrassed. Every card was signed by Regina. She checked to see his application for employment and he had been with the company for twelve years, was brought in by Mr. Marshall, Sr., and personally approved. Robin thought there is a story here, that she knew was interesting and she would get to the bottom of it. She wondered when Regina applied and pulled her application and saw she had been there ten years and she was promoted to accountant by Bill. Mr. Gulley was hired as a janitor, and became a naturalized citizen and he continued to study and was promoted to an interpreter and father Marshall paid for his education, he speaks three languages. Raul Gulley was the name given him by father Marshall, he is Chi Ho Young married and had two children but there are seven dependents listed. Robin had several problems with his treatment. She pulled his card and set it aside for review with Bob. Celia was straight because, Robin had handled her paper work, but she still double checked her payments.

There was a check due her that week. Robin looked at the salary and deductions and saw a discrepancy; must be a clerical error of two dependents, but Regina signed off on it. She made a note to straighten that out. She checked Maurice's application. He was hired as an electrical engineer, with credentials and excellent references with a generous starting pay. Married with three dependents and four at year end. Another Bill hire, with military experience in high tech. Four years employed with no pay raise since he was hired? Robin had a problem since he is head of Security and does Maintenance Supervision and other odd jobs, why is his salary the same, she wondered and checked for an attachment or codicil to his application but there was nothing mentioned. She went through every file even those who were deceased, quit or terminated and she stopped. No wonder this company has had so much trouble, when employees are mistreated, unless they are illegal and desperate, they quit, leaving positions high and dry. When she was checking into hiring, she remembered Regina's reaction to hiring Raymond and she understood why, now. Robin saw a MEO file and unfamiliar with the acronym she opened it to glean insight; it was a file of the vendors utilized by the company and its affiliates and took a closer look. When she was interrupted by Maurice. She put the file to the side and listened.

"It is clear in the bedroom, now, on this floor area I found eleven, repeat eleven bugs some older than the others, If I had to guess from my military experience, a couple were placed strategically in the father's command and the other's during Bill's, he said. I know that since we moved the furniture in one was placed in every room in this office, I'll stake my job on that," he said. "The bedroom was loaded. It is my opinion that whomever is listening decided most of the information would be relayed in the bedroom four bugs, one in kitchenette. Two in waiting area outside this door."

She said she didn't know there was a kitchenette in here.

"Everything is in here," he said. "The extravagance, that went into these two offices, is unbelievable. I spoke with Bob, earlier in here, and I must assume everything we said is now known. Yes, I have them all tucked away and as soon as I determine where the range ends, I can pinpoint who. I'm going to sweep the other phones, this is a direct number and if you haven't given it out, it's good to go. Just installed it today and I don't think anyone had access to this room today, but then, I was not on my posts."

"Check the bedroom in Mr. Marshall's apartment, I really need to know what is in there, I need a drink," she said.

"You need Bob," he said. "Excuse me if I am being impertinent."

"Right and right," she said and excused.

"You see that beautiful cabinet by the marble pole?" he asked.

"Yes," she said. "What about it."

"Go over and open the door," he said, "Tap three times."

She went over and opened the door and tapped three times and the panel moved and behind it was a bar and a safe.

"No, I do not have the combination and help yourself, while I complete my tasks," he said. "I know it is important to you, so as soon as I have the results for the apartment, I will let you know the truth."

"Thank you, Maurice. I really would appreciate your candor."

Robin looked at the bar and thought, all this expensive alcohol. Everything needed for the thirsty and desired to be inebriated. She took a bottle of Tonic Water and tapped and the panel closed as she closed the door and took her seat. She picked up the MEO file again and looked at it trying to pinpoint the culprit. Robin, was angry, too angry to drink, too angry to sleep and too angry to be understanding. Her primary thought was to clear up the problems and do it right or at least fair and just. She had to hire other people, but she also was accountable for righting the wrongs that were done to the old employees. She needed to know the vision behind the visionary for without a vision, the people perish. The true visionary wasn't the son, but was the first Mr. Marshall. Robin had to know him to expand on his vision until another was raised up to carry on, but she knew it would not be her.

Robin went through everything she could find with his signature, his thoughts. He kept extraordinary notes in a brown pouch that gave her tremendous insight into his life. He was happily married and worked hard to give his wife the best of everything, to make up for the years of lack she experienced with him. He was a religious man, not easily swayed by the lavish lifestyles of others, but loved people and it is at this point, that those after him missed the mark, she thought.

She looked for a connection with Raul, but she could not find it or she missed it. It was clear that there were many Raul's in his life of different nationalities and she deduced that he sponsored people to the United States and hired them to work for him and he helped them to become citizens and paid for their education. Robin thought about Raymond and the vision she was given regarding him and she said, "Yes, that was part of his vision."

Robin was excited. Where were the descendants of those he helped, and hired and why is there not one reminder of his good works available as a testimony of the hope he celebrated investing in people and products? These were questions she asked and planned to discuss with Raul Gulley also known as, Chin Ho Young.

Robin learned a lot, that night and she wanted to sleep on her revelation to activate the vision. She wondered if Maurice were still in the building and if Bob thought she was insane, but those thoughts were interrupted by Maurice.

"May I come in?" he asked.

"Of course," she said.

"Well, the good news is, I got them all, the bad news is there were six in the apartment new to very recent. I found no visuals, but every word uttered was heard," he said. "The kitchen was heavily bugged and the conference room as well, whom ever placed them, knew the layout of the building. The marks under the tables indicated they were replaced several times it reeks of insiders. How many total, rough estimate until actual counting, seventy-five, give or take two or three."

"I think it is an inside job as well. We need to speak with Bob tomorrow, right now, he probably thinks I have lost my mind, with my suspicions. I am disappointed that he didn't try to contact me, I will say this once, I love him," she said.

"I know love when I see it," he said. "And I see it on both of you. I wouldn't count him out, Robin, nor underestimate him."

"Never," she said. "Never!"

"There was no way to contact you here. The lines were disconnected, by me, once I discovered there was a problem," he said. "Once I checked your phone, I did reconnect it, but since you had not given out the number, I could not give it to him, after I messed up so badly earlier. I am hoping to redeem myself."

"Okay, okay, okay and soon," she said. "I appreciate your friendship, Maurice, but I must reprimand both my family and friends when they error or I am neither. Do have children?"

"I have one," he said.

"How old and boy or girl?"

"Ten and girl," he said.

"When she does things, she should not, do you just turn and walk away or do you show her the error of her ways?"

"I do the latter, because I love her and I am her father."

"I will finish that statement for you," she said. "And you would neither be a father nor love her, if you did not."

"Right, I understand," he said.

"I learned a lot tonight, for instance, you have worked here for four years hired by Bill, and you have never received a pay increase and you have three dependents for payroll and four for taxes. Will you tell me why?" she asked.

"Mr. Marshall paid me under the table too," he said. "I have exemptions and Regina placed the others and takes half the refund."

"Okay, I am so glad that you told me, because I am doing a review of your salary, unless you tell me not to, because as much as you do around here, your check should reflect it. Does it have anything to do with your pension?"

"No, I can make as much as I can, it just worked out better for me that way."

"But was it working well for the family? Regina, is a monster that really belongs behind bars. What if she were caught and she gave up all the employees, the doors of this building would be closed. That man Gulley has been here for twelve years he really has seven children and the only raise he received was from father Marshall and he has been living or trying to live on the same salary he originally received, it broke my heart to read all the things she did to employees and the company, that is why he always tries to get the leftovers, he's just trying to feed children and grandchildren. Is that fair?"

"I didn't know that, Robin, I feel badly about that. I was led to believe that he didn't have education was an illegal and the janitor."

"Let me guess, Regina told you that? He is a naturalized citizen, father Marshall paid for his education; he is an interpreter and speaks three different languages. He started off as a janitor, but was promoted and she never gave him his just wage and he never complained even though he catches hell from his wife about how he is treated. Now what do you think?"

"That is amazing," he said.

"He can't afford a decent suit to work in, but do you think if he were just an illegal ignorant immigrant he would be working in the cubicles up front? She really had you all snowed and I am so angry. That is why I said I need a drink, but after I saw all that alcohol and thought about how he asked for food, I just took the Tonic Water and closed the door. She had the nerve to call here and say she wants to talk to me, she'd do well to keep her distance!"

"Robin, she had us all deceived, and we were only thinking of ourselves. Now that she's no longer here, we're back where we started," he said.

"No, Maurice, you are not back where you started, you have enjoyed the ill-gotten fruits for an extended season, now, that the season is over, it is time to grow or stand still," she said. "The choice is yours, but as in all things that grow, there is pain; but once the pleasant fruit is harvested, the exceeding and eternal weight of glory will far surpass all you thought was plenty."

"I can live with and for that, Robin," he said.

"Good, Maurice, you've made me so proud of you. Redeemed," she said.

"Thank you, Robin."

"Thank you," she said. "Now let's solve this mystery so the business of business can roll on."

"I'll be working all night or as long as it takes," he said.
"So, will I, in my sleep I dream to reach decisions," she said. "I need a pen and paper so when I awaken, I can write down what needs to be done. One light is usually all I need but since I am a stranger in a foreign land, in here, I'll leave the lights on. Let's go to work now."

"Yes ma'am," he said.

Robin opened the bible and read one chapter and prayed and went to sleep.

She awoke and prayed and went to the shower. As she showered, she began to see and visualize the situation. She hurried and stepped out of the shower looked for a robe and forgot she wasn't home, she didn't even know where the towels were or where anything was, she went to the bedroom to see if there were clothes in the drawers or closets, she was in unfamiliar territory, she opened one more drawer and there were sheets, she took one out and wrapped herself in it and went to the office and picked up the MEO file, she zeroed in on the red mark and did a closer look at the vendors, she saw something that was significant then unbelievable and finally undeniable. She looked for clothes all she could find were men's pants and shirts, jackets and ties, they were of excellent material quality and she thought why not. She looked in the closet and saw that most of the clothing was matched and just ready to be put on. She wondered what really happened that these tops of the line clothes were left behind, but she stopped thinking about the clothes and focused again on what she discovered. She decided on a black velvet suit with a burgundy tie and burgundy striped shirt and kerchief. She put on the pants and the shirt, tucked in the shirt and put on her heels, tossed her hair and walked to the mirror and fixed her lip-gloss. She took the jacket and threw it over her shoulders and walked to the apartment the door was open; Robin walked into the bathroom and put on deodorant, walked to the bedroom and picked up the perfume and sprayed it and walked out. She felt different as she walked down the stairs just so far and saw the Donut Delivery man walking around the conference table; she cleared her throat and said, "Good morning, did you bring the donuts?"

"Yes," he said.

"Are you the same man who delivers daily?" she asked.

"No, he is sick today, and I made the delivery," he said.

"Well show them to me," she said. "I'm a little hungry, what do they call you?"

"I am Tito," he said.

"I am Robin," she said. "Pleased to meet you, Tito, will you be here in the morning?"

"Yes," he said as he walked close to her.

"At six," he said.

"I'll be here," she said. "Would you like a donut?"

"No, I've had two," he said. "But tomorrow I will not eat one."

"Ok, Tito," she said. "Six o'clock. Have a nice day."

"You, too," he said.

"Thank you," she said.

She wondered if Maurice got a picture of him and taped them. Robin was certain that the man was looking for the bugs, one thing of which she was sure, is he had no business in the conference room without Donuts! Robin took eight donuts and wrapped them up nicely and placed them in a bag, she looked in the freezer to see what was there and she saw a lot of lunchmeat, chicken and ham, she put all that in a bag and looked in the pantry to see what was there and to her delight, there were plenty of can goods. Robin took four cans of green beans, four of corn, four of carrots and peas and placed them in another bag. She put Raul's name on the bags and put the meat back in the freezer and the can goods on the counter. She went back upstairs and took three suits, shirts, ties and handkerchiefs in a suit bag from his closet looked for shoes and socks and placed them in the bag and took everything downstairs. She went back upstairs and picked out a brown suit and accessories and shoes and took them down, forgot the money, she went back up took out her wallet and took a twenty-dollar bill out and put her wallet back, locked the door and went back downstairs to see a white apron going out the door. Robin locked the door and picked up the bags and placed them on the counter and the brown suit and accessories on a chair in his cubicle, she put the money in her pocket and felt her ears, no earrings, she went back upstairs and unlocked the door, she put on her earrings and watch, bent over and brushed her hair, put on her jacket and walked down the stairs. She heard the door rattle and made a note not to have the doors on automatic open after tomorrow. It was difficult to believe that after all that had transpired, Maurice, deliberately left the doors opened, anyone could walk in and replace the bugs that were removed. She walked to the Security Office and knocked on the door. After a few minutes, the door opened and there he was.

"Maurice, were you taping the rooms this morning?"

"No," he said. "Why?"

"I found clothes to put on and went to the apartment to get deodorant," she said. And she whispered, "Get your machine out.

He beaconed for Robin to come in. She went in and said, "There was a man named Tito, from the bakery going around the table with his hand in the conference room; I asked him to take me to the donuts and he took me in the kitchen, I saw him walk out, but I did not hear a vehicle start up. Not thinking about it, because I told him I would see him tomorrow and he's going to eat donuts with me, I went upstairs to get somethings for Gulley came down the stairs and a white apron was going out the door. If he were new as he said, he would not be in the conference room with his hand under the table going around it with no donuts in the room."

"I agree," he said.

"How did the door open?" she asked. "Gulley said he waits until you come to get in the door because it is locked, this morning it was wide open I saw it. Explain, please?"

"I cannot," he said. "My readings say the doors are all locked and never been opened."

She said, "Get your equipment that works while I get a donut from the package I fixed for Gulley. Hurry before the people come and the door to the apartment was open too."

Robin went into the kitchen; the donuts were no longer there. She went into the freezer and took out the bag, she unwrapped the donuts and had one waiting for Maurice.

He said, "Yes."

Robin went to the door and tried to open it but it did not open. She looked out the window and there were no trucks outside, she went back to the kitchen and took the eight donuts and put them back in the freezer and looked to see if the bag was on the counter, the clothes were there. She walked to the cubicle and Raul's clothes were in his chair. She went into the conference room and looked in planters, vases, recorder, under chairs; he was standing when she saw him so whatever he planted he did standing. Robin waited for Maurice to return and when he did not she went to the apartment to see if he were there. She turned the knob, but it was locked. She went to get the keys. On her way down the stairs, she thought, something with a high pitch, opened the door or it was done by remote. Robin also was curious about who previously owned the building. She took a pad from supplies to communicate with, today, she was going to be death and dumb. It was clear to her that something nefarious was up. She didn't have any clothes of her own to wear and the suit was spiffy, sexy in a way because not only does a man make the clothes, a woman can make them shine and Robin made that suit shine, with the shirt open down the front just enough to show her cleavage, all she needed was a hat and she could be the cover girl of a magazine and sell a million of those suits without anyone questioning the price.

   Robin went to get the keys and she locked the door and walked to the bedroom turned on all the lights and looked in the closet, everything was so neat, then it hit her that the clothes that were laid out were clothes with trackers and body heat had to be the key activator to trigger something in the fabric that triggers a silent alarm alerting the enemy that their sleeper had arisen.

   She looked thru the clothes to see if there were any women's clothing. She opened every box, every bag and looked at pieces of paper and nothing looked like something until she came to the back of the closet and on the bottom of the wall something slightly stood out she hurried and took off the clothes and took her clothes from the previous day out of the bathroom, hoping they were dry, she put the suit in the freezer to stop the body heat and put on her clothes, she walked to the front and picked up her writing pad shook her hair out that she would not look like a man, put the rest of her clothes on and when she was satisfied that no one was out there she picked up the phone and called 911 and gave them the location of the building and said someone was being killed come quickly. She hung up the phone and went to the cabinet to get her purse and then checked again, she heard the sirens and ran to the closet pulled the box from the wall, placed it in her purse and she heard the knocking on the door, then glass shattering and a voice asking, "Anyone here!"

Robin was still leery, she heard them enter Mr. Marshall's apartment and someone yelled get the paramedics up here man down. Robin took out her I.D. and code pass and keys and placed the container under all the junk in her purse and she heard a voice ask, "Where is Robin?"

She ran from the room and said, "Robert, Robert."

He said, "I'm coming for you." But she refused to wait in that room another minute.

She went down the stairs and a shot rang out, she did a backwards dip and the bullet went over her head, a body was on top of her whispering, "Play dead, Robin." She held her breath as soon as he got up and said, "She's gone."

"I need to see," the voice said.

"You don't need to see her like this, Bill, no one does."

"Why did she have to meddle in things she didn't understand?" he asked.

"Why did you put her in that position, you knew she was braver than us all and she would never settle for half measures, she would find the truth, somehow! You knew how determined she was, why?"

"She was going to bring the world down on us!" he said.

"Who? Regina. Raul, Me and Maurice," he said.

"Going through files that were old and buried, the MEO file, especially, she was bound to find out that we were smuggling drugs and we had a good thing going until she started hiring people and throwing us off our schedule. Yesterday we lost millions while she let the new people go to the courthouse and Maurice couldn't make his pick up or deliveries. Juliette said, 'she had to go.' We sent a hit man to do the job, but someone dressed in good clothes was here and he couldn't make the hit. Then that new boy she hired came and we had to get rid of him and Maurice was asking too many questions, it was too dangerous for us. She helped us with Johanna and for that we'll give her a big send off."

"How did it come to this?" asked Bob.

"My father, kept sending for immigrants to help work and he was spending so much money with their education and health problems, like Raul, he came with his father, mother and cousins and the bills kept getting bigger and the income kept getting smaller and before we knew it, it was gone. I tried to run the business but all the killing was a little much so I brought in other people, to do that, until they were no longer useful then we'd get rid of them."

"Did you love Regina?" asked Bob.

"No, she was amusing for a while then she was greedy, then she was a pest and then she was gone."

"Gone where?"

"Dead!" he said. "Juliette invited her to the house and she had a fatal accident while riding. We did a fox hunt and she got in front of Juliette's rifle."

"Where do you go from here, my friend?" asked Bob.

"I'm going back to my Estate and tomorrow the cleaning crew will come out and we'll start fresh on Wednesday, replacing people and going on. You, my friend, are going to join your love forever. I'm afraid one day you may resent me for killing her and come for me, so I'm going to leave you with her and just a word of comfort for you, she really fell hard for you. I wish I had been lucky enough to find someone who loved me for me as you finally did, cause your ex-wife, was something else, I know, I had her every way I wanted."

"I know," said Bob.

"But it never would have happened with Robin," he said.

"You're right, and she was a fine, looking piece. Was she as good as she looked?" Robert was silent. "I hate I had to deprive you of Robin but now you'll be together forever. Goodbye, old friend," said Bill.

As he raised his gun, "Goodbye," said Bob.

A voice called out, "This is Officer Winter, of the CPD, drop your gun and raise your hands!" he said.

Bill turned around and said, "You drop yours or you'll have four more dead."

"Drop it, it's over now. You've killed enough people!" said Bob.

Chicago Police Department, "Drop your gun for the last time. We have your wife in custody and she's talking."

Bill shot in their direction and they returned the fire and he was pronounced dead at the scene.

Bob reached down and said, "We can go now, my love. We must wait until everyone is gone and the officer returns."

"My old office," she said. "It is a mess, but I'm not making excuses."

"And I'm not taking any," he said. "He will keep everyone away until we're upstairs."

"Would Officer Sam Winter, be the 'he'?" she asked.

"Yes," said Bob.

"Where is my purse?" she asked.

"There behind you," he replied.

He picked it up and they went to the office. "I need a drink now," he said.

"I will fix you whatever you want," she replied.

"Scotch neat, although a great brandy and a cigar would be great," he said.

Robin went over to the counter, opened the

door and tapped three times and the panel moved. "We have Scotch and we have Brandy, the very best," she said.

"Do we have cigars?" he asked.

"Will Cuban Pinar Del Rio work for you, dear?

"It certainly will, my love."

She handed him the cigar and clipper plus ash tray and then the glass of Brandy, "That's the best I can do without your robe and slippers. I think I'll watch you. Death missed me twice in the same day. I saw a bottle of an excellent Pinot Noir, while I uncork it, do you want to share how you knew?"

"Maurice called me and told me he found the bugs 'about seventy-five' he said. I called the officer I met here and shared with him your concerns, then he did a little digging and found out Bill's father was bankrupt from bringing immigrants here to work for him and because he loved people and tried to improve their plight, he invested in them by funding their education. He knew he had a selfish son and hoped that one day, if he needed help one of them would be there to help him. His father was a thorn in his side and warned him not to marry his wife, but he didn't listen. One day he just snapped and killed him pushed him down the stairs and called it an accident that he was sleep walking and fell down the stairs. No one questioned it. He needed money and used the immigrant connection to form his own drug farm. You were supposed to be killed this morning but dressing like a man threw them off."

"Who was in the room, Bob?"

"You heard him, Robin," "Maurice."

"Juliette was in on it, too?"

"She was probably the cause of all of it, she was just as greedy as my ex-wife," he said.

"Raul, was a real victim, too. Regina never reviewed him for a salary increase once in the ten years she was accountant," she said.

"I know, honey, but we'll never get the whole story about that."

"Where are we going, Bob?"

"To find that perfect world where we can live together and love each other until death do us part," he reached in his pocket and took out a lovely box, took the ring out. "Robin Watson, will you be my real wife?" he asked

"Only if you will be my real husband," she answered.

"Oh, I will," he said.

"That is a yes for me," she replied. He put the ring on her finger after he put the cigar down. She took the glass of brandy from his hand and placed it on the desk. She walked over and locked the door dropping pieces of clothing as she walked. He stood up and walked to her dropping clothing. They stood together taking off the other's clothes and finally there were no clothes, just skin.

He kissed her hands and said, "I am yours, Robin, completely for if we shall live, there will never be anyone who could touch me the way you do."

She considered his deep blue eyes and said, "I wish I had known you first, I would not have been as frigid as I am, but I thank God you came along in time to show me what love is, I really wanted to know."

She leaned into him as he caressed her silky heated skin and touched her with the touch of magic as he pulled her gently so close they breathed the same breath of air, so close their hearts beat as one, so close that there was no place to go but into each other, savoring every thrust as they moved slowly to a musical composition only the two of them composed. They danced horizontally trying to make the music last but the excitement, the thrill of it all, the ecstasy of the moment was building like a volcano ready to erupt, with its lava over flowing down the sides so did they and what an eruption it was. Their bodies shook and trembled as the fruit juices of their flower flowed down their legs as they moaned in unison, they held each other for what seemed like hours reveling in the knowledge that they have only just begun to turn their todays into tomorrows.

The box was a discussion for another day!

www.ingramcontent.com/pod-product-compliance
Lightning Source LLC
LaVergne TN
LVHW041539070426
835507LV00011B/827